MANDATE FOR CHANGE
The Impact of Law on
Educational Innovation

MANDATE FOR CHANGE
The Impact of Law on Educational Innovation

Joel F. Henning, *Project Director*
Charles White, *Writer/Editor*
Michael Sorgen, *Legal Research Director*
Leigh Stelzer, *Empirical Research Director*

ABA Special Committee
on Youth Education
for Citizenship

Social Science
Education
Consortium, Inc.

ERIC Clearinghouse
on Educational
Management

Printed in the United States of America
Produced by the ABA Press

Standard Book Number: 089707-010-0
Library of Congress Catalog Card Number: 79-89342

The American Bar Association,
1155 E. 60th Street, Chicago, IL 60637

Social Science Education Consortium, Inc.,
855 Broadway, Boulder, CO 80302

ERIC Clearinghouse on Educational Management,
University of Oregon, Eugene, OR 97403

This book was made possible by a grant from the
Ford Foundation

Contents

Foreword

America has long since run out of geography in which to expand. We are now discovering that there are limits on economic growth as well. In an era of limited growth, conflict inevitably increases.

The peaceful resolution of conflict was traditionally accomplished by the family, the church, the work place, the fraternal organization, the political party, and the governmental bureaucracy, among other social institutions. Today, however, the legitimacy of all institutions is under assualt and, as a result, citizens increasingly turn to lawyers and the courts for resolution of their disputes by impersonal third parties.

There appears to be only one remaining forum where moral issues find resolution, if it is found anywhere. Abortion, busing, affirmative action, obscenity, and other such matters invariably seem to end up, with other social conflicts, in the courts.

All of this legal activity is on the civil side, and ignores the appalling increase in crime and associated growth of the criminal justice field. Under the federal Speedy Trial Act and its counterparts in many states, criminal cases take priority on court dockets. Even so, criminal cases often drag on too long, results are perceived by many people as arbitrary, and plea bargaining remains a controversial means of diverting criminal cases from trial. The public appears vindictive toward those accused of crime, whether they are guilty or not, and therefore provides little support for improved correctional programs.

Legal activity is burgeoning at the bottom and top of the economic ladder. The federally-funded Legal Services Corporation receives approximately $300 million in appropriations, enough to provide salaries for two lawyers for every 10,000 citizens who cannot afford private counsel. Complex litigation preoccupies armies of corporate lawyers on behalf of giant enterprises such as AT&T, IBM, and Eastman Kodak. These cases often drag on for years, tying up judges and courts, and costing the parties millions of dollars.

Can our legal system survive all of these burdens which we have imposed upon it? I don't know. One thing is certain, however; it cannot survive unless the American people understand this system and the fundamental constitutional principles upon which it is based. Citizens must be able to recognize legal issues as they may affect them personally and cope with them effectively.

For better or worse, law is an important language of the modern era. Mathematics is also a language of the modern era. But students learn mathematics in systematic curricular programs throughout their elementary and secondary educations, while law has traditionally been relegated to formalistic and superficial treatment in civics and social studies classes, and an occasional exhortatory speech on Law Day. Surely no one believes that mathematics could be understood if it were given such short shrift in the schools.

Approximately a decade ago, the American Bar Association initiated steps to help America's citizens understand the legal system. It undertook to work with educators throughout the country in the development of a curriculum in law-related education that would help students from kindergarten through twelfth grade develop deep understanding of the legal system.

As the project got underway, it became clear that—however great the need—curricular reform in the schools would be as slow and difficult a process in this field as in every other. I had the good fortune to direct that project at its inception. With the enormous support of Edward J. Meade and Terry N. Saario of the Ford Foundation, we decided to analyze the legal ecology of curricular change, focusing on our own action project to integrate law-related education into the elementary and secondary curriculum. We felt it would be useful to compare curriculum laws with what actually happened in the classroom.

Was there a correlation between the two? Did the laws impede or encourage an innovation such as law-related education?

Thus, this project was born. Like so many research projects, it has taken much longer to complete than anticipated. Our first job was to research the laws and regulations touching upon curricular change in this field. In this work we were greatly assisted by Professor Michael Sorgen and his students at Hastings College of Law in San Francisco. Thereafter, political scientist Leigh Steltzer and his colleagues undertook empirical research in a selection of school districts through the country, to investigate the correlation between the laws and regulations on their face and their actual impact on the classroom. Charles White of the ABA staff worked on every aspect of the study and was responsible for writing and editing the final report.

This study is, as you will see, unique. As the first of its kind, we are aware that many questions are left unanswered and further questions raised by our research. Nevertheless, it has helped us and will, we hope, help others recognize that there is no shortcut to the reform of elementary and secondary curricula, even in a field as important as law. But it also demonstrates that positive change can be accomplished if all of the necessary components are assembled.

Mere legislative mandating of curriculum in any subject, including law, does not insure any meaningful classroom activity. In fact no law or regulation, unless integrated into a comprehensive program of public awareness, parent involvement, teacher education, and student engagement, will have impact on what students learn.

Reinforced with the results of this study, the American Bar Association plans to continue its work with educators and lawyers throughout the country to see that students are provided with engaging and useful curricula in law that will help prepare them to make informed and intelligent decisions as citizens. We hope that this study will encourage others to work at curriculum reform, equipped with more understanding of the process than we had at the outset. Finally, we hope that our efforts will lead to further enlightenment in this complex but important field.

JOEL HENNING

Preface

The law has become increasingly important to educators in recent years. More and more cases involving the schools are coming before the courts, both scholarly and journalistic writers on education are paying greater attention to law, and courses in education law are burgeoning at schools of education. However, this interest has been selective, with the greatest attention given to topical issues, such as busing, sexual equality, school financing, and student rights. The quieter, but perhaps even more pervasive, presence of law in other areas of education has been neglected.

For example, in every state in the United States there are laws directly affecting teaching and learning. Curriculum mandates influence the curriculum directly, either by stating general educational objectives or by specifying what shall or shall not be taught. The laws governing teacher certification specify what training is necessary for public school teachers, in effect determining who may teach and who may not. Laws specifying where schooling may take place may either facilitate or impede such innovations as work-study programs and internships, and laws governing instructional materials may exert a strong influence on the public school curriculum.

Given that it potentially may touch on many important aspects of teaching and learning, the law should be of great concern to educators.

1

However, the impact of education law on teaching and learning has received almost no scholarly attention, and little is known about the variations among laws in the various states; about the perceptions of these laws on the part of teachers, administrators, and others; about the effects of these various laws; and about the factors that might help explain their varying effects.

These questions are important because they concern not only the standing curriculum but also attempts at curricular innovation. If the law is an important determinant of the curriculum, then it is important to know what kinds of laws are efficacious, which kinds are conducive to curricular change, and which kinds impede it. Alternatively, if the laws are discovered to have little or no effect, this finding, too, will affect the strategy for change.

Since the American Bar Association's Special Committee on Youth Education for Citizenship (YEFC) seeks to further a curricular innovation known as law-related education, it has a clear interest in knowing how law affects curricular change. YEFC was established in 1971, under the leadership of Leon Jaworski, then president of the American Bar Association, to provide national leadership and direction to the movement to make the study of law and legal process part of elementary and secondary education in this country. (For more information on YEFC, see Appendix 1.) Research is one of YEFC's important activities, and a study of the effect of law on the adoption of law-related education advances YEFC's goal of stimulating law-related education programs.

Accordingly, in 1973 YEFC proposed to the Ford Foundation an investigation of the effect of law on the adoption of law-related education. The study was funded in 1974, and work continued from the fall of 1974 to the spring of 1978. As it turned out, looking at how law affected the introduction of law-related education necessarily entailed examining other factors that help explain the presence or absence of law-related studies. In addition, the study provided the occasion for the first in-depth survey of a group of teachers offering law-related education, giving us an understanding of the substance and pedagogy of law-related education as teachers report that it is practiced, as well as providing insights into the motivations of those teachers.

The study will also be useful to those not directly concerned with law-related education. For example, the report will be helpful to those seeking a better understanding of innovation in education generally. Since law-related education shares many characteristics with other recent innovations, our findings on the manner in which it does or does not become part of the curriculum may be of use to other curriculum innovators and to scholars studying the process of innovation.

The study also makes a contribution to the literature on civic education. Examination of the materials and methods used in courses devoted to law, as well as in social studies courses incorporating law topics, provides at least a partial picture of what is now happening in citizenship education. In addition, the questions we asked of teachers on the influence of the so-called hidden curriculum—that is, their feelings about the school's authority structure, their willingness to speak out on controversial issues inside the classroom and in the general community— may provide further data on the attitudes and behavior of teachers and suggest how these may influence both formal and informal curricula.

Finally, the report will be useful to persons who wish to influence the curriculum. We provide a number of recommendations both for those who make and implement education law, such as legislators and state department of education personnel, and for those who might seek to influence education policy, such as parents, community members, and others concerned with the school curriculum.

Because the report is intended for a large audience, including professionals in the field of law and education as well as a wide spectrum of policymakers and interested laypersons, we have made a concerted attempt to avoid overly technical or jargonistic reporting. That does not mean that we have oversimplified our findings or limited the scholarly rigor of our analysis. It means, rather, that we have tried to cut through the technical vocabulary of education, law, and social science research, expressing ourselves wherever possible in clear, direct prose. For instance, we have tried to avoid the passive voice and have substituted the collective "we" for the droning passive's impersonal phrases, such as "it is believed that," and "it was found that."

The project was directed by Joel Henning, YEFC staff director at the project's inception and now Assistant Executive Director—Communications and Education of the American Bar Association. The editor and assistant project director was Charles White of the YEFC staff.

Most of the legal research of this study was directed by Michael Sorgen, a specialist in education law who was at that time a professor at Hastings College of Law and is now legal advisor to the Oakland (California) Unified School District. Mr. Sorgen worked fulltime on the study from the fall of 1974 to the fall of 1975. The legal research is current through those years but does not take into account developments

3

that may have occurred since then. The legal research phase was principally concerned with state laws and state department of education regulations, since these are more central to teaching and learning than federal education law and more accessible than local regulations.[1] While local school boards are ultimately responsible for the curriculum, they are subordinate to state law. Given the more than 15,000 school districts in this country, we did not have the time or resources in this study to delve into local district policies and regulations.

Working with a team of law students, Mr. Sorgen compiled and analyzed the relevant constitutional provisions and statutes of each of the 50 states. In addition, he gathered information on state department of education regulations and attorney generals' opinions in many states. He also looked into the annotations and interpretations found in judicial decisions, an increasingly important source of law.

The goal of this portion of the study was (1) to gather as much information as possible about the various areas of law which might affect the curriculum; (2) to analyze that body of law on its face (for example, through the interpretations suggested by court cases, attorney generals' opinions, and the commentary of legal scholars), considering such factors as the constitutionality of various laws, trends in laws governing the curriculum, and the seeming effect of those laws; and (3) to suggest areas of inquiry for the second phase of the study, which was devoted to empirical research.

In the empirical research phase, teachers and administrators were interviewed to gather information on the actual effect of the laws—for example, how they were perceived by teachers, administrators, and other actors in the system; how, if at all, these laws were enforced; and how actors in the system felt the laws affected school practice. A second important purpose was to examine other factors that might explain the presence or absence of law-related education.

The empirical research phase was directed by Leigh Stelzer, formerly on the faculty of the Graduate School of Public Affairs, State University of New York at Albany, and a former special assistant to the chairman of the Education Committee of the New York State Assembly. The empirical research phase extended from the fall of 1975 to the spring of 1977.

This portion of the study focused on high school social studies in selected districts in five states—California, Georgia, Illinois, Pennsylvania, and Texas. We chose social studies because it is the curricular area most hospitable to law-related studies. We chose high schools be-

4

cause of a previous YEFC study[2] showed that law-related education is far more likely to be offered there than in the lower grades. We chose the five states because the legal phase had disclosed considerable differences in their education law, because our contacts with leaders in the field led us to believe that law-related education had been fostered and supported differently in each state, and because the states had wide geographic and demographic variety.

Within each state we selected a random sample of schools, but within each school interviewers sought social studies teachers who were already offering law-related education. Therefore, the teacher sample does not represent a random sample but rather is biased toward those interested in law-related education. We should emphasize that the data are based on the unverified reports of teachers and administrators. Independent observers might well see things differently. (See Appendix 2 for more information about the sampling technique and other aspects of our methodology in this portion of the study.)

The sample included a total of 78 schools. We interviewed a total of 214 secondary social studies teachers and 116 administrators: 73 principals and 43 superintendents. (See tabular material in Appendix 2 for the state-by-state distribution of the sample.)

We are aware that our sample is small, and with more funds we would have used a larger sample; however, we think that our sample was adequate for our purposes. For the most part we dealt with a highly specialized concern and a highly specialized group of people. Education in general and the social studies in particular have been influenced by certain factors that are similar from state to state. Teachers and administrators throughout the country tend to receive similar training, engage in similar experiences, deal with similar curricula, and use similar texts and methods.

Regions, states, and localities introduce some important variations, but they serve to make educators within a given region or state rather homogeneous. Most of the teachers we interviewed had received their education in the states in which they taught. Furthermore, within each state they were subject to the same state laws, policies, and pronouncements.

Given the general homogeneity of this population, the sample was large enough to permit cautious generalizations. However, the reader should remember that this is in many ways a pioneering study, and the smallness of the sample, along with such factors as the largely unexplored terrain we traveled, suggests that the findings and conclusions are not

5

definitive. Rather, the study should be viewed as a preliminary effort of which one principal purpose is to suggest questions for further study.

Michael Sorgen and Leigh Stelzer wrote separate reports on their research. A special subcommittee of YEFC and its Advisory Commission reviewed the draft manuscripts and suggested many useful changes. Composed of two members of the Special Committee (Isidore Starr and Donald Sandberg) and three members of the Advisory Commission (David Schimmel, James Shaver, and Judith Torney), this group included experts in education law, the social studies curriculum, survey research techniques, and other important areas, and their contributions have been felt in every chapter of this report.

The final report, a fusion of the legal and empirical research portions of the study, was prepared by Charles White from a design by Leigh Stelzer.

Many persons helped us at various stages of this project. We have already noted the contribution of our research directors and the invaluable oversight of the research subcommittee. Terry Saario of the Ford Foundation carefully reviewed draft outlines and drafts of large portions of the study, met with us on a number of occasions, and provided a great deal of help both in the methodology of the study and in suggesting the names of specialists who later served as consultants. Frances Zemans and Felice Levine of the American Bar Foundation, both of whom have an extensive background in law, legal socialization, and survey research techniques, gave generously of their time on more occasions than we can count.

In the very early stages of the project, a number of persons helped us clarify our concerns and shape our research design. Larry Freeman and Paul Olson of the Study Commission on Undergraduate Education and the Education of Teachers shared with us much of their research into legal factors shaping education and suggested many legal and educational scholars whose work proved very useful to us. Ron Anson, a lawyer on the staff of the National Institute of Education, proved a useful source of information on several matters. Mike Kirst of Stanford University and Dale Mann of Columbia University Teachers' College provided many insights into survey techniques and into the relationship between education and law. David Long of the Lawyers' Committee on Civil Rights Under Law generously shared with us findings of a study his group conducted on law and education. John Stanavage of the North Central Accrediting Association was also helpful. Don Moore and Sharon Weitzman of the Center for New Schools provided the perspec-

6

tive of those who are actively trying to bring about change in the schools. Finally, many leaders in law-related education gave us insights into the specific problems and opportunities of that curricular innovation. These included Wally Richter of the Missouri Bar, Jeannette Moon of Law Education in Atlanta's Public Schools, Bill Stevens of the Social Science Education Consortium, Chuck Quigley of the State Bar of California's Law in a Free Society project, and Todd Clark of the Constitutional Rights Foundation.

The legal phase of the study benefited from contributions by a great number of people. Among them were David White, an attorney associated with the Childhood and Government project of the University of California (Berkeley); Sheila Huff of the Educational Policy Research Center in Syracuse; Michael Rebell, a New York attorney who has done considerable research into education law; and Paul Tractenberg, an education law specialist on the faculty of Rutgers Law School.

In addition, our legal research benefited greatly from our meetings with Linda Perle, principal research lawyer for the study conducted by the Lawyers' Committee on Civil Rights Under Law; Bill Kaplin, a professor of law at Catholic University and a leading authority on legal issues of accreditation; Harold Orlans, principal author of a study on accreditation by the Brookings Institution; Bernard Rezabek of the National Council on the Accreditation of Teacher Education; Ron Pugsley and Les Ross of the staff of the Office of Education Accreditation and Institution Eligibility; Allen Schmeider of the U.S. Office of Education; and Carl Massanari of the American Association of Colleges for Teacher Education.

Other persons helpful in this portion of the study included Professor Matthew Finken of Southern Methodist University; David Rubin, chief counsel to the National Education Association; Geraldine Pershing, Margaret Knispel, and Enid Medas of the National Education Association; Brian Larkin of the National Council for the Social Studies; Wayne Mahood of the State University of New York; John Jehu, counsel to the New York State Department of Education; and New York Education Commissioner Ewald Nyquist.

Two highly useful resources for the legal research phase were Professor Tyll van Geel of the University of Rochester, who shared with us preliminary drafts of his extensive study of the curriculum laws of five selected states, and Dinah Shelton of the Berkeley Childhood and Government project, who supplied us with her preliminary research into state curriculum laws and the political socialization process.

7

Finally, members of our staff, on several occasions during this phase of the study, spoke with practitioners of law-related education. Included in this group were Virginia Franklin, a high school teacher of law-related courses who wrote her Ph.D. thesis on political socialization; Debra Weiner of Temple Law School; and Ed O'Brien of the National Street Law Institute.

Our greatest debt for the empirical research phase is to the hundreds of teachers and administrators who generously gave of their time to meet with our interviewers. Our interview schedules were long (approximately an hour for administrators and an hour and a half for teachers), a considerable demand in itself; nevertheless, many of our respondents not only completed the full interview but stayed on to talk informally with the interviewers and provide even more useful data. We thank them all. Without them this study would simply not have been possible.

Others who helped us during the empirical phase included such consultants as M. Kent Jennings, a political scientist at the University of Michigan; Donald Layton, a member of the Education Department at SUNY, Albany; and Fred Wirt, a political scientist at the University of Illinois. Other scholars who provided useful insights included Roberta Siegel, Donald Rosenthal, and Gerald Sullivan of Rutgers and Barbara Farah of the Survey Research Center of the University of Michigan. Coe Dexter and John Dority of the New York State Bureau of Social Studies helped us gain a greater understanding of the role of state departments of education. Early in the study we met with and observed the teaching of a number of high school teachers. These preliminary contacts were most useful to us as we set about constructing a questionnaire. We thank in particular James McDonnel and Joseph Cardone of Metuchin High School (New Jersey), Joson Okin, Tom Freeswhich, and Saul Kominski of Ramapo High School (New Jersey), John Walko (East Greenbush, New York), and Bob Neiderhoffer (Milne School, New York).

In addition, J. Robert Daggett, assistant to the commissioner, New York State Department of Education; Judith Gillespie, codirector, High School Political Science Curriculum Development Project; and Mervin Krimmins, principal, Olney High School (Philadelphia) assisted us greatly by giving their reactions to our presentation on the empirical research study, on April 7, 1977, at the Annual Meeting of the American Education Research Association in New York. Each of the three presented a number of insights that greatly aided our analysis of the data.

We also wish to express our gratitude to Louise Kaegi and Carol Kusnierek, who did an exceptional job of proofreading and copy editing

8

this report. Not only did they catch many errors of quotation and foot-noting, but they also corrected stylistic infelicities and clarified many obscure passages. Their care and perseverance is responsible for much of the merit this report may have.

Finally, we thank the people who typed and retyped this report. Of course we greatly appreciate their professionalism and accuracy, but we especially want to acknowledge the good humor they showed through the long process of writing and revision. Typists on preliminary drafts included Jane Koprowski and Eyvonne Watts of the YEFC staff; the final draft was the work of Carolyn Nichols of the ABA's WANG Word Processing Center.

If we have neglected to thank anyone who has helped us—and, in a study of this magnitude, it is almost inevitable that the acknowledgments will be incomplete—please be assured that the omission is not intended. We are deeply grateful for the help we received, and we take this opportunity to thank you, one and all.

Notes

[1] Education in this country has generally been a function of state and local governments, and therefore federal education law is relatively less important than state and local law. However, in recent years federal law and federal court decisions increasingly have been superceding state education law.

[2] *See* pp. 119–20 of YEFC's, LAW-RELATED EDUCATION IN AMERICA (St. Paul, Minn.: West Publishing Co., 1975).

Part I

CHAPTER 1

Introduction

Proponents of law-related education have a variety of goals in mind and a variety of purposes in urging this curricular innovation, and the major programs that have been developed differ somewhat in approach and emphasis. However, one goal probably common to all approaches in the field is to contribute to citizenship education through the study of law and the legal process.

A number of studies suggest that social studies, the citizenship portion of the school curriculum, simply is not doing the job. For example, reports in the 1960s by Langton and Jennings,[1] Hess and Torney,[2] Massialas,[3] Smith and Patrick,[4] and Shaver[5] indicate that citizenship students are alienated both by the method of learning—read and regurgitate—and by the content—platitudes, blind optimism, chauvinism, and naive descriptions of ideals rather than reality. The courses apparently do not increase students' ability to analyze political and legal phenomena. They have little impact at the time and virtually none afterward. Indeed, the most lasting effect may well be an *increase* in students' cynicism and alienation.[6]

Our interviewers' informal conversations with teachers during research conducted for this study lead us to think that frustration with the social studies curriculum is shared by students and faculty alike. Certainly, many teachers said that they sense the inadequacies of present citizenship courses, with their ritual exhortations to patriotism and their preoccupation with formal government structure.

Law-related education does not promise to solve all these problems, but it offers something very new in American education—an effort by the organized bar and others in the legal community to help educators strengthen a major portion of the curriculum. Those in law-related education do not want lawyers to replace teachers by offering courses and taking responsibility for a citizenship program. Rather, in most law-related programs, lawyers assist teachers in such matters as curriculum development, teacher training, materials selection, and evaluation. The primary responsibility remains where it should—with the teacher.

The law-related education movement has generated a lot of interest and excitement, and a number of programs have been established in this decade. Thousands of teachers have begun to offer courses in law or to add law-related units to existing courses. In addition, a recent ABA survey determined that more than 300 law-related projects are now in existence, compared with a little more than 100 in 1971.[7]

Although this record of accomplishment is impressive, it is clear that much remains to be done. Most projects are still pilot developments, which means that in most localities law-related education is an experiment rather than a permanent part of the curriculum. More importantly, the vast majority of the school systems in this country do not have a formal law-related project under way. While many courses and units seem to have developed spontaneously, without the intervention of a formal project, these individual efforts run the gamut from ambitious and well-conceived programs to civics under another name.

What accounts for this spotty development? Why is law-related education strong in some localities and weak (or nonexistent) in others? What factors influence the decision to adopt or not to adopt law-related education? Who makes these decisions? Is state education law important in furthering law-related education? What strategies suggest themselves to persons wishing to foster law-related education (and, by implication, other curricular innovations)? This study has sought to answer these questions and others like them.

What Law-Related Education Is—and Is Not

Law-related education seeks to improve the citizenship education of American youngsters by teaching them about law, the legal process, and the legal system. It attempts to give them another way of understanding our society and some tools with which they can constructively participate in the making and shaping of laws.

Law-related projects, courses, and units differ greatly in approach and emphasis. Practitioners could probably not agree on a precise definition of law-related education or on topics that must be included in courses or programs. Most practitioners, however, would probably agree on the following generalizations.

First, law-related education does not seek to make students amateur lawyers or to prepare them for a career in law—it is not legal education. Nor does it try to secure a public relations forum for the legal profession or to promote blind compliance to law by minimizing the faults of our legal system.

Second, law-related education is different from conventional social studies education. For example, although many civics and government courses devote some attention to law and the legal process, the stress is most often on the formal structure and functions of the three branches of government. Law-related education, on the other hand, defines the legal system more broadly, considering the roles of actors such as police, judges, prosecutors, public defenders, probation officers, and youth service workers. While many civics and government programs are relatively abstract, one major objective of law-related education programs is to make the study of law pertinent to students by focusing on issues that can be illustrated using their own experience, such as the conflict between rights and responsibilities and the interplay between society and the individual. Many law-related education programs take the issues of the street and examine them through case studies and role playing. To take another example from the social studies, in traditional history courses students frequently study the U.S. Constitution as a historical document, discussing its inception and surveying a few landmark decisions; law-related education tends to see it as a living document whose content has been and is still being shaped by legal cases raising significant issues that have troubled Americans for generations.

In technique, law-related education has incorporated some recent curricular innovations. For example, its emphasis on the inquiry method links it to a number of new social studies teaching strategies, its emphasis on the actual roles and behavior of people in the legal system links it to the recent attention given to political behavior in political science curricula, and its frequent use of the community (through legal intern-

13

ships and court observations, for instance) links it to recent citizen participation developments in citizenship education.

Law-related education seeks to build skills, improve understanding, and create constructive attitudes. The focus may be on such applied skills as how to read a contract and how to be a wiser consumer, or on such broad skills as analytical thinking, value analysis, the ability to persuade others, and the ability to reach decisions after having identified issues and weighed evidence. In trying to improve understanding, it seeks to provide a perspective on the clash of interests within society and the role of law in structuring society. Law-related education courses often examine such questions as the origins and purposes of law, alternatives to law and conventional legal processes, and limitations of law. In pursuing skill development, improved understanding, and inculcation of constructive attitudes, law-related education aims to prepare students to be knowledgeable, concerned, and active citizens.

Law-related education brings to traditional social studies subject matter new approaches and new insights into American institutions and behavior patterns. The law is replete with real, inescapable moral and social dilemmas in which important values conflict with each other. For example, how does a nation protect an individual's right to privacy or to a fair trial while guaranteeing a vigorous press and the public's right to be informed? How does a nation maintain the quality of its environment while promoting economic progress? How does a nation promote education and employment opportunities for minorities while guaranteeing those opportunities to all citizens? Techniques such as mock trials and real or hypothetical case studies can help students to confront, clarify, question, and challenge these fundamental concerns while at the same time providing them with an understanding of how our legal system operates.[8]

The Questions on Which the Study Was Built

This study was designed to answer three basic questions:

1. How does the high school social studies curriculum deal with law-related topics? We concentrated on the place of law-related education in both the overt and the "hidden" social studies curricula of public secondary schools in five sample states. In the overt curriculum, we sought to discover courses specifically devoted to law, as well as units on law in more broadly defined courses. To assess the implicit or hidden curriculum, we sought to explore the attitudes of teachers and administrators toward

14

law, authority, students as citizens, and many other questions impinging on our study. Such attitudes may be communicated informally and unintentionally to students and significantly shape their notions of citizenship.

2. What factors influence the presence or absence of law-related education? Our intent here was to see how the schools we studied changed (or did not change) as a result of the activities of such possible change agents as social studies teachers, school administrators, the state education department, and outside groups such as bar associations and parents' organizations.

3. What are the relevant state laws and what are their effects on the adoption and incorporation of law-related education? We looked first at laws governing the social studies curriculum and state department of education regulations implementing these laws. A principal means by which the state influences what is to be taught in local school systems, these laws and regulations could directly affect the adoption of curricular innovations such as law-related education.

We also looked at laws and regulations governing curricular materials, with particular attention to laws on adoption of textbooks. Laws specifying which textbooks are acceptable within a given state, or laws providing general guidelines to which materials must conform, may either impede or encourage law-related education and other curricular innovations.

And we looked at a wide assortment of laws and regulations that seek to define schooling, including those governing the length of the school day, places where schooling may take place, and individuals who are qualified to teach. We studied these laws because law-related education may involve learning that is outside the normal pattern of schooling. For example, law-related education may involve students leaving the school building to poll community members on their knowledge of law, working as interns in social service agencies, or visiting courts, correctional institutions, and other locations as part of their course work. Laws that seek to define schooling and regulate when and where it may take place (as well as who may offer it) may significantly affect innovations that stress alternative learning.

Organization of the Report

The report is divided into four parts. Part I consists of this introduction and a chapter describing what teachers told us about law-related education in the social studies curricula of the five states in which we conducted empirical research. Areas covered include the courses in which laws topics were found, methods and materials teachers reported using, and the goals of educators involved in this area.

Part II investigates how law-related education became a part of the social studies curriculum. Chapter 3 examines laws and regulations dealing with social studies and citizenship education. Chapter 4 reports on how teachers and administrators in the sample learn about such mandates and what effect they think the mandates have. Chapter 5 identifies other factors affecting the introduction of law-related education, in particular, the key actors in the innovation process (particularly teachers) and the factors that have influenced them. Chapter 6 focuses on elements of state law that may affect teachers' preparation to instruct about the law (for example, laws governing undergraduate education or in-service education). Chapter 7 explores how curricular materials are selected, considering the effect of state law and the roles of various actors. Chapter 8 deals with the use of the community in law-related education. It seeks to determine the impact of state law defining schooling, such as laws and regulations governing the community's access to the classroom and students' access to off-campus learning.

Part III of the report deals with what is often called the "hidden curriculum," that is, the implicit messages that may be conveyed by schooling. It examines the informal lessons that may be shaped by the attitudes and behaviors of professional teachers and school administrators, particularly implicit lessons about authority, rules and laws, and the rights and duties of citizens (and especially students as citizens). Chapter 9 provides the rationale for the section. Chapter 10 deals with the impact of recent judicial decisions on students' and teachers' rights in the school, focusing on how teachers and administrators view these decisions and what they think their effect has been on the schools. Chapter 11 examines the social studies teacher as a role model of the concerned, active, and informed citizen. Do teachers participate in the political system? What constraints do they feel within the classroom? How do they describe their role as employees? What do they feel are their rights? Chapter 12 focuses on the political life of high school students, as seen by teachers and administrators. How are schools governed? What is the general school treatment of student rights? What are the important issues in student rights controversies? What citizenship values are transmitted by schools?

Part IV contains our conclusions. It examines the central question

16

of the study—how state law influences law-related education—and suggests guidelines for lawmaking concerning the curriculum.

Notes

[1]Kenneth P. Langton and M. Kent Jennings, *Political Socialization and the High School Civics Curriculum,* THE AMERICAN POLITICAL SCIENCE REVIEW, 62 (1968): 852–67.

[2]ROBERT D. HESS AND JUDITH D. TORNEY, THE DEVELOPMENT OF POLITICAL ATTITUDES IN CHILDREN (Chicago: Aldine Publishing Company, 1967), pp. 32–59.

[3]Byron G. Massialas, *American Government: We Are the Greatest!* in BENJAMIN COX AND BYRON G. MASSIALAS, eds., SOCIAL STUDIES IN THE UNITED STATES (New York: Harcourt, Brace and World, Inc., 1967), pp. 167–95.

[4]Frederick R. Smith and John J. Patrick, *Civics: Relating Social Studies to Social Reality,* in COX AND MASSIALAS, SOCIAL STUDIES, pp. 105–27.

[5]James P. Shaver, *Reflective Thinking, Values, and Social Studies Textbooks,* SCHOOL REVIEW, 73 (Autumn 1965): 226–57.

[6]R. E. Cleary, *Are We Encouraging Political Cynicism in Our Schools?* PHI DELTA KAPPAN, 51 (June 1970), 450–553; R. D. Hess, *Political Socialization in the School,* HARVARD EDUCATION REVIEW, 38 (Summer 1968): 528–36.

[7]This survey was conducted during the 1976–77 school year; it was the basis of the third edition of YEFC's DIRECTORY OF LAW-RELATED EDUCATIONAL PROJECTS (Chicago: ABA Special Committee on Youth Education for Citizenship, 1978).

[8]For more detailed discussions of the rationale for law-related education, *see* YEFC's REFLECTIONS ON LAW-RELATED EDUCATION (Chicago: ABA Special Committee on Youth Education for Citizenship, 1973) and pp. 1–6 of YEFC's LAW-RELATED EDUCATION IN AMERICA (St. Paul, Minn: West Publishing Co., 1975). References to other rationales can be found on pages 62–63 of TEACHING TEACHERS ABOUT LAW: A GUIDE TO LAW-RELATED TEACHER EDUCATION PROGRAMS (Chicago: ABA Special Committee on Youth Education for Citizenship, 1976).

CHAPTER 2

The Nature and Scope of
Law-Related Education

This study found that law-related education is a vital and growing part of the high school social studies curriculum. This chapter provides a brief introduction to our findings about the place of law-related education in the social studies curriculum; its topics, methods, and materials; and the goals of teachers offering law-related education. We analyze these findings in later chapters; our purpose here is more descriptive than analytical. We want to provide the reader with a summary view of law-related education in the schools we studied.

Many proponents believe that law-related education could enrich other portions of the curriculum such as English, in a course on literature and the law, for instance, and the sciences, in a course such as environment and the law. However, we did not have the funds to examine the full high school curriculum. As indicated in Chapter 1, social studies, with its citizenship education focus, is a logical location for law-related education. We centered our study there, and our findings and discussion are restricted to law-related education in the social studies.

Some concern with the law has always been a part of the traditional social studies curriculum, in that civics courses and American history surveys have necessarily dealt with the Constitution or lawmaking or important Supreme Court decisions. However, in the past these courses generally did not systematically examine the law, the legal process, or the legal system. Studying the law was an adjunct, a means of illustrating certain political or historical developments. That seems to be no longer

18

the case. Our data suggest that in the last 10 years separate courses in law have come to be offered in many American high schools, and law topics have been added to many traditional courses, permitting students to closely scrutinize a wide range of law-related topics.

Courses Devoted to Law

The social studies curriculum has the potential for including a virtually unlimited number of law-related concerns in a variety of contexts and structures. In our research we sought to identify the specific law-related topics taught in particular social studies courses. We were especially interested in learning about courses specifically devoted to law as opposed to broader courses dealing in part with law.[1] We anticipated that the effort to pinpoint these courses would increase our understanding of how law-related education is introduced into the curriculum, what law topics are being taught, and what resources have been committed to law-related education.

In the sample of high schools in five states, 66 social studies teachers (30.8% of our sample) reported teaching 71 courses devoted to law. These reports indicated that courses devoted to law existed in 48 (63%) of the 78 schools our interviewers visited.[2] Quite frankly, this finding surprised us. While we knew that law-related education had grown dramatically in the 1970s, we did not expect to find that nearly two-thirds of the schools in our sample offered at least one course in law.

Remember, however, that this finding does not necessarily mean that courses devoted to law are as widespread elsewhere. One of the criteria for choosing these five states was the fact that each had at least one major law-related education project. So, while it is interesting to conjecture about the national implications of this finding, more informed generalizations will have to await future study.

Based on what teachers told us, the names of the courses devoted to law varied considerably. Eighteen of the reported courses were simply called "Law." Nineteen courses included the words "law," "justice," or "rights" in their titles (for example, "You and the Law," "Youth and the Law," "Youth and Justice," and "Law in American Society"). Twelve identified specific areas of law by key words in the title: "police" (2), "criminal" (3), "consumer" (5), and "business" (2). Although courses dealing with consumer and business law often dealt with non-legal issues, respondents indicated a strong legal focus. Twenty-two courses that teachers said were actually law courses had more traditional titles: "Civics" (4), "American Government" (9), and "The Constitution" (9).

19

When we analyzed the interview schedules, we assumed that the courses called "Law" and the courses that had key words such as "law" and "justice" in their titles were in fact law courses. However, we attempted to verify the law-related nature of the courses that had words such as "police" and "criminal" in the titles and courses that had more traditional titles. We carefully examined the interview schedules of these teachers, especially the lists of topics provided by the teachers of these courses, and the lists of materials they said they used. This examination convinced us that a number of these courses were not sufficiently law-related to be considered courses devoted to law, and so we dropped them from this group. We are reasonably confident that those that remain—these 71 courses—are in fact courses devoted to law.

Law-Related Education in General Courses

In addition to those teaching separate law courses, many teachers told the interviewers that they included law topics in their other, more general social studies courses. Given that most social studies courses must touch upon law topics, even in passing, this finding is not surprising. Indeed, only 3 of the 208 teachers who were interviewed said that they did not deal at all with law topics.

Teachers reported about three times more of these general courses with law topics than distinct law courses (244 to 71). Teachers said they had included law topics in a number of general courses, although, as Table 1 indicates, mainly in history and government courses.

What Topics Are Taught?

Our findings do not allow us to estimate how much time was being devoted to particular law topics in various social studies courses. We cannot answer such questions as, What approximate amount of time is spent on judicial review in American government courses? What percentage of the time in American history courses is devoted to the Constitution? What percentage of the time in courses devoted to law is given over to due process? One problem is that courses vary so much that they cannot be compared. For example, length of term and number of students vary greatly, and even a standard course such as "American History" can differ radically from school to school. More important, even when we were dealing with a particular course in a particular school, teachers were generally unable to distinguish time spent on law from time spent on other topics. Many told us that law studies pervaded their history and government courses, making it impossible to separate the legal aspects of a topic (say the causes of the Civil War) from its

TABLE 1
GENERAL COURSES REPORTED TO INCLUDE TOPICS
OR UNITS ON LAW

Course Title	Number of Courses
American government, civics, political science, state and local government, and miscellaneous government-related courses	80
American history	77
Problems, current affairs	18
Economics	15
Sociology	10
Social studies	8
American culture	7
World history, culture, politics	7
Other	22
Total number of courses	244

social, economic, and political aspects. When teachers were able to give a time estimate, it appeared to our interviewers that these were more a function of their concept of law studies (narrow or broad) and less a function of the actual time spent. In addition, many teachers told us that the time spent could vary from class to class, depending on students' interest, and from term to term, depending on current events such as elections, Watergate scandals, and various *causes célèbres*.

All the interviewers did, then, was ask teachers which law-related topics they included in their courses. To determine these topics, teachers completed a checklist of possible topics covered in their most law-related course. Since the information did not include the amount of time spent on each topic, there is no way of knowing which topics received the most attention. Teachers might well have indicated that they covered a topic if they spent half a class period on it. Furthermore, the financial constraints of the study made it impossible for us to verify the teachers' accounts by observing class sessions or examining syllabuses. The interviewers did note, however, that the teachers were very conscientious in filling out the checklist: they thought about the topics, had second thoughts, and asked for clarifications. Of course, teachers may have wanted to appear competent in this area and so exaggerated the number of topics they dealt with, but we believe that they were trying to be accurate, and consistencies in the data which we will discuss later suggest that this list of topics is reliable.

Table 2, comparing the incidence of specific topics in courses devoted

TABLE 2
LAW TOPICS REPORTED IN COURSES DEVOTED TO LAW AND IN GENERAL COURSES INCLUDING LAW TOPICS*

Topics	Percentage of Courses Devoted to Law (N = 66)**	Percentage of General Courses Including Law Topics*** (N = 139)**	Percentage Difference
The U.S. Constitution	88%	87%	1%
Environmental law	32	27	5
Basic legal concepts and terms (such as due process, felony equity, judicial review, double jeopardy, habeas corpus)	97	91	6
U.S. Constitution as a cornerstone of the legal system rather than of the political system	68	62	6
The state constitution	55	49	6
Organizational structure of the federal court system	85	78	7
Organizational structure of the state court system	68	61	7
Labor law	32	40	8
Local ordinances	65	56	9
Consumer law	59	50	9
Landmark constitutional cases	91	81	10
Drug law	61	51	10
Property law	47	37	10
State laws	77	65	12
Constitutional law and interpretation	83	67	16
Judicial process (courtroom actors, procedures, and behavior)	85	68	17
Defense rights and procedures	92	70	22

22

Police procedures	80	58	22
Case studies in state or local law	50	27	23
Landlord/tenant law	46	23	23
Criminal law	89	64	25
Careers in law and law enforcement	52	27	25
Juvenile law	89	63	26
Prosecution procedures	85	58	27
Correction practices and procedures	68	38	30
Tort law	52	17	35

*This table shows responses to a question on what topics teachers had dealt with in their single most law-related course. Thus, only one course per teacher is covered. We have no way of determining how much attention each of these topics received. It is possible that some were covered in passing.

**"N," which shows the total number of entities on which the percentage is based, is in this table based on each teacher's most law-related course. The 66 courses in column one are specifically devoted to law; the 139 in column two are more general courses which include some law topics.

***32% of the courses were American history and 33% were government.

to law and in general courses, provides us with a great deal of information about how the teachers in the sample perceived law-related education within the social studies curriculum. First, teachers of both law-specific and general courses said they included many law-related topics. Second, teachers of law courses and teachers of general courses said they included many of the same topics. There is no more than 10 percentage points difference for half the topics. According to the teachers, courses devoted to law and general courses dealt equally with such topics as national, state, and local law, the U.S. Constitution, basic legal concepts, and the federal court system.

Teachers of the two types of courses differed somewhat in indicating whether they dealt with such topics as legal procedure, such as prosecution procedures, and specific areas of law, such as torts. Teachers of courses devoted to law were more likely to say that they dealt with these topics, probably because they were more interested in law and focused on more legalistic issues. Perhaps they also sought to make law relevant to students by showing how it could affect them and other citizens.

Nevertheless, despite these differences, most teachers of general courses also said that they dealt with such topics as defense rights, criminal law, juvenile law, and police and prosecution procedures. Therefore, it seems to us that although teachers of the two types of courses differed somewhat in their orientation and subject matter, the similarities are striking.

Once again, however, we must caution that this table is based on the teachers' own perceptions, and that teachers could list topics no matter how little time they spent on them. Since some topics may have been covered for 10 minutes, and some for 10 weeks, it would be unwise to base extensive interpretations on these data.

Methods

As Table 3 shows, differences in the methods teachers reported they used tend to parallel the differences found in the topics. Just as teachers of courses devoted to law reported somewhat greater emphasis on examining substantive law and legal procedures, so they reported greater use of field observation, mock trials, outside speakers, studies of actual legal cases, and simulations. These techniques are frequently recommended in materials and curricula distributed by law-related projects.

However, despite these important differences, the teachers of both law-specific and general courses were very likely to report employing familiar methods such as research papers, and about half the teachers

TABLE 3
SPECIFIC METHODS TEACHERS REPORTED USING BY TYPE OF COURSE

Methods	Teachers of Courses Devoted to Law* (N = 66)**	Teachers of General Courses Including Law Topics* (N = 139)**	Percentage Difference
	50%	45%	5%
Examination of school government and disciplinary procedures to advance understanding of law and legal procedures	12	1	11
Internships in the legal-political community	70	56	14
Research papers	68	51	17
Games, simulations, or role plays	79	57	22
Speakers, panel discussions	79	57	22
Studies of legal cases	79	57	22
Mock trials	64	40	24
Field observation of legal practices and procedures	59	30	29

*Teacher often named more than one method, so the columns add up to more than 100%.
**"N" in this table is the number of teachers. Throughout the tables, "N" will mean the number of cases of whatever subject is indicated in the heading.

25

of both groups reported examining school disciplinary procedures as a means of casting light on law-related questions. Very few teachers in either group reported attempting to place students in internships or work-study programs in the justice system.

Materials

Tables 4 and 5 provide more information about the differences teachers reported between courses devoted to law and general courses which included law topics. Courses devoted to law were less often reported to rely on textbooks. The newness of the field and the limited number of formal texts probably explains why most teachers strung together a set of what would usually be called supplementary materials: films, paperbacks, and a variety of teacher-prepared materials.

Teachers of courses that included law topics used more texts, probably because these courses are broader and require materials with a broad focus. Most of these courses, as we noted earlier, were American history and government courses, and there are more texts available in these areas. However, only about 20 percent of the teachers of these courses relied exclusively on the text; most supplemented the text with a wide variety of other materials.

The content and form of specialized law-related materials vary greatly. Teachers reported using paperbacks designed for the popular

TABLE 4
MATERIALS REPORTED USED IN TEACHING ABOUT LAW

MATERIALS	TEACHERS OF COURSES DEVOTED TO LAW* (N = 72)	TEACHERS OF GENERAL COURSES INCLUDING LAW TOPICS* (N = 138)
Text exclusively	13%	21%
Text and supplementary published materials	39	36
Text and miscellaneous published materials, newspapers	13	25
Audiovisual materials	42	34
Teacher-prepared materials	25	10
Paperback books	22	11
Pamphlets	15	14

*Teachers often named more than one material, so columns add up to more than 100%.

26

market (Ramsey Clark's *Crime in America,* Vincent Bugliosi's *Helter Skelter),* paperbacks specifically designed for schools (John Paul Hanna's *Teenager and the Law,* Law in American Society's *Justice in Urban American* series), and Xerox Education Publication's *Public Issues* series, and special editions of magazines *(Senior Scholastic).* Many teachers reported using materials that are developed and distributed by law-related projects. In addition to the Law in American Society materials noted above, these include materials published by Project Benchmark of the Conference of California Judges and by the Constitutional Rights Foundation *(Bill of Rights in Action).* Some teachers reported using materials developed by local bar associations and justice agencies. State and local departments of education have also supplied teachers with law-related materials and resource guides, such as Pennsylvania's *Student Bill of Rights and Responsibilities,* Philadelphia's *Law-Related Education: A Teacher Resource Guide,* and Texas's *You and the Law.* No standard material or resource seems to have emerged, perhaps because interest in law studies is recent, perhaps because the field includes so many varied topics.

Teachers also said they used pamphlets, news articles, legal briefs and statutes, and excerpts from books which they reproduced on their mimeo and xerox machines. Some have been aided by commercial materials and materials put out by law-related projects, but others have acted almost entirely on their own. The interviewers reported that many

TABLE 5
TEACHERS' RANKING OF TYPES OF MATERIAL USED, BY TYPE OF COURSE

MOST IMPORTANT MATERIALS	TEACHERS OF COURSES DEVOTED TO LAW (N = 72)	TEACHERS OF GENERAL COURSES INCLUDING LAW TOPICS (N = 138)
Texts	42%	56%
Paperbacks, pamphlets, or supplementary published materials	31	18
Miscellaneous published materials, newspapers	11	11
Teacher-prepared materials	10	7
Audiovisual	4	4
Other	2	4
Total	100%	100%

teachers were not aware of the resources available or of specialized curriculum catalogs such as YEFC's *Biblography of Law-Related Curriculum Materials: Annotated* (second edition), *Media: An Annotated Catalogue of Law-Related Audio-Visual Materials,* and *Gaming: An Annotated Catalogue of Law-Related Games and Simulations.*

Teachers also reported using a wide variety of AV materials, which they learned of from distributors' catalogues, from other teachers, and from the lists of audiovisual materials put out by public libraries and school libraries. In some states, teachers reported finding good resources in the film libraries of the regional offices of the state department of education. Among the filmstrips teachers used were *You and the Law* and *This Honorable Court: The Supreme Court of the U.S.* (Guidance Associates), *Search and Seizure* (Xerox Education Publications), *The Teenager and the Police: Conflict and Paradox* (Coronet Instructional Media), and *The Justice Game* (Shloat). Films included *The Witches of Salem* (Learning Corporation of America), the films in the *Living Bill of Rights* series (Encyclopaedia Britannica), and *On Trial, Criminal Justice* (Westinghouse Learning Corp.). Games included *Law in American Society* (Law in American Society Foundation) and *Police Patrol* (Simile II). Some teachers in Texas reported using audio tapes that the state department of education distributes for the *You and the Law* program, and teachers in other states used such audio resources as the record *Law, You, the Police and Justice* (Scholastic) and a three-part series of tapes on Supreme Court cases (Educational Audio-Visual).

How Law Has Become Part of the Curriculum[3]

Our research findings suggest that most of the separate courses in law have been added to the curriculum in the 1970s (see Table 6). Seventy-nine percent of the courses devoted to law have originated since 1970; in contrast, only about a third of the general courses that included law topics have incorporated the law components since 1970. The creation of new law courses has resulted partly from a surge of interest in law topics and partly, our data suggest, from the greater number of specialized courses now offered by school systems.

As Table 6 suggests, the most active period for creating new courses devoted to law was the school year 1973–74. Perhaps that increase was caused by the tremendous interest in Watergate. More law topics were added to general courses in school years 1973–74 and 1974–75 than in other years in the 1970s, and this too may have resulted from interest stirred by Watergate.

28

TABLE 6
SCHOOL YEAR TEACHERS RECALL FIRST OFFERING
LAW COURSES OR FIRST ADDING LAW TOPICS
TO GENERAL COURSES

SCHOOL YEAR LAW FIRST OFFERED OR ADDED	TEACHERS OF COURSES DEVOTED TO LAW (N = 66)	TEACHERS OF GENERAL COURSES INCLUDING LAW TOPICS (N = 139)
1975-76	12%	4%
1974-75	9	7
1973-74	18	9
1972-73	14	4
1971-72	8	5
1970-71	12	4
Prior to 1970	14	58
Don't know	13	9
Total	100%	100%

Our research suggests that the creation of separate courses in law was facilitated by the new calendars many school systems adopted. We found that schools that had mini- or quarter-courses (that is, courses running from 9 to 12 weeks) were more than twice as likely to have courses devoted to law than schools that had terms running for a semester or a year. This happened because the introduction of mini-courses is often accomplished by breaking up traditional courses into discrete units and emphasizing subjects of interest to students and faculty. Thus many new law courses came into existence when broad history and government courses were divided into several mini-courses on particular topics.

Additional mini-courses often go in entirely new directions, and teachers in several schools described to us creative search processes to identify academically acceptable and popular subjects for mini-courses. These searches often revealed that students (and teachers) were interested in a wide variety of law topics. For example, when a western Illinois high school changed to a quarter system, teachers were asked to propose course titles, which were submitted to a student referendum. One respondent proposed a course called "Practical Law." He told us, "I put it down as a possibility. The students selected it as popular. So I went looking for materials and resources."

We have not found a perfect cause and effect correlation between a

29

mini-course structure and the presence of courses devoted to law. The structure only facilitates this type of innovation; it does not insure it. For example, findings for the schools we visited in Texas and Georgia suggest that a mini-course structure does not automatically lead to new content. State departments in both states have encouraged schools to reorganize their school terms into quarters. Yet these states are also the ones where we found the smallest proportion of separate law courses. We think this is because in other places with a mini- or quarter-course system the interest both in the new calendar and in new courses was generated within the school, and the two were closely linked in the minds of the innovators. By contrast, in Texas and Georgia impetus for the new calender came from above and tended to be separate from curricular innovation. As a result, in Texas and Georgia implementation of the quarter system appears to consist mainly of dividing year-long traditional courses into three parts. This yields shorter traditional courses rather than the specialized subject matter courses that we found in quarter systems in the three other states studied.

What Teachers Hope to Achieve Through Law-Related Education

As Table 7 shows, the goals reported by teachers of law courses differ somewhat from those of teachers who included law topics within a broader course. The teachers of courses devoted to law were more interested in skill development and, especially, in examining the issue of

TABLE 7
GOALS REPORTED MOTIVATING TEACHERS, BY TYPE OF COURSE

GOALS	TEACHERS OF COURSES DEVOTED TO LAW* (N = 71)	TEACHERS OF GENERAL COURSES INCLUDING LAW TOPICS* (N = 136)
Convey information about law	50%	51%
Convey information about government	6	18
Convey general information	5	9
Teach rights and/or responsibilities	53	34
Teach law-related skills	42	33
Teach general, political skills	8	6
Other	15	27

*Percentges are based on three responses and add up to more than 100%.

30

rights and responsibilities. As one might anticipate, the goals of the teachers in broader courses were less focused on law. Teachers in this group were more likely to say that their goals were teaching government or conveying general information about the law.

Teachers of both kinds of courses reported pursuing a variety of educational and intellectual goals. When asked what they hoped to achieve by teaching about law, 65 percent of teachers gave the interviewer two or more goals, and about half of this group gave three or more goals.

A few direct quotations from the interviews may convey a sense of the diverse goals. A teacher from western Pennsylvania offering a course called "Citizen Rights Under Law" said he hoped to teach his students

> more respect for the law; a working understanding of their rights—in school, as citizens, in a courtroom; awareness of occupations in the law field; to reason deductively through case studies; and to teach them that law has responsibilities also—it's a two-way street.

A teacher in a small Texas county said he tried to give students "a better understanding of law, the U.S. Government, their American heritage, and their rights as citizens." A teacher in California's wine country reported that his aim in teaching law was

> [t]o allow students to function more successfully in coping with the stresses of modern life: to examine areas of controversy where change may be warranted; to make students more effective participants in the political system; [to help] them deal more competently with personal and legal responsibilities.

Some teachers emphasized practical contact skills in describing their goals. A police officer teaching a course in one of the schools we visited said:

> My goals are multifold: to give a better understanding of the police role in society and the law kids have to abide by; to change the attitude of kids toward police; and to tell them the dangers of crime and narcotics. Ultimately, my goal is crime prevention.

A teacher from a middle-sized Texas city said he tried to give students a better understanding of the legal system, and added: "I don't preach, but tell students the penalties and law of drug abuse." A social studies department head in south Georgia said she hoped "to make better citizens, so at least they understand the law and legal procedures—a great many have scrapes with the law." And a Philadelphia teacher mentioned

31

that he hoped to "give students a stronger idea of their civil and criminal rights."

Some teachers stressed coping skills; others stressed giving students a handle on how to change things. A teacher from a middle-sized Texas city said he tried "to give students an understanding of why some things have happened, why things are the way they are, and how to change things they don't like."

Just as the goals were varied, so teachers of both kinds of courses reported trying to reach a very wide variety of students. Eighty-five percent of the teachers our interviewers talked to said that aside from grade level they had no type of student in mind when developing their law studies. Nine percent said that the courses or units were aimed at brighter students. The other 6 percent was composed of teachers who tried to reach students bored by the regular curriculum, kids in trouble, or some other specific group.

In the high schools our interviewers visited, juniors and seniors constituted the major clientele of law-related education. More than a third of both specialized and general courses were aimed specifically at juniors. Most of these courses, however, were open to students from other grades.

Conclusion

We are aware that our data do not answer many questions about how law-related education is being carried out today. Financial constraints forced us to rely solely on what teachers themselves told us, and, as we indicated, we were unable to pin down how much time was devoted to particular topics or to examine closely the methods and materials employed. The limitations of our research are especially evident in considering the general courses that included law topics, since we could not distinguish courses in which a law component was more or less *pro forma* from the courses in which the law component was a significant portion of the course of study.

However, we can draw some tentative conclusions. Nearly a third of the teachers of general courses reported having added law topics in this decade, and almost two-thirds of the schools visited had a separate course in law (most schools had added them in this decade), suggesting that law studies have received emphasis in recent years. Moreover, our data on the separate courses in law suggest that teachers of such courses have somewhat different goals, methods, topics, and materials from those who teach about law in a general history or government course. In particular, they place greater emphasis on teaching about legal procedures and rights and responsibilities, on imparting skills, and on examining the roles of actors in the legal system. It strikes us that this is entirely consistent with the experiential methods they employ. Finally, it appears that new course calendars and especially the opportunity to develop mini-courses enhance the teachers' opportunity to introduce law-related education.

Notes

[1] We relied on our teacher respondents to make the distinction but, as we suggest in the text, their responses indicated that they understood the differences between the two types of courses. For purposes of this discussion, "courses devoted to law," "separate courses in law," "law courses," and "distinct law courses" refer to the first group of courses; "general courses including law topics" refers to the second group.

[2] The proportion of teachers in our sample offering courses devoted to law varied by state: California (36%), Georgia (30%), Illinois (30%), Pennsylvania (42%), and Texas (16%).

[3] Chapter 5 of this report analyses extensively the processes and actors involved in introducing law topics into the curriculum. In this chapter, we give only a brief glance at this area.

Part II

CHAPTER 3
State Curriculum Mandates and Law-Related Education

The state's primary responsibility under each state constitution for establishing and maintaining a public school system includes a broad prerogative to specify what shall be taught in the schools. As a corollary to its power to require schooling each state has authority over educational policy, including selection of courses of study.[1] State legislatures have traditionally adopted statutes that specify what should be taught in the public schools. State education departments have traditionally taken the statutes and used them as a basis for developing rules and regulations governing the curriculum. Together, the statutes and regulations constitute the state's curriculum mandates.

We studied curriculum mandates to determine their effect on law-related education. Do the mandates encourage law-related education, do they impede it, or do they seem to have little or no effect either way? What kinds of curriculum mandates seem to have the most effect? What appears to account for their effectiveness? What is the role of the state department of education in interpreting mandates and transmitting them to local school districts?

We will try to answer these and other questions in the next two chapters. In this chapter we deal with the statutes in the 50 states and the regulations in a number of states.[2] In the next chapter, we will closely scrutinize the laws and regulations in our five sample states and report on how selected educators in those states understand these laws, how they became aware of them, and what they think their effect has been.

Mandated Subjects

Although they take many forms, there are statutes in every state designed to assure that all students acquire a basic familiarity with the legal-political framework of our governmental system. This is hardly surprising, since one of the original purposes of public education in America was to prepare citizens for democratic citizenship. This concern manifests itself in a variety of courses and approaches to citizenship education, but law-related education could very appropriately be a part of each of these courses or approaches. For example, history, government, and civics courses could quite appropriately include a systematic examination of important aspects of law, legal processes, and the legal system.

Since the federal constitution and state constitutions constitute the cornerstone of our legal-political system, it is not surprising that, as of our legal research conducted in 1974–75, statutes in 45 states prescribe study of constitutions. Of those, 41 prescribe study of state and federal constitutions, and 4 others of the U.S. Constitution only. (See Table 8 at the end of the chapter.[3])

Table 8 also shows that the study of history is another common approach to teaching the values of the nation and the importance of citizenship. As of 1974–75, statutes in 43 states prescribe courses in history—33 the history of the state and nation, the 10 others only the history of the United States.

A third common approach is to require courses in civics and the system of government. Table 8 shows that as of 1974–75, the laws of 38 states prescribe such courses, which generally focus on the state and federal levels. Of these, four limit the requirement to American government, while several others, including Georgia, Maryland, Michigan, and Mississippi, require additional study in community civics or local government. In Minnesota, the law specifies that "social problems" must be studied. We presume such a course might explore the role of government and law in meeting these problems. Although no statutes specify curriculum in civics or government in Alaska, North Carolina, and Kentucky, by statute the state education departments are authorized to (and do in fact) require these subjects in all public schools throughout the state.

In addition to these general requirements that provide opportunities for law-related studies, statutes and legislative resolutions of a few states explicitly require law-related education. In California, a statute (8571:1974) calls for "instruction in our American legal system, the operation of the juvenile and adult criminal justice systems and the rights and duties of citizens in the criminal and civil law and the State and Federal Constitutions." In Texas, a legislative resolution (HCR 46:1967) calls for a citizenship course "stressing the importance of law, the rights and responsibilities of citizens under it, and the possible long and short term consequences of violating it. . . ."[4] In Iowa, the state code, amended in 1975 (257.25[6][b] [Cum. Supp. 1978]) calls for inclusion of "family law."

Statutes in several states require particular attention to documents such as the *Federalist Papers* and the Declaration of Independence.[5] These too provide an obvious opportunity to explore many law-related topics.

The scope of the statutes—the range of courses or topics they prescribe—is only part of the story. To understand how the statutes might affect teaching and learning, we also need to know how specific they are. Do they explicitly detail courses of study or do they provide only general guidelines?

Our research revealed that only a few states specify in any detail what is to be taught. Texas statutes are quite explicit about several aspects of the social studies curriculum. Iowa law provides another example of specified content for the high school curriculum, indicating that required history courses must "reflect the achievement of women, minorities, and any others who, in the past, may have been ignored or overlooked." Iowa law also specifies that government courses must include instruction in voting statutes and procedures, voter registration requirements, and several other topics dealing with voting (257.25 [6] [b] [Cum. Supp. 1978]). The laws in six states seek to exercise supervision by requiring the state education agency to outline courses for study and by requiring written examinations that enforce adherence to the curriculum prescription.[6]

More often, however, state legislatures provide only the barest directives in the statutes, seldom going beyond listing broad subject areas. The legislatures have usually left the content and emphasis of instruction to professional educators in state departments and local districts.[7] None of the mandates precludes additional course offerings at local discretion. (See Tables 8–10 at the end of the chapter.)

37

For example, in New Mexico a statute, amended in 1969, simply instructs the state board of education to prescribe a course of instruction in the history of New Mexico (77–11–1 [Supp. 1975]). In North Carolina a statute instructs the state superintendent to include in a course of study for each grade outlines and suggestions for teaching the subject of "Americanism (115–37)." In Ohio, instead of instructing the state education department to pursue specifics, a statute calls on local boards of education to prescribe courses of study in a variety of subject areas including "geography, the history of the United States and Ohio, and national, state and local government in the United States" (3313:60 [B]). Just as legislatures usually are not specific about the content of mandated courses, they usually do not specify such details as grade level, time allotment, and teaching methods. A New York statute illustrates how much is left to the discretion of the Regents (the state department of education). The statute gives the Regents authority to prescribe courses, subjects to be included in courses, periods of study, grade levels, and attendance requirements of "courses of instruction in patriotism and citizenship (801.1)." In many other states, these details are unstated and tacitly left to the state department of education or to local discretion.

Statutes tend to distinguish between elementary and secondary grades. As Table 8 shows, although history is usually mandated for both elementary and secondary schools, only about half the states require a course on the Constitution at the elementary level and only 13 require a government course. Legislatures apparently hesitate in supporting instruction in the legal-political process earlier than the seventh grade, although they usually permit local discretion. The Illinois law, for example, while mandating the study of the Constitution above the seventh grade, specifically states, "This section does not prevent the study of such subjects in any of the lower grades..." (27–4). A couple of provisions include the self-evident stipulation that study be adapted to the age of the pupils.[8]

On the rare occasions when the laws provide details on instruction[9] it is sometimes difficult to see their utility. For example, a Florida statute would have the school's teaching staff "teach efficiently and faithfully, using the books and materials required, following the prescribed courses of study, and employing approved methods of instruction..." (231.09). This appears to communicate little other than the hope that teachers teach well. The provision continues with instructions

38

to school officials to "see that such subjects are efficiently taught by means of pictures, charts, oral instruction, lectures and other approved methods and required reports . . . to show the work which is being covered and the results being accomplished. . . ." There are specifics here, but we wonder if the statute really says more than that school officials are responsible for supervising instruction.

Values and Attitudes in the Mandates

Subject area requirements are but one part of statutes governing the curriculum. Legislatures often indicate which values and attitudes they wish to foster, particularly in statutes dealing with the social studies curriculum.

Thirty-eight states have statutes requiring the inculcation of specific values and attitudes. (See Table 9 at the end of the chapter.) Of these 38 states, at least 12 charge teachers with responsibility for building the moral character of their students. Statutes dating back several generations tend to stress, in rather quaint language, such characteristics as piety, truth, benevolence, sobriety, frugality, and similar virtues. For example, a California statute calls on teachers to teach their students to avoid "idleness, profanity, and falsehood, and to instruct them in manners and morals. . ." (8553). Similarly a Maine statute calls on educators to "impress on the minds" of their students: "the principles of morality and justice and a sacred regard for truth; love of country, humanity and a universal benevolence; sobriety, industry and frugality; chastity, moderation and temperance" (20:1221).[10]

Statutes in a number of states also endorse "civic virtues." The Maine statute quoted above goes on to link moral characteristics with their tendency "to preserve and perfect a republican constitution, secure the blessings of liberty and to promote students' future happiness." At least 12 states seek to instill "patriotism," "loyalty," "love of country" or "devotion to American institutions and ideals." Indiana, South Carolina, and Vermont statutes speak of "good" citizenship or behavior.[11]

The codes tend to stress the duties, responsibilities, and obligations of citizenship much more often than they enumerate the rights of citizens. When "law" is mentioned, it is normally preceded by "obedience to" and commingled with "respect for" the flag, the Constitution, and other fundamental values or symbols of our states and nation.[12] The New York statute previously quoted is a good example of how citizenship statutes generally identify good citizenship with respect and obedience.

Several specific provisions seek to have the student's value orientation and world view formed through what is taught about certain political doctrines. Seven states mandate teaching about communism in language that suggests its "evil nature," "destructive effects," or "threat to our system." The Florida statute prescribes teaching "Americanism vs. Communism," details the expected approach and teaching materials, and then specifies that the primary purpose is to instill in students' minds "greater appreciation of democratic processes, freedom under law, and the will to preserve that freedom" (233.064). Nebraska requires a course in "the benefits . . . of our form of government and the dangers and fallacies of fascism and communism. . ." (79–213 [5] [b]). Still other provisions take a more positive approach and require teaching the "benefits of the free enterprise system"[13] and the "development of our economic system and the role of the entrepreneur" (California, 8571).

Statutes concerning forbidden subjects are supplemented by prohibitions against indoctrination in the classroom. In New Hampshire teachers may not advocate "communism as a political doctrine or any other doctrine which includes the overthrow by force of the government of the United States or of this state. . ." (191.1). California does not prevent teaching the facts of communism, but only teaching "with intent to indoctrinate any pupil with, or inculcate a preference in the mind of any pupil for, communism" (9031).[14]

An Ohio statute is interesting for its suggestions of priorities and sequence of course study. With a "first things first" authority it states:

> Basic instruction in geography, United States history, the government of the United States, the government of the state of Ohio, local government in Ohio, the Declaration of Independence, the United States Constitution and the Constitution of the state of Ohio shall be required before pupils may participate in courses involving the study of social problems, economics, foreign affairs, United Nations, world government, socialism and communism. (3313.60)

The most common statutory proscriptions bar sectarian, denominational, and partisan teachings and influences. These provisions are generally aimed at preventing teachers from advocating particular religions or political parties. While some may view these provisions as deterrents to dealing with controversial issues in the schools, generally the intent has been to proscribe advocacy by teachers. The proscription

40

of advocacy is, of course, a tenet of the professional ethics of social studies teachers.

Many laws deal with commemorative ceremonies. Generally, these ceremonies seek to inculcate patriotic attitudes. Beyond the daily pledge of allegiance to the flag provided in many states codes,[15] there are numerous provisions for patriotic exercises. All students in Minnesota schools are required by law to engage in patriotic exercises for one half-hour each week, including "the singing of patriotic songs, readings from American history and from the biographies of American states-men and patriots" (126.08). Nebraska's elementary students must devote one hour per week to such exercises, and all Nebraska schools must offer appropriate commemorative programs on Lincoln's birth-day, Washington's birthday, Flag Day, Memorial Day, and Armistice Day, or the day preceding or following such holidays (79–213 [3], 79–213 [6]).

Because they are isolated events, not integrally related to regular courses of study, these required exercises have not been included in Table 9. They may, however, be an important part of students' learning. Commemorative ceremonies may, according to Hess and Torney, "establish an emotional orientation toward country and flag even though an understanding of the meaning of the words and actions has not been developed. These seem to be indoctrinating acts that cue and reinforce feelings of loyalty and patriotism."[16] These required ceremonies also tell us a great deal about the basic citizenship goals of legislators.

Skills Specified in the Statues

Although one might expect a major goal of social studies education to be the development of an individual's ability to perform effectively in society, this objective is rarely specifically addressed in state curriculum laws. Perhaps legislators believe that they lack competence in the area and are willing to leave these considerations to professional educators. However, the recent concern of legislators and educators for "output" measures has led to increased emphasis on skills in both statutes and state department of education regulations, including encouragement of such skill-related learning as consumer, career, and law-related edu-cation.[17]

Voting skills have traditionally been the citizenship skills specified in the statutes. Illinois and Iowa require instruction in voting methods.[18] Pennsylvania law seeks to instill in youth the obligation to vote (24:16–

1605).[19] Indiana mandates five full recitation periods of class discussion on voting, the party system, and "responsibilities of citizenship participation" within two weeks immediately preceding any general, congressional, or state election (20–10–12–1).

Some states have identified additional citizenship skills. For example, a regulation of the Hawaii Department of Education calls for instruction in which "stress shall be placed on learning how to make judgments based on facts."[20] Three other states put decision-making skills into the context of public participation. For example, the student should "become an effective and responsible contributor to the decision-making processes of political and other institutions of the community, state, country and the world" (New Jersey); should have "proficiency in operating in a democratic situation in a manner appropriate to age and ability" (Colorado); and should develop "skill for participating in the processes of public and private political organizations and for influencing decisions made by such organizations" (Texas). Only rarely do these goal statements explicitly mention participation in the affairs of the school itself. Rhode Island encourages civic education "by continuous actual participation throughout the entire educational experience," West Virginia desires each student to be "an active participant in the student government of his school," and Tennessee wants each child to learn "his legal rights and responsibilities as a student and as a citizen."[21] A recent goal statement of the Michigan Department of Education brings it all together:

> Michigan education must assure the development of mature and responsible citizens, with the full sense of social awareness and moral and ethical values needed in a heterogeneous society. It must encourage critical but constructive thinking and responsible involvement, with consideration for the rights of all, in the resolution of the problems of our society. It must create within the school system an atmosphere of social justice, responsibility, and equality which will enable students to carry a positive and constructive attitude about human differences and similarities into their working or community relationships in later life.[22]

However, we must stress again that these statutes and regulations are unusual. By and large, mandates have not suggested that students be taught petitioning, public speaking, debating, bargaining, or decision making. The focus of citizenship education is still more on conveying certain information and on fostering certain attitudes than on giving

42

students such skills as perceiving and defining problems and making appropriate decisions.

Enforcing the Mandates

Another concern of this study was the means by which states might enforce laws and regulations governing the curriculum. Of course, the presence of potential sanctions does not indicate whether they are used or the degree to which they influence local school practices. In fact, our interviewers' reports of conversations with state department of education officials in the five sample states suggest that state officials are generally reluctant to impose sanctions on local districts. In the first place, state officials say that the need seldom arises. Second, state departments are not set up for active supervision of the local curriculum. Third, state law, tradition, and extensive court decisions generally uphold wide areas of discretion for local districts, especially discretion to act above and beyond state curriculum pronouncements. Finally, many state laws and court decisions uphold the rights of local districts to undertake a wide variety of curricular innovations.[23] We decided to discuss these enforcement mechanisms, however, because they are on the books, and, since they could at some point be brought into play, our discussion of curriculum mandates would not be complete without considering them.

The principle that underlies these various enforcement provisions is that local districts are subordinate agencies of the state in matters of education. They are expected to conform to curriculum mandates and state directives regarding materials and approach.[24] Even an alleged lack of sufficient funds is not good reason for a local board to fail to offer a statutorily required program.[25] Moreover, even the extensive local discretion to supplement state-wide minimum requirements must be exercised in conformity with state regulations or guidelines.[26]

In most of the states there are sanctions for not complying with mandates. (See Table 10 at the end of the chapter.) A number of the enforcement provisions are directed to local school districts or to educators employed by these districts. In some states, the education agency has authority to visit, inspect, and examine local school districts (for example New York Education Law Article 5 section 215 [McKinney 1969]), but more often enforcement is anticipated through extensive reporting requirements. In California, for example, teachers must report under oath that they have complied with all rules and regulations pertaining to

43

courses of study and approved textbooks before their final paycheck of the year can be approved by the superintendent (13529). High school principals must make a similar report, with failure to do so punishable by fine (13567). County superintendents must inspect each school district under their jurisdiction and assure the state superintendent of compliance with curriculum mandates (802).

In these and other states failure of teachers and principals to perform all prescribed duties can lead to withholding of pay, fine, dismissal from position, and even revocation of credentials. In Texas a teacher can be fined up to $500 for not teaching "patriotism" for 10 minutes each day, and up to $200 for not teaching Texas history (416). In Arkansas any teacher or other school official violating the curriculum requirements can be liable for a fine up to $500 or subject to imprisonment in the county jail for a term between 30 days and 6 months, in addition to discharge or removal from the position (80–1616). Teachers and principals in Indiana who do not include the federal and state constitutions in their civics instruction are subject to fine and license revocation (20–10–11–1). Michigan school officials not only must offer required subjects but must, at the risk of misdemeanor penalities, assure that every student recommended for graduation has complied with all course requirements (388.373).

Many states have provisions that directly penalize noncomplying districts by permitting the state education agency or the commissioner to withhold state funds or revoke accreditation for failure to offer required courses. For example, New York gives the commissioner of education power to withhold funds from local districts that do not conform to the "patriotism and citizenship" requirement:

> The commissioner may, in his discretion, cause all or a portion of the public school money to be apportioned to a district or city to be withheld for failure of the school authorities of such district or city to provide instruction in such courses and to compel attendance upon such instruction, as herein prescribed, and for a non-compliance with the rules of the regents adopted as herein provided. (801.3 ([McKinney])

In addition to the sanctions directed toward the faculty and administration, there are others, such as promotion and graduation requirements, more directly aimed at students. Very few states have promotion requirements, and those are generally found in regulations rather than in statutes. They range from quantifiable criteria, such as a minimum

44

number of days of school attendance, to more subjective kinds of standards, such as whether the child has "progressed within the limits of his ability." At the lower grade levels the rules look to general performance rather than to achievement in any particular subject.[27]

On the other hand, high school graduation requirements often do include specific law-related course requirements. All but nine states have laws precluding from graduation any student who has not taken required courses in such areas as the state or federal constitution, history, or civics. Compliance with these provisions generally requires the counting of academic units rather than an attempt to measure students' level of understanding acquired in these subjects. Only eight states require students to pass an examination before they can graduate. (In South Carolina a student must not only pass a test on the United States Constitution but also satisfy the examiner of his loyalty thereto [43–259].) Six other states waive the required course of study for students who can pass an equivalent examination. New Jersey gives credit for study carried out in the armed forces, and Michigan exempts from the civics requirement those students who have enlisted or have been inducted into military service (388.371). This suggests the close link in legislators' minds between civil education and patriotism.

There are, then, a wide variety of potential sanctions that the state might impose against local school districts or individual educators. We stress again, however, that we have no evidence on the extent to which these sanctions are brought into play, if ever.

Specific Authorization for Innovation

A number of statutory and regulatory provisions explicitly recognize that the intent of state law is not to stifle local innovation. One approach is to stipulate that rules and standards that might otherwise constrain imagination and initiative should be administered with sufficient flexibility. For instance, the New York regulations provide:

Nothing herein contained, however, shall prevent a board of education from making such curriculum adaptations as are necessary to meet local needs and conducting such experimentation as may be approved by the commissioner. This principle of flexibility shall apply to every area of curriculum. The exercise of initiative and responsibility on the part of local school authorities in the administration of the curriculum is encouraged.[28]

State laws are replete with exemptions from state accreditation requirements when necessary to facilitate nontraditional programs.[29] These include waiver of required teaching materials, permission to offer courses beyond the areas for which teachers are certified, the use of paraprofessionals or teacher aides, and demonstration programs for experimentation in the organization and methods of instruction.[30] Similarly, standards set by the six private regional accrediting associations, on which state departments often rely in examining secondary schools, do not ostensibly inhibit innovation.[31] Their guidelines frequently contain statements indicating that they seek to assure minimum quality, not to impose uniformity or to discourage experimentation.[32]

State laws often include provisions for research and evaluation of new concepts and programs. New Jersey has established centers for educational research and demonstration, which are to test and evalute "unproven educational ideas, equipment, methods and approaches, and newly developed curriculum materials" to ascertain their value to local districts (18 A–6–72 [West Cum. Supp. 1978]).[33] In Ohio the results of assessment can lead to experimental courses' becoming a permanent part of the curriculum. In Pennsylvania, assessment can lead to discretionary termination of a program.[34] A provision in Louisiana couples evaluation with a yearly renewal of innovative programs (17–31–1 [(1969]).[35] Illinois has created a Department of Urban Education to implement experiments in school governance, in areas such as staffing, curriculum, and accountability (ch. 122:10–23.9, 2–3.37 [1967]). Such a provision might potentially prove a useful vehicle for increasing student and community participation in school operations or for designing courses focusing on the school as a model of justice. A Florida rule that authorizes and funds experimental programs requires local districts to furnish data, in the approval application, on the use of school and community facilities.[36]

Summary

Our analysis of state social studies mandates suggests that they facilitate and encourage law-related education. Every state in the United States requires teaching in at least one of the major citizenship areas (the constitutions, history, government, or civics). Some mandates call for teaching such fundamental documents as the Bill of Rights and the Declaration of Independence, providing yet more opportunities for law-

46

related education. And, of course, several states have specifically mandated the study of law.

By and large, educators should not feel constrained by the requirements contained in the statutes, since for the most part they merely specify a subject or a course title and indicate that it be taught for a certain period of time (and sometimes at a certain grade level). The language of the reporting and inspection provisions of these laws suggests that the state is not expected to actually supervise actual content of classroom instruction but rather to use the sanctions of fine, imprisonment, or removal from office only when the required course is not offered at all. Local districts have a wide flexibility in implementing mandates and could very appropriately include a number of law-related topics in courses.

Furthermore, although many of the laws do suggest goals (knowledge, values, attitudes) that are to be furthered through the requirements, these are often very general and would rarely constitute serious constraints on local districts. In addition, these goals often suggest concerns to which law-related courses could legitimately address themselves.

Finally, there is a tradition of local flexibility in implementing state requirements explicit in some statutes and endorsed in judicial decisions. Thus, local districts are free to infuse in existing courses a wide variety of law-related topics and materials.

Notes

[1] *See* Tyll van Geel, *Authority to Control the School Curriculum: An Appraisal of Rights in Conflict,* 1975 (Report of a project conducted under Grant #NE-G-00-3-0069, awarded by the National Institute of Education). This report was largely incorporated in van Geel's AUTHORITY TO CONTROL THE SCHOOL PROGRAM (Lexington, Mass.: Lexington Books, 1976).

[2] Although we have sought to locate all mandates that might affect law-related education, we have found that most relevant ones deal with the social studies curriculum. We were able to examine the statutes of every state, but we were not able to examine the department of education regulations in all the states. As a result, most of the discussion in this chapter concerns the statutes.

[3] In Table 8 we have omitted the statutory citations. In the text of this chapter, we have not footnoted information that is found in Table 8 except when the law provides more information than is included in Table 8 or

when we quote from a particular code section; in these cases we provide a parenthetical reference in the text or a footnote with the section number. Where pertinent, we have added the date of amendment.

[4]California and Texas are two of our five sample states. We discuss their statutes and regulations extensively in the next chapter. Tables 11, 14, 17, 20, and 23 indicate the titles, relevant section numbers, and sources of the statutes and regulations in the five sample states.

[5]*E.g.*, LA. REV. STAT. ANN. § 17–268 (West 1963) and MINN. STAT. ANN. 126.06 requiring study of the Declaration of Independence and other documents such as the *Federalist Papers*.

[6]*E.g.*, IND. CODE ANN. §§ 20–10–14–1, 20–10–14–3 (Burns 1973), NEB. REV. STAT. § 79–213 (1974); OR. REV. STAT. § 337.260 (1971); ARIZ. REV. STAT. § 15–1022 (1975); UTAH CODE ANN. § 53–14–11 (1974); CONN. GEN. STAT. ANN. § 10–8 (West 1977), which directs the state board to make sample teaching materials available on request of the local board. (All above statutes relate to mandated courses on the state and federal constitutions.) The Virginia statute is a good example:

> In preparing the course of study in civics and history in both the elementary and high school grades, the State Board shall give careful directions for, and shall require, the teaching of the Declaration of American Independence, the Virginia Statute of Religious Freedom, and the Virginia Bill of Rights which subjects shall be carefully read and studied, thoroughly explained and taught by teachers to all pupils in accordance with the State course of study, which course of study shall require written examinations as to each of the last three mentioned great documents of Virginia's history at the end of the term in which the course is given. An outline shall likewise be given of the Constitution of the United States and the general principles of the Constitution shall be carefully explained.

(VA. CODE § 22–234 [1973])

See also NEW YORK STATE EDUCATION DEPARTMENT, MINIMUM REQUIREMENTS FOR SCHOOLS IN NEW YORK STATE, 1973, pp. 8–9.

[7]In the words of Tyll van Geel "curriculum law is basically a body of law concerned with the allocation of authority and secondarily a body of substantive principles spelling out what the content of the curriculum should be." *Authority to Control the School Curriculum*, p. 5.

[8]*E.g.*, PA. STAT. ANN. tit. 24 § 15–1512 (Purdon 1962).

[9]"If there is one area of the school curriculum that seems to have been left entirely in the hands of the local district, it is the choice over methods of instruction. . ." (van Geel, *Authority to Control the School Curriculum*, p. 11).

[10]*See also* MASS. GEN. LAWS ANN. ch. 71 § 30 (1978); N.D. CENT. CODE 15–38–10 (1960); and KY. REV. STAT. § 158.190 (1971) prohibiting books of "infidel or immoral character."

[11]IND. CODE ANN § 20–10–9–1 (Burns 1973); S.C. CODE § 59–29–10; VT. STAT. ANN. tit. 16, 906 (1968).

[12]IND. CODE ANN. § 20–10–14–1 (Burns 1973); FLA. STAT. ANN. § 233–065 (West 1977); MISS. CODE ANN. § 37–13–5 (1973); NEB. REV. STAT. § 79–214 (1974); OR. REV. STAT. § 336.067 (1971); UTAH CODE ANN. § 53–14–10 (1974).

[13]ARIZ. REV. STAT. § 15–1025 (1975); LA. REV. STAT. ANN. § 17–274 (West Cum. Supp. 1978); N.C. GEN. STAT. § 115–37 (1978); TEX. EDUC. CODE ANN. tit. 2 § 21–1031 (Vernon Cum. Supp. 1978).

[14]See also VT. STAT. ANN. tit. 16 § 4(b) and CAL. EDUC. CODE §§ 8454, 9759 prohibiting "propaganda injurious to the welfare of the public."

[15]E.g., N.Y. EDUC. LAW § 802 (1) (McKinney 1969).

[16]ROBERT D. HESS AND JUDITH V. TORNEY, THE DEVELOPMENT OF POLITICAL ATTITUDES IN CHILDREN, pp. 106–108.

[17]Tyll van Geel observes:

> There is evidence to indicate that states are moving toward a radically different approach to the control of the curriculum; namely, states are attempting to regulate not what goes into the school program but what comes out, that is, achievement in certain basic subjects. . . . Over half the states have now adopted legislation designed to pursue education accountability. AUTHORITY TO CONTROL THE SCHOOL PROGRAM, (Lexington, Mass.: D.C. Health & Co., 1976) page 85.

The movement toward educational accountability, van Geel goes on to note, has often resulted in statewide testing, and raises the strong possibility of greater state influence over the curriculm. This is one of the trends which has led him to conclude that "increasingly the establishment of curriculum policy is being undertaken at the legislative level through the adoption of laws which constrain the discretion of other participants in the policy-making process" (*Authority to Control the School Curriculum*, p. 5). So far, however, such statewide tests are generally advisory and the movement toward education accountability has yet to be widely felt in statutes regarding social studies (it would appear to be much more widespread in state department of education regulations).

[18]See ILL. ANN. STAT. ch. 122 § 27–3 (Smith-Hurd 1962).

[19]See also ME. REV. STAT. tit. 20 § 102(7) (1965).

[20]See, e.g., HAWAII DEPARTMENT OF EDUCATION, POLICIES AND REGULATIONS FOR INSTRUCTION (1970), § 2320.1: "Stress shall be placed on learning how to make judgments based on facts."

[21]These goal statements are collected (without comment or analysis) in COOPERATIVE ACCOUNTABILITY PROJECT, EDUCATION IN FOCUS: A COLLECTION OF STATE GOALS FOR ELEMENTARY AND SECONDARY EDUCATION, Alan Zimmerman, ed., Denver, Colorado (1952). The quotations cited here are in Goal Area: *Citizenship and Political Understanding*, pp. 14–17.

[22]MICHIGAN DEPARTMENT OF EDUCATION, THE COMMON GOALS OF MICHIGAN EDUCATION, Lansing, Sept. 1971, Goal 2: CITIZENSHIP AND SOCIAL RESPONSIBILITY, p. 4. *See also* HAWAII DEPARTMENT OF EDUCATION, POLICIES AND REGULATIONS: "Democracy demands a citizen who has positive attitudes toward learning and inquiring, who communicates effectively, and who is guided in making his choices from critically determined and commonly shared values."

[23]According to van Geel, "the state agencies have not attempted to exercise their authority to mandate minimum educational requirements. States have confined the vigorous exercise of these powers to driver education and physical education. . . . It can be concluded that state agencies tend to have more formal authority than they generally exercise with regard to the content of the school program" (van Geel, *Authority to Control the School Curriculum*, p. 19).

[24]*See, e.g.,* Ehret v. Sch. Dist. Kulomont 5 A.2d 188, 333 Pa. 518 (1939); Ring v. City of Woburn 311 Mass. 679, 43 N.E.2d 8 (1942).

[25]In Board of Education of Aberdeen-Huntington Local School District v. State Bd. of Ed., 116 Ohio App. 515, 189 N.E. 2d 81, 85 (1962), the court surmised that the district's failure to meet academic standards resulted from lack of funds, but affirmed the charter revocation because "both the reins of power and the purse strings are in the grasp of the Legislature." The Court added the following admonition: "This same Legislature should remember that when standards are raised the purse strings must be loosened proportionately as nonincome producing real estate (homes) and low-income producing real estate (farms) are now being taxed beyond the owners' ability to pay. The Legislature has now reached the point of no return. It soon must face a moment of truth on this score and realize that an increase in the state's contribution to local school districts is long overdue." *See, also,* Bd. Sch. Cmsrs v. State 129 Ind. 14, 28 N.E. 61 (1891).

[26]Gearhart v. Kentucky State Bd. of Educ. 355 S.W.2d 667 (Kentucky, 1962); Wagner v. Royal-Westland Publishing Co. 78 Pac. 1096, 36 Washington 399 (1904).

[27]LAWYERS' COMMITTEE FOR CIVIL RIGHTS UNDER LAW, A STUDY OF STATE LEGAL STANDARDS FOR THE PROVISION OF PUBLIC EDUCATION (Wash., D.C.: Lawyers' Committee for Civil Rights Under Law, 1974) pp. 50–51; *but see* ILL. ANN. STAT. ch. 122 § 27–21 (Smith-Hurd 1962) requiring evidence of comprehensive knowledge of U.S. history to graduate from eighth grade.

[28]NEW YORK REGENTS REGULATIONS, § 100.2 (b); *see also,* NEW HAMPSHIRE STATE DEPARTMENT OF EDUCATION STANDARDS.

[29]PENNSYLVANIA STATE DEPARTMENT OF EDUCATION, REGULATIONS, § 5.4a (waiver of "any and all requirements"); COLO. REV. STAT. § 22–21–102

et seq. (1974); ALABAMA STATE DEPARTMENT OF EDUCATION, ACCREDITA-
TION STANDARDS FOR HIGH SCHOOLS, 1966; PRINCIPLES AND STANDARDS FOR
PUBLIC SECONDARY EDUCATION IN MARYLAND, 1964; HAWAII DEPARTMENT
OF EDUCATION, POLICIES AND REGULATIONS, §§ 2430, 2430.1.

[30]INDIANA ADMINISTRATION HANDBOOK, 52 ch. 1 G 12, 52 ch. 364–12
waives the limitation of courses to certification area as well as rules for
teaching materials. See Chapter 8 later for more discussion on flexibility in
teacher selection; see Chapter 1 for analysis of laws designed to improve
teachers' instructional abilities in specific areas.

[31]Robert Armstrong, *Do NCA Accreditation Standards Inhibit Innovation?*
NCA QUARTERLY 47 (1972) 255–58.

[32]Aside from general statements encouraging innovations, there are specific
provisions permitting noncertified personnel "in courses of an interdisciplinary or specialized nature" (*Standards for Accreditation of Junior High
Schools,* Northwest Assn., 1974) or promoting use of the community in educational programs (*North Central Association Standards* [1974] p. 16, Southern Association, *Standards, Policies and Procedures of the Commission on
Secondary Schools* (1974)).

[33]*See also* COLO. REV. STAT. § 22–21–104 (1973); N.M. STAT. ANN. §
77–11–18 (1972).

[34]*Minimum Standards for Ohio Schools,* 1968 Ed 6–403–01K, Ed 6–405–
01 (K); Pennsylvania State Department of Education, *Accreditation Requirements,* sec. 4.

[35]LOUISIANA HANDBOOK FOR SCHOOL ADMINISTRATORS (August 1973),
p. 78.

[36]FLORIDA EDUCATION DEPARTMENT, REGULATIONS (1971), § 9.611.

TABLE 8
LAW-RELATED SUBJECTS MANDATED BY STATUTE IN EACH STATE

STATE	U.S. AND STATE CONSTITUTION*	U.S. AND STATE HISTORY**	CIVIC, GOVERNMENTAL SYSTEM***
ALABAMA	U.S. Constitution only at elementary level, both at secondary level	Both at elementary level	Both at secondary level
ALASKA	No specific statute but State Board of Education authorized to prescribe courses		
ARIZONA	Both at elementary and secondary levels	Both at elementary and secondary levels	Both at secondary level
ARKANSAS	—	U.S. history only at elementary level; State history only at secondary level	Both at secondary level
CALIFORNIA	Both, 6-12	Both at elementary level	Both 6-12, also legal system
COLORADO	Both, 7-12	U.S. history only at elementary level, both at secondary level	Both at secondary level
CONNECTICUT	—	U.S. history only at elementary level, both at secondary level	Both at secondary level
DELAWARE	Both, 8-12	—	—
FLORIDA	U.S. Constitution only at elementary level, both at secondary level	Both at elementary and secondary levels	Both at secondary level
GEORGIA	Both at elementary and secondary levels	Both at elementary and secondary levels	Both at secondary level

State			
HAWAII	Both at elementary and secondary levels	—	—
IDAHO	U.S. Constitution only at elementary level, both at secondary level	Both at elementary and secondary levels	—
ILLINOIS	Both at elementary and secondary levels	U.S. history, also history of Negro race	Both at secondary level, and principles of representative government and method of voting
INDIANA	Both, 6-12	Both at elementary and secondary levels	—
IOWA	Both, 8-12	Both at secondary level	Both at secondary level
KANSAS	Both at secondary level	Both at elementary and secondary levels	—
KENTUCKY	Both at elementary and secondary levels	Both and American traditions at elementary and secondary levels	—
LOUISIANA	Both, 8-12	U.S. history (*Federalist Papers* and Declaration of Independence) specified at elementary level only	—
MAINE	Both at elementary and secondary levels—included in Foundations of American Freedom	Both at elementary level, U.S. history only at secondary level	Both at elementary and secondary levels
MARYLAND	—	Both at elementary level, U.S. history only at secondary level	Community civics

53

TABLE 8 (Continued)

STATE	U.S. AND STATE CONSTITUTION*	U.S. AND STATE HISTORY**	CIVIC, GOVERNMENTAL SYSTEM***
MASSACHU-SETTS	Both at elementary and secondary levels	Both at elementary and secondary level, also local history	Both at elementary and secondary levels
MICHIGAN	Both, 8-12	Both at elementary and secondary levels	Both at secondary level, also local government
MINNESOTA	Both, 8-12	Both at elementary level, U.S. history only at secondary level	Social problems at secondary level
MISSISSIPPI	Both at secondary level	Both at elementary and secondary levels	Both at elementary and secondary levels, also local government
MISSOURI	Both, 7-12	Both, 7-12	U.S. government system at secondary level only
MONTANA	——	Both at elementary and secondary levels	U.S. government system at secondary level only
NEBRASKA	Both at elementary and secondary levels	Both at elementary level, U.S. history only at secondary level	U.S. government system at secondary level only
NEVADA	Both at elementary and secondary levels	Both at elementary and secondary levels	Both at elementary and secondary levels
NEW HAMPSHIRE	Both, 8-12	U.S. history at secondary level only	——
NEW JERSEY	Both, 7-12	Both at elementary and secondary levels	Both at elementary level
NEW MEXICO	State Board of Education prescribes grades	Both and Declaration of Independence at elementary and secondary levels	State Board of Education prescribes grades

54

State			
NEW YORK	Both at elementary and secondary levels	Both at elementary and secondary levels	—
NORTH CAROLINA	State Board of Education authority to prescribe course.		
NORTH DAKOTA	Both, 7-12	Both at elementary level, U.S. history at secondary level only	Both at secondary level
OHIO	Both at elementary and secondary levels	Both at elementary and secondary levels	Both at elementary and secondary levels, also local government
OKLAHOMA	—	Both at elementary and secondary levels	Both at elementary and secondary levels
OREGON	Both at elementary grade 8, U.S. Constitution only at secondary level	—	—
PENNSYLVANIA	Both, 7-12	Both at elementary and secondary levels	Both at elementary and secondary levels
RHODE ISLAND	Both at secondary level	Both, 4-12	Both at elementary and secondary levels
SOUTH CAROLINA	Both at elementary and secondary levels	Both at elementary and secondary levels	—
SOUTH DAKOTA	Both, 8-12	—	—
TENNESSEE	Both at secondary level	Both at elementary and secondary levels, also Negro history	U.S. government system at secondary level only

TABLE 8 (Continued)

STATE	U.S. AND STATE CONSTITUTION*	U.S. AND STATE HISTORY**	CIVIC, GOVERNMENTAL SYSTEM***
TEXAS	Both at elementary level, U.S. Constitution only at secondary level	—	—
VERMONT	Both at elementary and secondary levels	Both at elementary level	Both at elementary and secondary levels
VIRGINIA	Both at elementary and secondary levels	Both at elementary and secondary levels	Both at secondary level
WASHINGTON	Both at elementary and secondary levels	Both at elementary and secondary levels	Both at secondary level
WEST VIRGINIA	Both at elementary and secondary levels	Both at elementary and secondary levels	Both at elementary and secondary levels
WISCONSIN	Both at secondary level	Both at elementary and secondary levels	—
WYOMING	Both at elementary and secondary levels	—	—

NOTE: This table includes only statewide mandates. Nothing precludes additional course offerings at local discretion.

*Explicit requirements to teach about constitutions.
**Explicit requirement to teach history; includes mandates on use of specific historical documents (e.g., Declaration of Independence, *Federalist Papers*).
***Explicit requirement to teach civics, government system and process; includes also California provision on legal system.

TABLE 9
VALUE SYSTEMS TO BE TAUGHT OR AVOIDED, AS MANDATED BY STATUTE IN EACH STATE

STATE	INDIVIDUAL RIGHTS, RESPONSIBILITIES, ATTITUDES; MORAL AND CITIZENSHIP EDUCATION*	SPECIFIC DOCTRINE**
ALABAMA	——	Evils of communism
ALASKA	No specific statute but State Board of Education authorized to prescribe courses	
ARIZONA	——	Free enterprise, no racism
ARKANSAS	——	——
CALIFORNIA	Morality, K-6; legal rights and duties, 7-12	Problems of communism: no racism or sexism
COLORADO	——	——
CONNECTICUT	Duties, responsibilities and rights of citizenship, at elementary and secondary level	No racism
DELAWARE	——	——
FLORIDA	Morality	Americanism vs. communism
GEORGIA	Devotion to American institutions and ideals	——
HAWAII	——	——
IDAHO	Citizenship at secondary level only	No sectarianism
ILLINOIS	Morality at elementary and secondary level, patriotism	No racism
INDIANA	Morality, obedience to law at elementary and secondary level; good behavior at elementary level only	No racism
IOWA	Citizenship	——
KANSAS	Patriotism and duties of citizens	No sectarianism
KENTUCKY	Morality, rights and duties in this democracy at elementary and secondary levels	——
LOUISIANA	——	Evils of socialism and communism, benefits of free enterprise system

57

TABLE 9 (Continued)

STATE	INDIVIDUAL RIGHTS, RESPONSIBILITIES, ATTITUDES; MORAL AND CITIZENSHIP EDUCATION*	SPECIFIC DOCTRINE**
MAINE	Morality, privileges and responsibilities of citizenship, and importance of voting	——
MARYLAND	——	——
MASSACHU-SETTS	Morality, justice, and Bill of Rights	——
MICHIGAN	Morality, justice, rights and responsibilities of citizens	No racism
MINNESOTA	Citizenship at elementary and secondary levels	——
MISSISSIPPI	Duties and obligations of citizenship, patriotism, respect for and obedience to law	Americanism, nature and threat of communism; no doctrinal, sectarian denominational doctrine
MISSOURI	——	——
MONTANA	Duties of citizenship	Benefits of U.S. form of government, dangers and fallacies of nazism, communism
NEBRASKA	Morality, obedience to law and citizenship	——
NEVADA	Duties, citizenship, love of country and loyalty	No sectarian, denominational doctrine
NEW HAMPSHIRE	——	No subversive doctrine
NEW JERSEY	Voting privilege	——
NEW MEXICO	——	——
NEW YORK	Patriotism, citizenship and Bill of Rights week	Communism: methods and destructive effects
NORTH CAROLINA	——	Americanism and free enterprise system
NORTH DAKOTA	Patriotism	——
OHIO	——	——

58

TABLE 9 (Continued)

STATE	INDIVIDUAL RIGHTS, RESPONSIBILITIES, ATTITUDES; MORAL AND CITIZENSHIP EDUCATION*	SPECIFIC DOCTRINE**
OKLAHOMA	Citizenship and obedience to law	——
OREGON	Morality, respect for Constitution, obedience to law and citizenship	——
PENNSYL-VANIA	Loyalty, solemn duty to exercise voting privilege	——
RHODE ISLAND	Morality	——
SOUTH CAROLINA	Good behavior and loyalty	——
SOUTH DAKOTA	Patriotism	——
TENNESSEE	Skills basic to citizenship in American democracy—privileges and duties	——
TEXAS	Patriotism (10 minutes instruction per day)	Benefits of free enterprise system
UTAH	Morality, obedience to law, habits and qualities of upright and desirable citizenry	——
VERMONT	Patriotism, loyalty, and good citizenship	No propaganda or subversion
VIRGINIA	Bill of Rights	——
WASHINGTON	——	——
WEST VIRGINIA	——	——
WISCONSIN	Citizenship	——
WYOMING	Devotion to American ideals	——

NOTE: This table includes only statewide mandates. Nothing precludes additional course offerings at local discretion.

*Explicit requirements dealing with moral and citizenship education; includes specifically enumerated attitudes and principles; individual rights, duties, responsibilities; loyalty, obedience, respect. The wording is indicated in the table. Also includes "importance of voting" because this pertains to attitude formation and skill development, but note that Illinois "method of voting" is placed in Table 8 (third column) because it is related to understanding of government process.

**Explicit requirements dealing with teaching about political, economic, and social doctrines, such as Americanism, communism, free enterprise; and prohibitions of racism, sectarianism, partisanship, and the like.

59

TABLE 10
COMPLIANCE MEASURES AND SANCTIONS FOR FAILURE
TO COMPLY, AS PROVIDED BY STATUTE IN EACH STATE

STATE	COURSE REQUIREMENTS FOR PROMOTION AND GRADUATION*	SANCTIONS**
ALABAMA	U.S. government and civics	Reports
ALASKA	Prescribed offerings (or equivalent)	Accreditation granted or withheld, State Department of Education investigates, may order school to cease conferring diplomas
ARIZONA	History, constitutions, and free enterprise	——
ARKANSAS	History, civics	Teachers and school officials can be fined, imprisoned, removed; school charters can be revoked
CALIFORNIA	U.S. history, U.S. government (or equivalent)	Reports, inspection, accreditation withheld
COLORADO	——	——
CONNECTICUT	History, government, citizenship (or equivalent)	Reports
DELAWARE	Social studies	——
FLORIDA	U.S. history, U.S. government, Americanism vs. communism	Accreditation withheld
GEORGIA	History, government (test)	——
HAWAII	State Department of Education authorization	——
IDAHO	U.S. history, U.S. government	Accreditation withheld
ILLINOIS	Patriotism, representative government, U.S. history at elementary level only (test)	Reports, reduction in teacher pay
INDIANA	Government, citizenship, and U.S. history	Fine teachers or principals, revoke licenses
IOWA	Government, history	——
KANSAS	U.S. Constitution, government	——
KENTUCKY	Social studies (or equivalent)	Reports, state can withhold funds
LOUISIANA	U.S. history, constitutions, and communism	——

60

TABLE 10 (Continued)

STATE	COURSE REQUIREMENTS FOR PROMOTION AND GRADUATION*	SANCTIONS**
MAINE	U.S. history, U.S. government, and constitutions	——
MARYLAND	U.S. history	——
MASSACHU-SETTS	——	State Board of Education can withhold funds
MICHIGAN	Citizenship, constitutions (waiver for military service)	Misdemeanor to recommend for graduation a student who hasn't complied with course requirements
MINNESOTA	U.S. history, citizenship, and social problems	——
MISSISSIPPI	Communism, history, and constitutions	——
MISSOURI	Constitutions, history, and government	Willful failure of teacher, principal, or superintendent cause for termination
MONTANA	U.S. history and U.S. government	——
NEBRASKA	——	Misdemeanor, fine, imprisonment
NEVADA	Social studies (test) (or equivalent)	State can withhold funds
NEW HAMPSHIRE	U.S. history, social studies	Teachers can be dismissed or fined; accreditation withheld
NEW JERSEY	Constitutions, history, civics (equivalent), credit for instruction in armed forces	Inspection, approval withheld
NEW MEXICO	U.S. history, social studies elective	Reports
NEW YORK	All required courses (test)	Inspection, reports, affidavit, license revoked, no state aid and accreditation withheld
NORTH CAROLINA	Social studies	Report
NORTH DAKOTA	——	Accreditation withheld
OHIO	All required courses	——
OKLAHOMA	History, government	——

TABLE 10 (Continued)

STATE	COURSE REQUIREMENTS FOR PROMOTION AND GRADUATION*	SANCTIONS**
OREGON	Citizenship, social studies	——
PENNSYL-VANIA	Social studies	——
RHODE ISLAND	——	——
SOUTH CAROLINA	U.S. Constitution, history, loyalty (test)	Teachers, principals, and superintendents can be dismissed or removed
SOUTH DAKOTA	——	——
TEXAS	Constitutions, history, government (test)	Any school employee can be fined or removed from office
TENNESSEE	U.S. history	Misdemeanor for principals; teachers can lose license; school accreditation withheld
UTAH	——	——
VERMONT	Constitutions, civics, history (equivalent)	——
VIRGINIA	——	——
WASHINGTON	Civics, history, government, constitutions	——
WEST VIRGINIA	Required courses	School employee can be fined or removed
WISCONSIN	——	——
WYOMING	Constitutions (test)	School employee can be removed

NOTE: This table includes only statewide mandates. Nothing precludes additional course offerings at local discretion.

*With the exception of Ilinois, these are all high school graduation requirements. "Test" indicates that the student must have taken the courses and passed a standardardized examination in lieu of the required course. Michigan and New Jersey waive requirements for those who have served in the military, as noted in text and in table.

**Sanctions include only those found in statutes applying to the mandates. This listing is incomplete because sanctions such as reporting, inspection, and accreditation may be found in other parts of state codes.

CHAPTER 4

How Teachers Perceive Curriculum Mandates

In the previous chapter, we discussed curriculum mandates and made generalizations about their content and possible impact. But that kind of approach can tell us only so much. For example, it may indicate what interpretation is apt to be placed on statutes and regulations, and it can suggest what effect they are likely to have in practice, but it cannot tell us what effect they actually have. Other questions remain. How, if at all, do teachers and administrators find out about curriculum mandates? What is the role of the state department of education in conveying information about the mandates? What do educators think of the mandates, and how much are they influenced by them in planning and carrying out courses and units?

To answer questions of this sort, we conducted a five-state study of curriculum laws and regulations and how they are perceived. (For information on how we selected the states and drew our sample, see Chapter 1 and Appendix 2.) First, our staff looked carefully at the laws, regulations, and state department of education (SDE) documents in each state. Then our interviewers asked teachers a series of questions designed to probe their awareness of the mandates and to determine the extent to which they thought the mandates had influenced teaching and learning.

We discuss each state separately, drawing some general conclusions at the close of the chapter. We first discuss states having rather specific requirements and centralized authority, then move to states with lesser requirements and more relaxed authority.

TEXAS
Mandates

As the first column of Table 11 shows, the Texas legislature has passed many laws dealing with the citizenship component of the curriculum. As a result of four legislative acts passed in 1905, 1917, 1918, and 1929, Texas secondary schools must offer instruction in U.S. history, Texas history (at least two hours a week, and only in history courses), civil government, the federal and state constitutions (a separate course), and "intelligent patriotism" (at least ten minutes a day). (See Table 11 at the end of the chapter; Tables 14, 17, 20, and 23 are also at the end of the chapter.)

Two of Texas's statutes and resolutions do not add anything new to the curriculum but rather indicate how a previously mandated subject is to be implemented. Thus the original (1905) mandate for Texas history was first clarified (in 1917) by a requirement that schools offer at least two hours a week of Texas history in history courses. A 1951 resolution provided further clarification by specifying a half-semester of Texas history to be completed in high school.

Statutes and resolutions passed between 1967 and 1974 *require* law-related education (a 16-hour unit in junior high school), a course in the free enterprise system, and teaching about the "dangers of crime and narcotics"; statutes passed between 1967 and 1975 *permit* electives in consumer education and police and fire protection administration.

The legislative acts of the 1960s and 1970s focus on new curricular areas and, unlike earlier statutes, generally ask the Texas Education Agency (TEA) to develop curricula and teaching materials.

Regulations

The second column of Table 11 shows how the TEA has taken the legislative mandates and transformed them into a series of core courses that schools must offer. Another core course, world history or world geography, has been mandated not by the legislature but rather by the state board of education, an elected body that is "the policy-forming and planning body for the public school system of the state" (2:11.24).

The TEA also has made American history, American government, and world history or world geography requirements for graduation (TEA regulation 31725 1). Of course, schools could make additional TEA-approved social studies courses a requirement for graduation, but they must require the mandated courses.

Data maintained by the TEA show that core courses for grades 7–12 have far greater enrollments than other courses.[1] Presumably requirements that do not entail separate courses, such as the mandate to teach about the danger of crime and narcotics, are met through units in existing courses.

In addition to the core courses, the TEA has approved various social studies electives that the schools may offer. These include Advanced Texas Studies, courses on a variety of ethnic groups, and introductions to such social science disciplines as anthropology and economics. If a school wishes to offer a course whose title does not appear on this list, it must first gain the approval of the TEA.

The TEA does not prepare detailed curriculum guides for all approved courses.[2] Its basic document, *Framework for the Social Studies, Grades K–12,* provides a general overview of the K–12 social studies program and then briefly describes each approved course, including short paragraphs on the purpose of the course, its content, the values it is to further, and appropriate teaching strategies. According to a TEA official,[3] school districts are free to take the general provisions and fashion them into courses of their own.

And the detailed curriculum guides that are available allow plenty of freedom. For example, though the course guide for the free enterprise course is quite lengthy (62 pages of rationales, objectives, outlines, learning activities, and references to materials), it too is intended not to be prescriptive but rather to provide information and suggestions to help local districts set up their own courses.[4] However, as we will see in Chapter 7, Texas's law on curricular materials, which provides state funds only for a small group of approved texts for each course, might limit local districts' freedom in practice.

Enforcement Provisions and Inducements to Comply

The TEA's curriculum documents call attention to many statutes and regulations that inform educators of their responsibilities under the law. For example, the *Framework for the Social Studies, Grades K-12* reprints in full the two resolutions dealing with the social studies curriculum as well as the 1929 law on the constitutions and a section of the 1917 law on Texas history.

A separate document on the rules governing the social studies curriculum in Texas includes excerpts from four regulations and nine statutes. These excerpts convey some, but not all, of the enforcement provisions. For example, the regulation on the Constitution Test is included but not the penalty for supervisors who fail to comply with the provision on Texas history. This document provides a table that correlates each approved course or topic with its statutory authorization.

This document also shows how each course or topic fulfills Texas's standards for accrediting elementary and secondary schools. These standards are quite general. For example, Standard 3 of Principle 6 reads in part:

> Emphasis is placed upon teaching the facts of and developing appreciation for, all phases of the American heritage, nicluding culture, language, and life style diversities.
>
> Teachers plan activities designed to develop understanding and appreciation of American history and traditions. . . .
>
> Pupils participate in meaningful patriotic ceremonies. . . .

By linking courses and standards, the TEA indicates to schools that offering the core courses (and stressing the required content and values) will help them become accredited, thus providing an inducement to comply.

Texas Educators and Mandates

The Texas mandates are very broad, dealing with many subject areas and topics. But at the same time, they are unusually specific, detailing grade levels and the time to be allotted to courses.

The TEA has followed through by creating a framework of core courses that embody the specific requirements of the mandates. The TEA's basic document, the *Framework,* conveys the language of some of the statutes and regulations, and its special document on the regulations dealing with the social studies curriculum contains excerpts from many relevant laws and resolutions. The mandated courses are also linked to state accreditation standards.

All in all, then, the Texas legislature and the TEA seem to have created a comprehensive framework for social studies programs for grades 7–12. On paper, this seems a good example of a system by which curriculum directives made at the top (by the state board of education and legislature) are funneled through the state department of education to local school districts.

Does this hierarchical model work in practice? Do individual educators understand what is required of them and do they carry out the intent of curriculum laws and regulations? On the basis of our limited sample, it seems that the answer is yes and no. As Table 11 shows, more than half of the teachers interviewed knew that American history and American government were mandated courses, but fewer than half were aware that state history and government, world history, and free enterprise were mandated.[5]

Does it matter if teachers know what portions of the curriculum are mandated? Must mandates themselves come to teachers' attention, or is it sufficient if the mandates reach teachers through curriculum guides, standard syllabuses, and textbooks? These questions, because they are fundamental to our discussion of the responses of teachers in Texas and in each of the other states we surveyed, call for extensive discussion here.

It might be argued that teachers in any state need not know the mandates to implement them. After all, teachers receive direction from state education departments and the staff of their local school system and may get additional help from textbooks and teachers' guides. Not only might it not be necessary for individual teachers to have direct knowledge of state statutes and regulations, it is easy to understand why they might not get this information Teacher education courses may not inform prospective teachers about the law, and when teachers begin teaching they are not asked to check the law to see what to include in their courses. Their supervisors provide information on the school's curriculum, and teachers naturally assume that the supervisors are conforming to the law. Teachers would have a hard time finding the laws and regulations, which are scattered throughout the educational code, because they usually do not have access to law books and state department regulations. Finally, school districts may have no procedures for informing teachers about mandates.

On the other hand, our data on how law-related education is introduced into the curriculum (see Chapter 5) suggest that the teacher is a crucial actor in creating and designing new courses. The self-created courses are generally not at all influenced by a curriculum guide, a state-selected textbook, or a district-wide syllabus. In fact, most of the teachers our interviewers talked to, in Texas and in the other states, reported that even when they taught standard courses such as American government or American history, they did not rely on a system-wide syllabus or the state's curriculum guide. They reported considerable flexibility in deciding what to teach and how. They occasionally felt limited by a departmental syllabus—a course of study devised by teachers as a group—but they almost never felt limited by directives from administrators. Even in states with limited selection of textbooks, some teachers said they paid little attention to the standard text for their course, relying instead on paperbacks, films, and other supplementary materials. These findings suggest that mandates may not filter down to teachers and that mandated sujects may not get taught when teachers are unaware of what is mandated. Therefore, it is important to know whether teachers do know about the mandates directly.

Turning to the findings on Texas, we note that there is some evidence that Texas educators do implement the mandates without having direct knowledge of them or without even knowing that there are mandates. For example, 25 percent of Texas teachers told our interviewers that they did not know what was mandated, easily the highest percentage in this category in our five states. That does not mean, however, that the mandates had no effect on these teachers. A number of them, even though they could not give us a list of specifics, said they taught the subjects they were told to teach, or that they taught according to the *Framework*. Many told us they followed the curriculum guide and the textbook. Since local school districts in Texas must choose their textbooks from a small list of four or five state-approved texts for each course, teachers who followed the text would probably teach many of the mandated topics.

In Texas, then, many teachers said they did not know the mandates; however, they may have been implementing many of them merely by following the text or the directives of their superiors.

However, a further look at the data suggests that some mandates may not be getting through to. teachers, even indirectly. For example, Texas teachers tended to respond to our question by listing the required *courses* contained in the TEA's *Framework,* beginning with American history and then naming world culture and American government, but they tended to leave out such mandated *topics* as study of the constitutions, patriotism, and state history and government.

The effectiveness of getting subjects taught by mandating courses rather than just topics is suggested by the fact that the five most frequently named mandates in Texas (American history, American govern-

68

ment, world history or world geography, state history and government, and free enterprise) are mandates associated with specific courses. That is, even though the mandate for a free enterprise course is new (the statute mandating it was passed in 1974), and even though it had not been fully implemented at the time of our interviews with Texas teachers (about midway through the 1975–76 school year), more teachers knew the subject was required than knew that study of the constitutions or promotion of patriotism were required, even though these have been statutorily mandated for decades and have also been the subject of a legislative resolution.

So, to return to the question that began this discussion, does it matter whether teachers know what is mandated? Without further study, we simply cannot answer that question, and we suggest that new research, in Texas and elsewhere, include an examination of curriculum guides, texts, teachers' guides, and course syllabuses, as well as classroom observation, to determine the extent to which mandated topics filter down to teachers and actually become part of the course of study.

Learning About the Mandates

The respondents in Texas and the other states who knew about the mandates were asked how they had become aware of them.[6] Their answers help us understand how mandates are conveyed to teachers. As Table 12 shows, the state department of education in Texas is a somewhat more important source of information on mandates than is the department of education in any other state. This suggests that the hierarchical administrative model, in which information flows from the top down, works better in Texas than in the other states we studied. However, even in Texas more administrators and teachers in our sample learned through "professional experience," drawing on informal sources such as conversations with their colleagues and an understanding of the traditions of the school or the system. Even in a state with as many mandates as Texas, and with as active a state department of education, the diffusion of information is rather hit or miss.

The Effect of the Mandates

Texas administrators and teachers reported that mandates have some effect. Table 13 shows that Texas educators were somewhat more convinced than educators in other states that the mandates have had a beneficial influence. Texas teachers were most likely to say that the mandates helped by telling what was expected. Texas administrators

TABLE 12
HOW RESPONDENTS IN TEXAS LEARNED OF THE MANDATES

SOURCE OF INFORMATION ON MANDATES	TEACHERS IN TEXAS* (N = 35)	TEACHERS IN ALL FIVE STATES* (N = 184)	ADMINISTRATORS IN TEXAS* (N = 22)	ADMINISTRATORS IN ALL FIVE STATES* (N = 105)
School administration	40%	43%	15%	15%
Professional experience	26	28	45	42
State department of education	23	16	35	30
School courses	14	16	0	18
Other	11	12	20	15

*Percentages are based on two responses and add up to more than 100%.

TABLE 13
HOW RESPONDENTS IN TEXAS PERCEIVED
THE EFFECT OF SOCIAL STUDIES MANDATES

Influence of Social Studies Mandates	Teachers in Texas* (N = 37)	Teachers in All Five States* (N = 197)	Administrators in Texas* (N = 20)	Administrators in All Five States* (N = 96)
No Influence				
They have no influence	41%	43%	6%	25%
Some Influence				
Mandates reinforce teaching. The subjects would be taught anyway	13	12	35	10
Mandates help by telling what is expected	23	13	12	13
Mandates tell what is expected but leave a lot of room for additions	15	16	12	24
Considerable Influence				
The subjects are taught *because* they are required	13	17	29	17
Mandates limit teaching by requiring subjects that are not always relevant or important	3	3	0	4
Other	5	5	6	7

*Percentages are based on two responses and add up to more than 100%.

71

were far less likely than administrators in the other sample states to say that mandates have no influence and far more likely to say that subjects are taught because they are required.

Two more pieces of data suggest that Texas teachers want to comply with requirements. One is a small substudy we did of how eighth-grade Texas teachers implemented the 16-hour unit on law mandated by the Texas legislature. We discuss this substudy in some detail in the final chapter, but it is relevant here that every one of the teachers we talked to had taught the unit.

The second piece of data came up in response to a question, asked of teachers in all five states, on how law-related education had first entered the curriculum. Forty-six percent of Texas high school teachers said law entered as a result of state requirements. This was three to nine times the proportions from other states who responded similarly.[7] However, there is no explicit law-related mandate for grades 9–12. Texas mandates for these grades, like mandates from many states, merely call for teaching about constitutions, patriotism, and respect for law. Furthermore, the Texas secondary teachers we talked to were not aware of the resolution explicitly calling for law in the eighth grade, and only 5 percent said that law was mandated. The difference is not in the laws but in the teachers' perceptions. Texas teachers view their teaching as a response to state directives. Generally, they say they teach what they are told to teach.

ILLINOIS
Mandates

As Table 14 shows, the Illinois School Code, like that of Texas, contains many provisions giving form and substance to the social studies curriculum. The mandates include the values and information the legislature hopes schools will impart, specifying also that schools teach the contributions of blacks and of many specified ethnic groups. They enumerate three documents deserving of study—the Declaration of Independence and the constitutions of the United States and Illinois—and call for teaching about such law-related topics as justice, understanding of law, and consumer matters.

Regulations

The Illinois state department's *Program for Evaluation, Supervision and Recognition of Schools* is the basis for evaluating schools.[8] The *Program* suggests a "basic curriculum" designed "to meet the minimum program defined by The School Code of Illinois." As Table 14 shows, the paragraph on social studies and history (6–11.1) contains excerpts from the two major statutes dealing with social studies, conveying some of the exact language but omitting several specifics, including the one-hour minimum a week in all grades to be devoted to patriotic studies, the proper use of the flag, and the method of voting. Only in the area of consumer education has the state department provided much detail.

The Illinois regulations contrast with those of Texas. The TEA gives mandates greater specificity through course requirements; the Illinois Office of Education (IOE) requires only one course (American history and government). Basically, the IOE regulations simply transmit some of the language of the mandates, providing no additional details such as the number of hours, grade level, or amount of time to be devoted to history, the constitutions, or government. And the Illinois *Program* explicitly rejects a uniform curriculum and tries to encourage diversity.[9] Interestingly, the one specific requirement the program transmits—that students must pass the Constitution Test if they are to graduate—is readily picked up by the schools.

Enforcement Provisions and Inducements to Comply

Some provisions are directed at school officials. A statute (27–16) calls on principals or teachers to state in monthly reports whether they have complied with the provisions on moral and humane education, and teachers who knowingly violate the provisions are subpect to fines. However, we have learned that the Illinois Office of Education does not collect these monthly reports.[10]

The Illinois Office of Education has developed a mechanism for determining compliance which we did not find in the other four states. Every three years a visiting team of teachers evaluates the teaching program of each public secondary school. The social studies evaluator uses a checklist that includes the question, "To what extent are the mandated requirements of American history, the federal and state constitutions, and ethnic studies being met?"

The Constitution Test is another means of inducing compliance. The "Constitution Test" or the "Public Law Test" is usually administered during the required course in American history. This test is developed locally by the teacher or the social studies department. In most of the schools we visited students had to pass the Constitution Test to pass the course, but a few schools allowed successful completion of the course in lieu of a Constitution Test.

73

The state department has not developed a uniform test, probably so as not to interfere with its goal of giving local school districts flexibility. Similarly, teachers and administrators told us that the three-year evaluations do not measure schools against a prearranged standard but rather encourage schools to undertake a self-evaluation of how their instructional programs are meeting their own goals and objectives. In short, the system looks compliance-oriented only at first glance. The Illinois Office of Education is more a facilitator than a policeman.

Illinois Educators and the Mandates

As the third column of Table 14 shows, Illinois teachers and administrators are very likely to know of the American history and constitution requirements but are far less likely to be aware of such additional topics as American government, citizenship, and minority studies. These findings show the efficacy of embodying the mandates in required courses and calling on schools to take such specific action as giving the Constitution Test.

It is quite possible that these other topics that are not perceived as mandates are taught anyhow in broader courses. However, only 30 percent of Illinois educators knew that consumer education was mandated, suggesting that the legislative message may not be getting through and affecting the curriculum.

The IOE has made a concerted effort to have schools implement the consumer education mandate, giving schools the option of requiring a separate course or including consumer education in other courses. Schools must "maintain evidence which shows that each student has received adequate instruction in consumer education as required by law." Of course, it is possible that school districts have met this mandate in departments other than social studies. However, it may also be that a considerable number of teachers and administrators simply do not know about this mandate. We again suggest further study to determine the extent to which this and other mandates have reached teachers and administrators and have affected teaching.

Learning About the Mandates

As Table 15 shows, Illinois educators were less likely to learn of the mandates from the state than were educators in the other states of our study, a rather odd finding considering that the state's curriculum documents are assiduous in linking regulations to specific provisions in the law. It may suggest that these curriculum documents are not being

74

widely disseminated, and it may help explain why knowledge about such mandates as consumer education seems slow in spreading.

The Effect of the Mandates

Table 16 shows that Illinois teachers and administrators generally had views on the mandates that were similar to those of educators in the other four states of our study. Illinois educators in our survey, however, were somewhat more likely than their counterparts in other states to credit the mandates with considerable influence, probably because of the Constitution Test.[11]

So in Illinois as in Texas the record is mixed. Mandates that result in the required course or a specific action appear to have an effect; other topics, even including one that has received as much attention as consumer education, may not have penetrated.

GEORGIA

Mandates

As Table 17 shows, a single section of the Georgia Education Code prescribes the core of the social studies curriculum, courses in state and U.S. history and in the state and U.S. constitutions. This section of the code consolidates two sections of an earlier version (1953) which were repealed in 1974. The new section did away with the requirement that students pass an exam in U.S. and Georgia history and constitutions.

The Georgia curriculum statutes, unlike those of Texas or Illinois, contain a narrow range of topics, including no reference to the values that the legislature wishes to foster, no emphasis on the role of minorities in American life, and no reference to such specific subjects as consumer education or free enterprise education. Although they are specific on course subjects, the statutory mandates leave it to the Georgia Department of Education to define the length of the course, the grade level, and the topics.

Regulations

The regulations provide that to graduate, students must take a minimum of three years of social studies in grades 9 through 12. One year is to be devoted to United States history and government (a course designed to meet the requirements), and two years are elective.

The state board's 1972 course outline begins with a reprinting of the relevant sections of the Georgia Code. As Table 17 shows, the foreword

TABLE 15
HOW RESPONDENTS IN ILLINOIS LEARNED OF THE MANDATES

Source of Information on Mandates	Teachers in Illinois* (N = 41)	Teachers in All Five States* (N = 184)	Administrators in Illinois* (N = 22)	Administrators in All Five States* (N = 105)
School administration	46%	43%	17%	15%
Professional experience	22	28	29	42
State department of education	7	16	21	30
School courses	15	16	29	18
Other	17	12	21	15

*Percentages are based on two responses and add up to more than 100%.

TABLE 16
HOW RESPONDENTS IN ILLINOIS PERCEIVED
THE EFFECT OF SOCIAL STUDIES MANDATES

Influence of Social Studies Mandates	Teachers in Illinois* (N = 41)	Teachers in All Five States* (N = 197)	Administrators in Illinois* (N = 21)	Administrators in All Five States* (N = 96)
No Influence				
They have no influence	36%	43%	22%	25%
Some Influence				
Mandates reinforce teaching. The subjects would be taught anyway	18	12	12	10
Mandates help by telling what is expected	8	13	22	13
Mandates tell what is expected but leave a lot of room for additions	15	16	9	24
Considerable Influence				
The subjects are taught *because they are required*	23	17	22	17
Mandates limit teaching by requiring subjects that are not always relevant or important	5	3	9	4
Other	5	5	4	7

*Percentages are based on two responses and add up to more than 100%.

to the curriculum outline suggests such heritage values for the course as pride in state and nation. The eight-page curriculum suggests major topics. It is far less elaborate than the recent Texas guide to the free enterprise course but more detailed than the guidelines adopted earlier for the other Texas courses.

Enforcement Provisions and Inducements to Comply

Enforcement provisions and inducements to comply are written into the law. Schools that do not comply risk losing all or a portion of their funding from the state,[12] and students must pass the required course if they want to graduate.

Georgia Educators and the Mandates

As Table 17 suggests, four out of five interviewed Georgia teachers knew that American history was required, and almost half knew that state history and government were required. Perhaps American government was not widely recognized as a mandate because it is not stressed in the state board of education course outline.

Once again, we must ask whether it matters if educators know what is mandated, since they might well teach mandated topics without realizing that they are teaching courses set up in response to a state requirement. For example, the Georgia Department of Education's suggested outline for the American history and government course devotes considerable attention to the constitutions, so it is possible that these documents are covered by teachers who are unaware that they are mandated. However, we do not know whether the outline has influenced the teaching of the course. Furthermore, Georgia's textbook law permits a wide selection of texts for the course, so it is also possible that these topics might not enter the course through this means. Thus, only further study can determine if, or how, the legislative intent reaches teachers and influences teaching.

Finding Out About the Mandates

As Table 18 shows, Georgia teachers in our sample were more likely to say they learned of the mandates from their local school administrators than were teachers in other states, and Georgia administrators were somewhat more likely to have learned of the mandates from the state department of education than were administrators in other states. These findings suggest that the hierarchical model works well in Georgia. Perhaps this is because the Georgia mandates are the simplest of the five states we studied, perhaps because the suggested course outline reprints the relevant laws. Note, however, that a large minority of the Georgia administrators and teachers appeared to learn by the hit-or-miss method of general experience.

The Effect of the Mandates

As Table 19 shows, Georgia teachers viewed the effect of the mandates as teachers in the other states did. However, Georgia administrators were more likely to say that the mandates had no influence or had a minor influence of helping by telling what was expected. They were less likely to say that the mandates had considerable influence.

Administrators may feel this way because the main Georgia statute is limited and because the Georgia Department of Education has allowed great latitude in the remainder of the social studies curriculum.

PENNSYLVANIA

Mandates

As Table 20 shows, Pennsylvania, like Georgia, details the core of the social studies curriculum in a single section (24:16–1605) of the public school code. However, the provision, unlike the one in Georgia, not only specifies the time to be devoted to the subject (at least four semesters of U.S. and Pennsylvania government and history in grades 7–12) but also suggests a variety of American foundation documents as the basis of instruction. In another contrast, the provision contains explicit references to the values the legislature wishes to promote, essentially "the good, worthwhile and best features" of the American experience. This provision also stresses the importance of patriotic attitudes and voting skills. A second value-laden section (24:7–771) links patriotic lessons to the display of the American flag.

Regulations

As Table 20 shows, the Commonwealth of Pennsylvania Department of Education specifies[13] that schools offer six units (semesters) of social studies during grades 7–12, of which four are in required subjects—two of world cultures and two of American culture—and two in electives (Regulation 7–153). The department provides an extensive rationale for the American culture and world cultures courses, calling them "interdisciplinary studies taken from the social sciences (anthropology, economics, geography, history, philosophy, political science, psychology, and sociology)." The department does not provide outlines for these courses or describe them in any detail, leaving much to the discretion of local districts. A department of education curriculum

79

TABLE 18
HOW RESPONDENTS IN GEORGIA LEARNED OF THE MANDATES

Source of Information on Mandates	Teachers in Georgia* (N = 30)	Teachers in All Five States* (N = 184)	Administrators in Georgia* (N = 19)	Administrators in All Five States* (N = 105)
School administration	63%	43%	20%	15%
Professional experience	30	28	45	42
State department of education	13	16	40	30
School courses	10	16	5	18
Other..............................	3	12	20	15

*Percentages are based on two responses and add up to more than 100%.

TABLE 19
HOW RESPONDENTS IN GEORGIA PERCEIVED
THE EFFECT OF SOCIAL STUDIES MANDATES

INFLUENCE OF SOCIAL STUDIES MANDATES	TEACHERS IN GEORGIA* (N = 34)	TEACHERS IN ALL FIVE STATES* (N = 197)	ADMINISTRATORS IN GEORGIA* (N = 16)	ADMINISTRATORS IN ALL FIVE STATES* (N = 96)
No Influence				
They have no influence	36%	43%	35%	25%
Some Influence				
Mandates reinforce teaching. The subjects would be taught anyway	14	12	0	10
Mandates help by telling what is expected	19	13	29	13
Mandates tell what is expected but leave a lot of room for additions	11	16	18	24
Considerable Influence				
The subjects are taught *because they are required*	19	17	12	17
Mandates limit teaching by requiring subjects that are not always relevant or important	5	3	0	4
Other	5	5	6	7

*Percentages are based on two responses and add up to more than 100%.

document stresses that "these regulations represent minimum requirements by the State. School districts may and are encouraged to require students to take more than the mandated . . . units."[14]

The department apparently intends the American culture course to fulfill the legislative mandate. As Table 20 shows, the department transmits some of the language of the act in its rationale for the social studies program. However, the department's guidelines appear to differ significantly from the statute. Whereas the statute calls for four semesters of U.S. and commonwealth history and government, the department calls for only two semesters of American culture and an additional two of world culture.[15] The new emphasis encompasses values rather different from those described in the statute.

Enforcement Provisions and Inducements to Comply

Besides requiring *schools* to offer six semesters of social studies in grades 7–12, the department requires high school *students* to take two semesters in order to graduate. These may be in world history, American culture, or an elective.

In addition to this compliance required of students, the department has authority to withhold a district's entire share of its state appropriation for a year if the district has not provided "competent teachers to teach the several branches required in this act" (24:10–1005 [Cum. Supp. 1978]), and the programs of all schools, public and private, are subject to evaluation by the superintendent of public instruction. Program approval is necessary if a school is to qualify for state reimbursement and if the diplomas issued by such a school are to "constitute valid preprofessional credentials."[16]

However, the department's curriculum documents downplay the enforcement provisions and put greater emphasis on encouraging districts to create flexible curricula.[17] A striking example can be found in the department's 1971 booklet, *Social Studies Today: Guidelines for a Curriculum Improvement,* which tries to provide "positive stimulation, suggestion and support of curriculum revision at the local level." The booklet offers guidelines and suggestions on the process of curricular innovation but does not provide objectives or teaching techniques themselves. Though it includes excerpts from statute requiring social studies instruction, its entire tone is characterized by the statement that ends the first chapter: "State requirements for the social studies are fortunately minimal, allowing school districts much freedom to experiment and innovate."[18]

Pennsylvania Educators and the Mandates

As Table 20 shows, more than half of our sample of Pennsylvania teachers believed that world culture and American history were required, but slightly more than a fourth each mentioned American government, social studies, and American culture. The responses of Pennsylvania administrators were not so scattered, but over half thought that "social studies" was mandated. Perhaps social studies as a rather vague category in their minds encompassed many of the more specific alternatives.

The broad variation in the responses may be due to the Pennsylvania department's loose interpretation of the legislative mandates. The state department has faithfully transmitted the time requirement but has broadened the content. Pennsylvania statutes are noteworthy for describing American life in almost loving detail and specifying the principles and ideals legislators wish to have fostered. However, the department has not transmitted most of these details. Furthermore, the commonwealth's board of education has made additions (such as intergroup education and racial, ethnic, and women's studies) which are general guidelines rather than detailed directives. In other words, the curriculum prescriptions in Pennsylvania are essentially empty baskets that local districts can fill in a wide variety of ways.

Probably as a result, few teachers seem aware of the specific topics, values, and goals in the mandates. Only two respondents mentioned the minority studies requirements, only one mentioned patriotism, and none mentioned voting. These topics may be in the courses, but they do not represent a conscious response by teachers to state requirements.

Finding Out About the Mandates

As Table 21 shows, the department's relaxed attitudes affect how Pennsylvania teachers and administrators find out about the mandates. Pennsylvania teachers and Pennsylvania administrators surveyed in our study were far more likely to say that they learned of the mandates through general experience—informal, on the job learning—than were their counterparts in other states.

The Effect of the Mandates

Table 22 shows that the Pennsylvania educators we interviewed tended to say either that the mandates had no influence or that they had the minor influence of telling what was expected but leaving a lot of room for additions. Pennsylvania educators did not see the

TABLE 21
HOW RESPONDENTS IN PENNSYLVANIA
LEARNED OF THE MANDATES

Source of Information on Mandates	Teachers in Pennsylvania* (N = 38)	Teachers in All Five States* (N = 184)	Administrators in Pennsylvania* (N = 21)	Administrators in All Five States* (N = 105)
School administration	26%	43%	14%	15%
Professional experience	42	28	52	42
State department of education	18	16	29	30
School courses	23	16	19	18
Other	13	12	5	15

*Percentages are based on two responses and add up to more than 100%.

TABLE 22
HOW RESPONDENTS IN PENNSYLVANIA PERCEIVED THE EFFECT OF SOCIAL STUDIES MANDATES

INFLUENCE OF SOCIAL STUDIES MANDATES	TEACHERS IN PENNSYLVANIA* (N = 41)	TEACHERS IN ALL FIVE STATES* (N = 197)	ADMINISTRATORS IN PENNSYLVANIA* (N = 21)	ADMINISTRATORS IN ALL FIVE STATES* (N = 96)
No Influence				
They have no influence	46%	43%	29%	25%
Some Influence				
Mandates reinforce teaching. The subjects would be taught anyway	2	12	5	10
Mandates help by telling what is expected	5	13	0	13
Mandates tell what is expected but leave a lot of room for additions ...	32	16	48	24
Considerable Influence				
The subjects are taught *because* they are required	12	17	0	17
Mandates limit teaching by requiring subjects that are not always relevant or important	2	3	9	4
Other	2	5	9	7

*Percentages are based on two responses and add up to more than 100%.

mandates as constricting and generally did not find them a particularly important determinant. In other words, they view the mandates much as the Pennsylvania department does.

CALIFORNIA

Mandates

The California legislature has been nearly as active as the Texas legislature in indicating which subjects are to be studied. As the first column of Table 23 shows, the basic statute (8571:1974) defines the social sciences broadly, noting that they are to draw on many disciplines, that they are to include "instruction in the American legal system" and the economic system, and that they are to include such specialized topics as Eastern and Western cultures and contemporary issues. Other provisions mandate the study of women and members of ethnic groups, and prohibit instruction "reflecting adversely on persons because of their race, sex, color, creed, national origin or ancestry."

Besides these substantive provisions, several statutes deal with the problem of maintaining general state authority over the curriculum while preserving the autonomy of local school districts. The basic statute recognizes the legitimate interests of both groups:

> The Legislature hereby recognizes that because of the common needs and interests of citizens of this state and the nation, there is a need to establish a common state curriculum for the public schools, but that, because of economic, geographic, physical, political and social diversity, there is a need for the development of educational programs at the local level. . . . Therefore, it is the intent of the Legislature to set broad minimum standards and guidelines for educational programs, and to encourage local districts to develop programs that will best fit the needs and interests of the pupils. . . . [7502:1970]

The legislature explicitly takes responsibility for prescribing certain basic courses that all high school students must take and authorizes the state department of education to set broad guidelines for local districts and, "as may be required," approve local programs. However, the state board of education is explicitly *not* authorized to establish minimum academic standards for high school graduation (a stricture prohibiting, presumably, the setting of statewide tests for graduation). Thus the state requires American history and American government for graduation and exercises very general supervisory authority, but leaves it to local school districts to create these courses and to establish their

86

own standards for determining who is deserving of the high school diploma. Similarly, the legislature requires social sciences in grades 7–12 but defines the subject very broadly and leaves all details (such as courses and grade levels) to local districts.

Regulations

The California State Board of Education has prepared only general guidelines for local social studies programs. The *Social Sciences Education Framework for California Public Schools,* often referred to as the *Framework,* is explicitly committed to local flexibility.

Although it summarizes the Education Code's "requirements affecting social science education," the *Framework* is really more a lengthy statement of some general goals than it is a course of study. For each goal, it provides general questions that teachers at various grade levels might wish to take into account. Like the Pennsylvania curriculum guide, it is clearly designed to help develop a teaching program rather than to be one.

Enforcement Provisions and Inducements to Comply

Like Pennsylvania, California is not compliance-oriented.[19] A statute (8058:1968) regarding curriculum flexibility is similar to the Pennsylvania regulations on experimental programs. It provides that the state board of education may exempt a local district from course of study requirements, as long as the exemption is "an essential part of a planned experimental curriculum project which . . . will adequately fit the educational needs and interests of the pupils."

California's annual reporting system, the "October Report," also shows that the state is not compliance-oriented. The report asks schools to list the titles and grade levels of courses "in which required instruction is included," and each topic on the form—for example, "manners, morals, and citizenship"—is linked to the relevant section of the education code. Schools are also asked to indicate the total number of semester hours in American history and American government required for graduation. However, the "October Report" is merely to gather information, and the state department has no sanctions to apply to a district found not in compliance.[20]

California Educators and the Mandates

As Table 23 shows, administrators and teachers in California generally identified only American history and American government as state mandates.

87

These findings suggest a familiar pattern. Subjects and topics embodied in required courses are more or less well known; subjects and topics not given courses of their own are simply not recognized as mandates.

Finding Out About the Mandates/The Effect of the Mandates

Table 24 shows that California educators were very similar to their counterparts in our five-state sample in how they learned of the mandates. As Table 25 shows, teachers were more likely than their counterparts in other states to say that the mandates had no influence, and administrators were rather likely to say either that they had no influence or that they left plenty of room for other courses. As in Pennsylvania, the state department has encouraged diversity and local planning, and California educators reflect the department's generally relaxed attitudes toward mandates.

WHAT EDUCATORS KNOW ABOUT THE MANDATES

We have discussed the mandates and educators' perceptions state by state. Now it is time to look at the data as a whole and to draw some conclusions.

Teachers in the various sample states differ on how they perceive state mandates, and these differences appear to be closely related to differences in the laws and regulations. In Pennsylvania, teachers think American and world cultures are mandated; in Illinois, teachers mention the Constitution Test and consumer education; in Georgia and Texas, teachers mention state government.

As Table 26 shows, however, despite these differences teachers in our five states generally agree on what constitutes the mandated social studies. American history is the core of the national social studies, government an important satellite that is sometimes spun off on its own and other times brought back into history, and the constitutions, civics, and culture are often synonyms for history and government. Other subjects exist on the peripheries. Fad and fortune periodically draw attention to these shooting stars.

Understandably, teachers seldom have first-hand knowledge of curriculum laws. Few teachers have picked up the rhetoric and goals of the statutes. Generally, the teacher's rendition of the mandates is dependent on the state department's rendition of the statutes. In states such as Texas, Illinois, and Georgia, where the state department has transmitted

TABLE 24
HOW RESPONDENTS IN CALIFORNIA
LEARNED OF THE MANDATES

SOURCE OF INFORMATION ON MANDATES	TEACHERS IN CALIFORNIA* (N = 40)	TEACHERS IN ALL FIVE STATES* (N = 184)	ADMINISTRATORS IN CALIFORNIA* (N = 21)	ADMINISTRATORS IN ALL FIVE STATES* (N = 105)
School administration	43%	43%	10%	15%
Professional experience	23	28	40	42
State department of education	20	16	25	30
School courses	15	16	35	18
Other	15	12	10	15

*Percentages are based on two responses and add up to more than 100%.

89

TABLE 25
HOW RESPONDENTS IN CALIFORNIA PERCEIVED
THE EFFECT OF SOCIAL STUDIES MANDATES

INFLUENCE OF SOCIAL STUDIES MANDATES	TEACHERS IN CALIFORNIA* (N = 44)	TEACHERS IN ALL FIVE STATES* (N = 197)	ADMINISTRATORS IN CALIFORNIA* (N = 18)	ADMINISTRATORS IN ALL FIVE STATES* (N = 96)
No Influence				
They have no influence	52%	43%	33%	25%
Some Influence				
Mandates reinforce teaching. The subjects would be taught anyway	14	12	0	10
Mandates help by telling what is expected	12	13	0	13
Mandates tell what is expected but leave a lot of room for additions ...	7	16	33	24
Considerable Influence				
The subjects are taught *because* they are required	17	17	23	17
Mandates limit teaching by requiring subjects that are not always relevant or important	0	3	0	4
Other	5	5	11	7

*Percentages are based on two responses and add up to more than 100%.

90

TABLE 26
COURSES OR TOPICS SOCIAL STUDIES TEACHERS BELIEVED WERE MANDATED IN THEIR STATE

COURSES OR TOPICS	CALIFORNIA* (N = 46)	GEORGIA* (N = 36)	ILLINOIS* (N = 43)	PENNSYLVANIA* (N = 42)	TEXAS* (N = 42)	ALL* (N = 209)
American history	63%	81%	81%	52%	62%	68%
American government	54	19	5	29	56	33
American culture	0	0	0	26	0	5
State history, state government, state studies	19	47	12	19	28	24
Federal or state constitution	2	5	81	0	10	21
Citizenship, patriotism	9	3	7	2	8	6
Law	11	0	0	0	5	3
Social studies	4	19	5	26	3	11
World history or culture	6	5	0	62	36	10
Consumer education	4	3	28	14	5	11
Free enterprise education	0	0	0	0	20	4
Minority studies	11	0	16	5	3	7
Don't know	11	14	0	7	23	10

*Percentages are based on four responses and add up to more than 100%.

the mandates in some detail, and where there is a strong action component to the mandates, teachers have a clearer idea of them than do teachers in states that have not turned mandates into courses.

A lack of specificity and explicit action components may explain why teachers fail to note requirements to teach such topics as consumerism, minorities, patriotism, citizenship, constitutions (except Illinois), environment, drugs, and law. Some of these do not have to be taught in social studies, and schools may have found it easier to locate them in science, health, home economics, and business. Furthermore, the legislation sometimes does not specify whether schools must offer the subjects and whether students must take them; whether separate courses or passing attention are required; and whether the legislature merely wants to encourage the subjects or wants to see them fully incorporated into the curriculum.

LEARNING ABOUT THE MANDATES

There are several ways for mandates (laws and regulations) to reach teachers. Mandated topics might filter down to teachers through established district courses, standard syllabuses, state-approved texts, or state department of education curriculum guides, and teachers could teach these topics without being aware that they are mandated. Or teachers and their supervisors might be systematically informed of the mandates and consciously implement them. We do not know to what extent mandates filter down, but it appears that educators are not systematically informed of them. Our findings suggest that some information is conveyed through formal courses, some from the administrative hierarchy, and some from educators' general experience, including conversations with colleagues or the way things have always been done in the school.

As Table 27 shows, only 16 percent of the teachers became aware of the mandates through the state department of education's publications. Formal education also is relatively unimportant. Only 16 percent of the teachers recalled gaining information about the mandates from college courses, even though 80 percent went to college in the states where they now teach.[21]

A more significant source is teachers' experience on the job. Twenty-eight percent said they picked up information on the mandates while teaching, counseling, administering a project, revising the curriculum, or, as a teacher from southern Illinois told us, "somewhere along the line."[22] Many teachers who said they picked up information informally

TABLE 27
SOURCES OF INFORMATION ON SOCIAL STUDIES MANDATES AND CHANGES IN THE MANDATES

Sources of Information	Social Studies Mandates		Changes in Mandates	
	Teachers' Sources* (N = 184)	Administrators' Sources* (N = 105)	Teachers' Sources* (N = 177)	Administrators' Sources* (N = 104)
School administration	43%	15%	81%	33%
Professional experience	28	44	0	0
State department of education	16	30	10	78
College and post-graduate courses ...	16	20	0	0
High school courses	5	4	0	0
Professional associations	1	2	11	14
Reading, looked it up	2	7	0	0
Colleagues	2	0	0	0
Media, press	0	0	5	6
Other	0	3	11	6
Don't know	4	3	0	2

*Percentages are based on two responses and add up to more than 100%.

on the job did not remember who told them about the mandates. When asked how he had become aware of the mandates, a California teacher told us "I'll be damned if I know." A teacher from a Chicago suburb responded, "It's common knowledge."

The largest number of teachers, 43 percent, learned from administrators in their district. They credited their department head, curriculum orientations, or handbooks distributed by their schools. This proportion differs considerably by state. Sixty-three percent of Georgia teachers credited the administration, but only 26 percent of Pennsylvania teachers did. The proportions in Illinois (46%), California (42%), and Texas (38%) hover around the average.

Teachers frequently do not learn of the mandates systematically. The second most important source, professional experience, is a grab bag that includes all sorts of informal learning. The most important source, the school administration, may be somewhat more formal and systematic, but even so more than half of the teachers (57%) did not gain information about the mandates from this source, and a large proportion of the interviewed administrators (40%) said that they had done nothing to acquaint teachers with curriculum mandates.[23]

And how do administrators themselves learn of the mandates? Only a handful credited other administrators, with a much larger proportion (29%) crediting state publications and guidelines. They are thus about twice as likely as teachers to have the state education department as a source.

The largest porportion of administrators (46%) said they learned about mandates from their own experience. As with teachers, the administrators' experiences are a grab bag of on-the-job encounters with the mandates. A principal said he learned the mandates when he was a social studies teacher. A superintendent learned them when he was a principal. A third administrator told us "They've been there for as long as I can remember." A fourth succinctly stated "word-of-mouth."

Most education administrators begin their careers as teachers. If they are like the teachers in our sample, they have obtained rather spotty information about the social studies mandates from administrators and other teachers. Now that they have become administrators, they may pass on this information to another generation of teachers. Looking at the whole process, we get a sense of the mandates as a kind of lore passed on by successive generations of administrators and teachers.

As Table 27 suggests, there is a much more formal process to inform teachers and administrators of *changes* in the mandates. When teachers were asked how they became aware of changes in the mandates, 81 percent gave administrators as a source for such information, about twice as many as credited administrators with informing them of the mandates themselves.

The interviewed administrators, in turn, learned about changes through the state education department. Practically all the superintendents gave the state as their source, and two-thirds of the principals did so. In addition, 40 percent of the principals said that they learned about mandate changes through the administrative hierarchy. Thus principals said they learned both directly from the state and indirectly through the hierarchy.

The professional organizations of administrators (superintendents, principals, curriculum supervisors) seem to serve as an alternative means of transmitting information about changes in the state requirements. As Table 27 shows, 14 percent of administrators credit a professional organization with informing them of new requirements.

In general, our data provide some evidence that educators learn of the mandates from their supervisors or the state department of education, but informal sources seem important too. The formal model of information transmittal (that is, information systematically diffused from the top down) does not seem to be fully operative.

THE INFLUENCE OF STATE MANDATES

Table 28, which shows various influences on teachers in each state, indicates that the mandates do have some effect. The most striking differences are between Texas and the other four states. As we noted earlier, teachers in our Texas sample were far more likely to say that law-related education originated with state requirements and far less likely to say that they made the crucial decisions themselves. Half of our respondents said they played no role in developing law-related offerings. They "covered the text"—which had been selected from a short list of state approved books. They did not develop separate and distinct courses because it was difficult to find places for them in the state-prescribed curriculum.

Georgia, like Texas but unlike the other three states in our sample, has a statewide list of textbooks that are "acceptable." Because the books are screened, teachers may tend to accept the texts as the

95

TABLE 28
HOW TEACHERS REPORT ORIGINS OF LAW STUDIES, BY STATE

ORIGIN OF LAW-RELATED EDUCATION	CALIFORNIA* (N = 44)	GEORGIA* (N = 36)	ILLINOIS* (N = 40)	PENNSYLVANIA* (N = 39)	TEXAS* (N = 41)	ALL* (N = 200)
Teacher's own interest	36%	33%	50%	33%	12%	33%
Curriculum revision	11	19	7	23	7	13
Teachers collectively, other teacher(s)	14	14	10	20	2	12
Administration	0	3	3	0	5	2
Students	16	14	25	31	2	17
Tradition	27	22	10	10	22	19
State requirements	7	8	15	5	46	17
Textbook	2	17	5	0	12	8
Law-related group	5	17	17	8	2	7

*Percentages are based on three responses and add up to more than 100%.

approved program, including what the texts include and excluding what the texts exclude. Thus, as Table 28 shows, 17 percent of Georgia teachers apparently see the law-related topics in the texts as notice that the state wants them to teach these topics.

In Illinois, the state has taken a different approach to regulating part of the social studies curriculum. It requires students to pass a "Constitution Test," thus requiring a certain amount of material to be developed on the U.S. and Illinois constitutions and the Bill of Rights. Though the tests are developed locally and teachers are encouraged to teach the subject according to their own interests, some Illinois teachers see this mandate as the origin of law studies.

In Pennsylvania and California, teachers generally do not report that the mandates have influenced law studies even though, as we have seen, law-related education is explicitly recognized by statute in California as part of the social studies. The California findings may be in part because the mandate is new (1974), in part because it has no action component—no mandated course, graduation requirement, or statewide test.

When interviewers asked teachers and administrators about the general effect of the mandates, they found some interesting variations state by state. In California, where the mandates are unspecific, a high of 52 percent of the teachers said they ignored the mandates. No Californians said they were limited by the mandates. By contrast, in Georgia and Illinois, where the mandates are quite specific, lows of 36 percent said they ignored the mandates. These same states had the largest proportion who said that they teach the subjects because they are required. Texas (23%), with the most specific set of requirements, and Georgia (19%) had the largest proportions of teachers who said that the requirements helped them in their teaching. Pennsylvania, where the mandates are essentially empty baskets, had the largest proportion (32%) who said that the mandates leave a lot of room.

Table 29 shows how the whole sample (that is, the five-state totals) perceived the effects of the mandates. Some educators thought social studies mandates had not influenced teaching at all. Some respondents gave the interviewers short answers such as "no way," "haven't," "none." Others, like a teacher in a middle-sized Texas city, told us "I pick the ones I want and like, the rest I just forget about." Another from California told us: "They have a minimal effect. There is no enforcement. No one checks."

Administrators are less likely than teachers to say that mandates have

TABLE 29
HOW TEACHERS AND ADMINISTRATORS
(SUPERINTENDENTS AND PRINCIPALS) PRECEIVED
THE INFLUENCE OF SOCIAL STUDIES
MANDATES ON TEACHING

INFLUENCE OF SOCIAL STUDIES MANDATES	TEACHERS* (N = 197)	ADMINISTRATORS (N = 96)
No Influence		
They have no influence.	43%	25%
Some Influence		
Mandates reinforce teaching. The subjects would be taught anyway.	12	10
Mandates help by telling what is expected	13	13
Mandates tell what is expected but leave a lot of room for additions	16	24
Considerable Influence		
The subjects are taught *because* they are required.	17	17
Mandates limit teaching by requiring subjects that are not always relevant or important	3	4
Other	5	7

*Percentages based on two responses.

no effect, and they are more likely to see the mandates as a minimum requirement leaving room for a great number of local options. A Pennsylvania principal said,

> Until we wised up, they were sort of limiting, but it was just us. What happens is we become tradition bound. They came out with the title "World History," and we taught the course World History. But we've realized that there is actually a lot of flexibility in 9–18 week courses. We can cover more interesting topics that are still under the umbrella of the law.

At the other extreme, less than a fifth of teachers and administrators said that topics were specifically included in response to state requirements. One south Georgia principal said that his school had to conform to the mandates. "We get some dictation regarding funding and accreditation. We must do this [conform to the mandates]. We can't get students into college if the school is not accredited by the state." This was one of very few responses suggesting the possibility of sanctions for failure to teach requirements.

Perhaps some teachers told us a little more than they intended when they praised the state requirements. A teacher in the San Antonio area told us, "I abide by them and I agree that they are good. They tell you when there should be changes or additions to a course." A teacher in the Atlanta area told us how state requirements had changed his life:

I've become more aware of social problems. They have increased my understanding of the relationship between the state, local, national, and international government. I've taken more interest since I've been teaching social studies. Since it's a state requirement, a lot of emphasis is put on it. I don't see why world history is a requirement.

There are many gradations between ignoring the mandates and following them to the letter. Sometimes respondents told us the situation was a little of both and some of another. A superintendent from southeast Texas said:

We follow state guidelines. The teacher will teach much the same with or without the laws.

A principal from a suburb south of Chicago spoke more broadly about the effects of the mandates.

They have quite an effect on the social studies offering. We have to teach the Constitution on the state and federal levels. We have to make the test easier and easier because everyone has to pass it to graduate. No one's going to hold a kid back from graduating because he didn't pass the Constitution Test, because then you're liable for obstruction of the right to an education and ruining job opportunities, and on and on.

A principal from a Los Angeles suburb was a little more direct.

I do not feel bound by state requirements. I do feel bound, however, by the community.

In general educators said they did not think social studies mandates were a major factor in shaping the curriculum. Many said that they ignored them. But about two-thirds felt the mandates had some effect— helping, directing, reinforcing, requiring. When we asked teachers familiar with the mandates if they were "very important, moderately important, of minor importance, or not important at all to what you teach and how you teach," a third said they were very important. (Again, the proportions were greater in Georgia and Texas.) Another

99

third said they were moderately important, and a final third said they were of minor or no importance.

The data suggest that teachers do not see the mandates as an imposititon. On the contrary, those who report an effect are more likely to see it as beneficial. By a three-to-one margin teachers and administrators suggested the mandates helped their teaching or supported a sound curriculum.

Finally, interviewers asked respondents, "If you had the opportunity, how might you change the state social studies requirements?" The single most frequent response of both teachers (25%) and administrators (43%) was "no change," and there seems to be little consensus about suggested changes, with responses all over the field.

While there was little argeement on changes, a few patterns did emerge from the responses. First, by a three-to-one margin teachers and administrators were more interested in increasing requirements than in decreasing them. One southern California teacher told us, "I would fight like hell to get more. The cutting of requirements hurts my teaching by not allowing me the time needed to cover materials adequately." Teachers most often mentioned the desirability of increased requirements in government (13%), law (9%), and economics (8%). Seven percent, all from Texas and Georgia, wanted a change in the grade level at which courses are taught. A tenth of the Illinois teachers wanted the Constitution Test eliminated.

A theme underlying the responses of those who reject change is that tinkering can only make a good situation bad or a bad situation worse. A department head from a small district on the northern California coast told us, "Leave it as it is. There is plenty to teach. Schools are the dumping grounds for all new ideas. There has to be an atmosphere of school rather than a testing ground." The principal of that school came to the same conclusion from a slightly different perspective. "I don't think I would change them at all. They allow for the different needs of the community; each community is a little different. We have the opportunity to fill needs we can identify here." A suburban Chicago principal echoed these feelings: "There would be possibly some local needs that don't necessarily apply statewide. You'll find you limit by mandating too much."

All in all, then, teachers and administrators reported being rather comfortable with their states' mandates. They are not fully aware of them and do not think mandates have a very strong influence, but they support the *idea* of mandates.

Since legislatures do not seem inclined to eliminate mandates—Tyll van Geel suggests, in fact, that they are generally adding to them—and since teachers are not dissatisfied with them, mandates will probably be a part of the education landscape for some time to come.

Naturally, mandates interest proponents of law-related education and other curricular innovations. They seem, at first glance, an easy way to get an innovation adopted throughout a state. However, as we have seen, much depends on how specific the mandate is, on whether it has an action component, and on how effectively it is transmitted to teachers. We will make a number of recommendations on each of these points in the concluding chapter of this study.

Notes

[1] A survey conducted by the TEA and reported in the document "Social Studies Enrollment Grades 7–12, State Totals," disclosed that in the spring of the 1974–75 school year, 215,980 students were enrolled in Texas history and geography (grade 7), 209,131 in American history and citizenship (grade 8), 194,163 in American history (grades 9–12), a total of 196,722 in either world history studies or world geography studies (grades 9–12), and 87,504 in American government (grades 10–12). By contrast, the largest enrollment in any course not required was only 11,752 (economics). The survey shows that only 1,700 students took free enterprise. Presumably most schools had not yet implemented this new course. Although the act that mandated instruction in free enterprise was to apply to the 1974–75 school year, the TEA curriculum guide on free enterprise did not appear until June, 1975.

[2] The TEA does prepare "resource guides" for some of the courses. For example, AMERICAN GOVERNMENT: A RESOURCE GUIDE (Austin, Texas: TEA, 1973) is a 54-page document containing several questioning strategies, reports of research, reprints of articles from social studies magazines, and suggestions for further reading. It is, then, a resource for teachers rather than a day-by-day guide for their teaching. It does include the two legislative resolutions on social studies education, as well as a section from the 1929 law on teaching constitutions.

[3] Interview with Elvin Tyrone, Consultant, Social Studies Section, Division of Curriculum Development, Texas Education Agency. The interview took place on November 4, 1977.

[4] See Purposes of This Course Guide, FUNDAMENTALS OF THE FREE ENTERPRISE SYSTEM: COURSE GUIDE, (Austin, Texas: TEA, June 1975, p. 3).

[5] Teachers were responding to the following question: "Almost all states prescribe some elements of the social studies curriculum. Do you know, in a general way, what is mandated in the social studies area?" If teachers answered "yes," we asked them to tell us what was mandated.

[6] If respondents answered that they knew what was mandated in the social

studies area, we asked them "How did you originally learn of those state requirements?"

[7]Only 5% of Pennsylvania teachers gave this response. The figures for the other states are California (7%), Georgia (8%), and Illinois (15%).

[8]"Recognition is the process by which the (state board of education) . . . certifies that a local school district has met efficient and adequate basic standards for the quality of the instructional program. . . ." Foreword to the *Program* (Springfield, Illinois: The Office of the Superintendent of Public Instruction, 1974), p. ii. It may seem that the state is exercising close supervision, but the foreword says that "every effort should be made to revitalize the local district's capability to chart its own future" (p. ii), and the guide is intended to help local districts successfully plan and evaluate their own programs.

[9]As the *Program* itself states, "the central goal is to assist school districts in the improvement of their program."

[10]Letter from Joseph Cronin, August 12, 1976. Superintendent Cronin wrote that since the statute dealing with the reports does not specify that they be submitted to the central office, and since requiring them would result in a "monumental flow of paper," compliance "is regulated at the local level."

[11]Illinois educators are also relatively likely to say that law studies entered the curriculum as a result of mandates.

[12]Section 32–669a, Withholding of Funds from Local Units, reads in part:

In the event a local unit of administration shall fail to comply with any provision of rules, regulations, policies, standards or requirements established by the State Board, the State Board may, in its discretion, withhold from such local unit all or any part of the State-contributed Adequate Program for Education in Georgia funds allotted to such local unit under provisions of this Chapter until such time as full compliance is made by the local unit.

[13]REGULATIONS OF THE STATE BOARD OF EDUCATION OF PENNSYLVANIA, GENERAL CURRICULUM REGULATIONS, Chapter 7 (March 14, 1969); *Social Studies Curriculum Requirements in Pennsylvania* (May 1973).

[14]*Social Studies Curriculum Requirements in Pennsylvania* (May 1973), p. 2.

[15]Note that in Texas the required course in world history or world geography is also not mandated legislatively but is rather the result of a policy adopted by the state board of education. The Pennsylvania Department of Education says that world history was traditional in Pennsylvania and that a 1961 state board mandate broadened it to include world cultures. The department adds that the required course in American and Pennsylvania history and government became the American culture course as a result of a 1969 state board policy. (*Social Studies Today: Guidelines for Curriculum Im-*

provement, Pennsylvania Department of Education, 1971).

[16]*Regulations of the State Board of Education of Pennsylvania,* "General Curriculum Regulations," Chapter 7 (March 14, 1969); "Social Studies Curriculum Requirements in Pennsylvania" (May 1973).

[17]For example, the first regulation in the chapter on the curriculum regulations states that "it shall be the policy of the State Board of Education. . . to delegate to local districts the greatest possible flexibility in curriculum planning consistent with the high quality of education for every pupil in the Commonwealth" (8–100). This is immediately followed by provisions that authorize the superintendent of public instruction to grant exceptions to the regulations in this chapter "where necessary to adapt these regulations to school district curriculum needs" (7–111) and that authorize the superintendent to "waive any or all the regulations contained in this chapter for experimental programs" (7–112).

[18]SOCIAL STUDIES TODAY, pp. v–vi, 1–6.

[19]There is, however, a statute (1242) that is similar to statutes found in many states. It provides that districts which have neglected or refused to establish courses of study approved by the state board will lose 10% of all apportionments from the state school fund.

[20]Interview with John R. Eales, Office of Curriculum Services, California State Department of Education, April 21, 1976.

[21]There is, however, a slight relationship between the proportion who attend college within the state and the proportion who regard their college courses as a source of learning about mandates. In Pennsylvania, where a high of 91% of teachers attend college within the state, a high of 24% credited their college courses as the source of information about mandates. Georgia teachers, by contrast, were less likely to have attended college within the state (70%) and less likely to mention courses as a source (10%).

[22]This proportion varies a bit by state: Pennsylvania (42%), Georgia (30%), Texas (24%), California (22%), and Illinois (22%).

[23]We compared each teacher in the sample with his or her principal to see the relationship between what the principals said they did to acquaint teachers with the mandates and what teachers recalled of administrative sources of information. Of those teachers whose principals said they had acquainted teachers with the mandates, only 40% credited the administration. Of those teachers whose principals did not claim a role, 34% credited the administration. These data are hardly conclusive. It is possible that principals exaggerated their roles somewhat, or perhaps they were ineffective in conveying information about the mandates, but it is also possible that teachers whose principals had acquainted them with the mandates may have had other sources that were more compelling, or that teachers whose principals had not acquainted them with mandates may have had other administrative sources.

TABLE 11
TEXAS SOCIAL STUDIES MANDATES AND
WHAT TEACHERS AND SCHOOL ADMINISTRATORS
BELIEVED WERE MANDATED

Statutes*	State Regulations**
§ 21.101. Courses of Study All public free schools in this state shall be required to offer instruction in the following subjects: English grammer, reading in English, orthography, penmanship, composition, arithmetic, mental arithmetic, United States history, Texas history, modern geography, civil government, physiology and hygiene, physical education, and, in all grades, a course or courses in which some attention is given to the effects of alcohol and narcotics. Such subjects shall be taught in compliance with any applicable provision of this subchapter. (Enacted in 1905.)	The TEA prescribes the following social studies curriculum. Texas History and Geography (Grade 7), American History and Citizenship (Grade 8), American History (usually Grades 9 or 10), World History or World Geography (usually Grades 10 or 11), and American Government (Grade 12). By a policy of the TEA (3172 1), all pupils who wish to graduate must complete at least one unit (1 year) of American History, one unit of World History or World Geography, and one unit of American Government.
§ 21.102. Patriotism The daily program of every public school shall be so formulated by the teacher, principal, or superintendent as to include at least 10 minutes for the teaching of intelligent patriotism, including the needs of the state and federal governments, the duty of the citizen to the state, and the obligation of the state to the citizen. (Enacted in 1917.)	[no specific TEA directive regarding this provision; presumably it could be met by any of the required courses except World History]
§ 21.103. Texas History The history of Texas shall be taught in all public schools in and only in the history courses of all such schools. The course shall be taught for not less than two hours in any one week. The commissioner of education shall notify the different county, city, and district superintendents as to how the course may be divided. (Enacted in 1918.)	Texas History and Geography (grade 7)
§ 21.106. Constitution All public free high schools in this state shall teach and require a course of instruction in the constitutions of the United States and the State of Texas. The course shall be a combined course in both constitutions, and shall be given for at least one-half hour each week in	American Government (Grade 12)

TABLE 11 (continued)

Statutes	State Regulations

the school year or at least one hour each week for one-half of the school year, or the equivalent thereof. No student shall be graduated from any public free high school in this state who has not passed a satisfactory examination in the course of instruction herein described. (Enacted in 1929.)

HCR 53 (American Citizenship)

WHEREAS, the Legislature finds that public schools are doing commendable work with the youth of this state in stressing good citizenship and the responsibilities of citizenship in a free society, and

WHEREAS, the Legislature finds that even greater emphasis upon the fundamental principles upon which the American way of life is founded is necessary in order to achieve stronger state and national unity to meet the tests that lie ahead; now, therefore, be it

RESOLVED by the House of Representatives, the State of Texas, concurring, that the Central Education Agency, with the objective of further encouraging and promoting state and national unity through a more adequate knowledge and appreciation of the fundamental principles and ideals of the Constitution of the United States and of the State of Texas, advise and counsel with the public free school system of this state to the end that in the education and teaching of the youth of this state the Constitutions and the Bills of Rights therein contained as the source of all liberties, citizen responsibilities, freedoms and rights enjoyed in the United States of America and in the State of Texas be more strongly emphasized, and be it further

RESOLVED, that a one-year course in American Citizenship be offered in the high schools of this state, which courses shall include a study of government, civics, the Constitutions and other historic documents, and that a one-half semester in the study of Texas history be given during the course of High-

[no specific TEA directive; presumably American Government and the optional high school Texas History course meet this requirement]

105

TABLE 11 (continued)

Statutes	State Regulations
school study. (Acts 1951, 52nd Legislature.)	

HCR 46 (16 Lessons in Citizenship)

WHEREAS, Rapid change, growing complexity, and dissolution of the family unit are generally accepted characteristics of contemporary American life; and

American History and Citizenship (Grade 8); Special unit, You and the Law

WHEREAS, This has resulted in widespread ignorance, especially among juveniles, of the laws, a person's rights and responsibilities under them, and the possible consequences of violating them; and

WHEREAS, This is one of the major factors contributing to the rise in juvenile crime; now, therefore, be it

RESOLVED by the House of Representives of the State of Texas, the Senate concurring, That the Texas Education Agency, in cooperation with the Texas Youth Council, the Department of Public Welfare, the Department of Public Safety, and the Texas Department of Corrections, be, and is hereby, directed to develop a course of instruction, of at least 16 classroom hours in length to be taught in the sixth or seventh grades [see annotation on p. 295], to teach the basic elements of good citizenship, stressing the importance of the law, the rights and responsibilities of citizens under it, and the possible long and short term consequences of violating it; and, be it further

RESOLVED, That the Texas Education Agency prepare and develop all such texts, course outlines, visual teaching aids, and other materials as are necessary to teaching this course of instruction; and, be it further

RESOLVED, That the Texas Education Agency, in developing this unit, consider the value of including programs such as "Operation Teen-ager," put on by inmates in the Texas prison system, as part of this course of instruction; and, be it further

RESOLVED, That the Texas Edu-

106

TABLE 11 (continued)

| Statutes | State Regulations |

cation Agency, is encouraged to solicit the services of the State Bar Association, the Texas Congress of Parents and Teachers, the Hogg Foundation for Mental Health, and other public service organizations in developing this course of instruction; and, be it further

RESOLVED, That the Texas Education Agency develop this course of instruction, along with the necessary texts, course outlines, and teaching materials, and make them available to all school districts teaching a sixth or seventh grade no later than September 1, 1968; and, be it further

RESOLVED, That the Texas Education Agency report to the 61st Legislature its recommendations as to the legislation needed to require all school districts in Texas teaching a sixth or seventh grade to offer this course of instruction; and, be it further

RESOLVED, That, for the purposes of this Resolution, the Texas Education Agency is hereby authorized to expend money from its general operating fund. (Acts 1967, 60th Legislature)

§ 21.1031. Instruction in Free Enterprise System

(a) All public high schools shall give instruction on the essentials and benefits of the free enterprise system. Instruction shall be given in accordance with the course of study prescribed by the State Board of Education for at least one semester or quarter, equal to one-half unit of credit. The State Board of Education shall prescribe suitable teaching material for the instruction.

(b) As used in this section 'free enterprise' means an economic system characterized by private or corporate ownership of capital goods, by investments that are determined by private decision rather than by state control, and by prices, production, and the distribution of goods that are determined in a free manner.

This act applies beginning with the 1974-75 school year.

Fundamentals of the Free Enterprise System (new required course, with extensive TEA course guide)

107

TABLE 11 (continued)

Statutes   **State Regulations**

§ 21.119. Consumer Education

(a) The Central Education Agency shall develop curricula and teaching materials for a unit of study in consumer education. The unit shall include study of installment purchasing, budgeting, and price comparison.

(b) Beginning with the 1975-76 school year, any public school in the State may offer consumer education as an option unit of study. Added by Acts 1973, 63rd Leg., p. 763, ch. 337, § 1, eff. June 12, 1973.

§ 21.113. Dangers of Crime and Narcotics

The Central Education Agency shall develop curricula and teaching materials for units of study on the dangers of crime and narcotics. The units of study shall be required for all students each academic year for grades 5 through 12. Added by Acts 1971, 62nd Leg., p. 1514, ch. 405, § 44, eff. May 26, 1971.

§ 21.112. Police Administration and Fire Protection Administration

Beginning with the 1967-1968 school year, every independent school district in a county having a population of 200,000 or more, according to the last preceding federal census, may offer in each high school for senior students a one-semester course in police administration and a one-semester course in fire protection administration, to be conducted according to the State Department of Education's requirements relating to curricula and teaching materials. Such courses, if offered, shall be elective courses.

*SOURCE: *Vernon's Annotated Statutes of Texas.*
**SOURCE: *Framework for the Social Studies, K-12; Regulations Regarding the Social Studies.*

TABLE 11 (continued)

WHAT TEXAS RESPONDENTS BELIEVED THE MANDATES WERE

COURSES OR TOPICS	TEACHERS* (N = 39)	ADMINISTRATORS* (N = 23)
American history	62%	87%
American government	56	57
American culture	0	0
State history, state government state studies	28	48
Federal or state constitution	10	4
Citizenship, patriotism	8	9
Law	5	9
Social studies	3	4
World history or culture	36	39
Consumer education	5	13
Free enterprise education	20	26
Minority studies	3	4
Don't know	23	17

*Percentages are based on four responses and add up to more than 100%.

TABLE 14

ILLINOIS SOCIAL STUDIES MANDATES AND WHAT TEACHERS AND SCHOOL ADMINISTRATORS BELIEVED WERE MANDATED

Statutes*

§ 27–3. Patriotism and Principles of Representative Government—Proper Use of Flag—Method of Voting

American patriotism and the principles of representative government, as enunciated in the American Declaration of Independence, the Constitution of the United States of America and the Constitution of the State of Illinois, and the proper use and display of the American flag, shall be taught in all public schools and other educational institutions supported or maintained in whole or in part by public funds. No student shall receive a certificate of graduation without passing a satisfactory examination upon such subjects.

Instruction shall be given in all such schools and institutions in the method of voting at elections by means of the Australian Ballot system and the method of the counting of votes for candidates. 1961, March 18, Laws 1961. p. 31. § 27–3.

(The original law dates from 1921. The voting method provision was added in 1943, the constitution test requirement in 1953.)

TABLE 14 (Continued)

Statutes*

§ 27-4. Time Devoted to Subjects Mentioned in Section 27-3

Not less than one hour of each school week shall be devoted to the study of the subject mentioned in Section 27-3 in the seventh and eighth grades or their equivalent, and not less than one hour of each school week to the advanced study thereof in all high school grades, in the public schools and other institutions mentioned in such section. This section does not prevent the study of such subjects in any of the lower grades in such schools or institutions. 1961, March 18, Laws 1961; p. 31, § 27-4.
(The original law dates from 1921.)

§ 27-12. Honesty, Kindness, Justice and Moral Courage

Every public school teacher shall teach the pupils honesty, kindness, justice and moral courage for the purpose of lessening crime and raising the standard of good citizenship. 1961, March 18, Laws 1961, p. 31, § 27-12.
(The original law dates from 1909.)

§ 27-21. History of United States

History of the United States shall be taught in all public schools and in all other educational institutions in this State supported or maintained, in whole or in part, by public funds. The teaching of history shall have as one of its objectives the imparting to pupils of a comprehensive idea of our democratic form of government and the principles for which our government stands as regards other nations, including the studying of the place of our government in world-wide movements and the leaders therof, with particular stress upon the basic principles and ideals of our representative form of government. The teaching of history shall include a study of the role and contributions of American Negroes and other ethnic groups including but not restricted to Polish, Lithuanian, German, Hungarian, Irish, Bohemian, Russian, Albanian, Italian, Czechoslavakian, French, Scots, etc. in the history of this country and this State. No pupils shall be graduated from the eighth grade of any public school unless he has received such instruction in the history of the United States and gives evidence of having a comprehensive knowledge thereof.
As amended 1967, June 26, Laws 1967, p. 815, § 1.
(The original law dates from 1909.)

§ 27-20.1 Illinois Law Week

The Governor shall annually designate by official proclamation one week in May to be known as "Illinois Law Week" to be observed throughout the State to foster the importance of law and the respect thereof in Illinois. Dur-

110

ing that week, the public schools may devote appropriate time, instruction, study, and exercises in the procedures of the legislature and the enactment of laws, the courts and the administration of justice, the police and the enforcement of law, citizen responsibilities, and other principles and ideals to promote the importance of government under law in the State.

1961, March 18, Laws 1961, p. 31, § 27–20.1, added by P.A. 76–1183, § 1, eff. Sept. 4, 1969.

§ 27–13.1 Consumer Education

Pupils in the public schools in grades 8 through 12 shall be taught and be required to study courses which include instruction in the area of consumer education, including but not necessarily limited to installment purchasing, budgeting and comparison of prices. The Superintendent of Public Instruction shall devise or approve the consumer education curriculum for grades 10 through 12 and specify the minimum amount of instruction to be devoted thereto.

1961, March 18, Laws 1961, p. 31, § 27–12.1, added 1967, Aug. 11, Laws 1967 p. 2000, § 3.

State Regulations**

6-4 Additional criteria for secondary schools

    6-4.1 The district must provide a comprehensive curriculum, including the following as a minimum program of offerings:

Language Arts	Health Education
Science	Physical Education
Mathematics	Conservation
Social Studies and	Consumer Education
History of the	Special Education
United States	Driver Education (high school only)
Foreign Language	Vocational and Technical Skill
Music	Development (high school only)
Art	Safety Education
Career Development—	
Orientation and	
Preparation	

    6-4.7 Specific minimum requirements for graduation: 16 units or the equivalent in grades 9-12 if a 4-year high school and 12 units in grades 10-12 if a 3-year high school

      In either of the above, one must be in American History, or American

111

TABLE 14 (Continued)

State Regulations

History and Government. In a 4-year high school 3 units must be in English. In a 3-year high school 2 units must be in English.

In addition to the foregoing, all graduates are required by law to have had adequate instruction in American patriotism and representative government, proper use and display of the American flag, honesty, justice, moral courage, humane education, safety education, health education, The Illinois Vehicle Code, conservation, consumer education, physical education, and others mandated in Section 27.

Social Studies and History

6-11.1 Each school system shall provide history and social studies which do the following: critically analyze not only the principles of representative government, the Constitution of the United States and of the State of Illinois, and proper use of the flag, but also how these concepts have related, and presently do relate, in actual practice to our world. The teaching of history shall include a study of the role and contributions of ethnic groups in the history of this country and the State (Sec. 27-21). No student shall receive a certificate of graduation without passing a satisfactory examination upon such subjects. (Sec. 27-3).

6-9 Consumer Education and Protection

6-9.1 Pupils in the public school systems in grades 8-12 shall be taught and be required to study courses which include instruction in consumer education, including, but not necessarily limited to, installment purchasing, budgeting, and comparison of prices (Section 27-12.1).

a. A course in consumer education shall include: the individual consumer in the marketplace, money management, consumer credit, buying goods and services, housing, food, transportation, clothing, health services, drugs, cosmetics, recreation, furnishings and appliances, insurance savings and investments, taxes, and the consumer in society.

. . . .

c. The Superintendent of each school district shall maintain evidence which shows that each student has received adequate instruction in consumer education as required by law (installment purchasing, budgeting, and comparison of prices) prior to the completion of the 12th grade. For grades 8, 9, 10, 11, and 12, consumer education may be included in

112

course content of other courses or it may be taught as a separate required course.

. . . .

e. Each district shall use as a minimum guideline the standards set forth in Guidelines for Consumer Education issued by the Office of Public Instruction 1972.

EVALUATION CRITERIA FOR SOCIAL STUDIES (SA-23)

District Name and Number	County

. . . .

Program Offerings

20. To what extent are the mandated requirements of American History, the federal and state constitutions and ethnic studies being met?

21. To what extent is there a variety of social studies course offerings on the secondary level?

22. To what extent is career education integrated into the social studies program?

23. To what extent is there evidence of a sequential and coordinated curriculum with regard to content and skills?

24. To what extent are students encouraged to form concepts and generalizations from experiences in and/or outside the classroom?

25. To what extent are students being helped to deal with current and controversial issues?

*SOURCE: *Illinois Annotated Statutes*, Chapter 122, Schools.
**SOURCE: *The Illinois Program for Evaluation, Supervision and Recognition of Schools;* Circular Series A, Number 160, Revised 1974.

What Illinois Respondents Believed the Mandates Were

COURSES OR TOPICS	TEACHERS* (N = 43)	ADMINISTRATORS* (N = 25)
American history	81%	92%
American government	5	12
American culture	0	0
State history, state government, state studies	12	4
Federal or state constitution	81	84
Citizenship, patriotism	7	12
Law	0	0
Social studies	5	20
World history or culture	0	0
Consumer education	28	32
Free enterprise education	0	0
Minority studies	16	4
Don't know	0	4

*Percentages are based on four responses and add up to more than 100%.

113

TABLE 17
GEORGIA SOCIAL STUDIES MANDATES AND WHAT TEACHERS AND SCHOOL ADMINISTRATORS BELIEVED WERE MANDATED

Statutes*

32–657a Required Curriculum; Instruction in Municipal, County, State and Federal Governments; Instruction in the Essentials of the United States and Georgia Histories and Constitutions

All elementary and secondary schools which receive in any manner funds from the State shall provide the following course offerings and in the manner prescribed by the State Board of Education. (a) The State Board of Education shall prescribe a course of study in the background, history and development of the Federal and State Governments. The course in the study of Federal and State Governments shall be supplemented in each high school by a study of the local and county and municipal governments. No student shall be eligible to receive a diploma from high school unless said student has successfully completed the course in government as provided for by this section.

(b) The State Board of Education shall prescribe a course of study in the history of the United States and in the history of Georgia, and in the essentials of the United States and Georgia Constitutions, including the study of American institutions and ideals to be offered at the high school level. No student shall be eligible to receive a diploma from a high school, unless said student has successfully completed the courses in history and Constitutions provided for this section.

32–664a Voter Registration

Each student in the public schools of the State of Georgia, upon attaining the age of 18 years, shall be apprised of his right to register as an elector and vote in elections upon attaining the age of 18 years. The State Board of Education shall promulgate rules and regulations to carry out the provisions of this section.

32–664a.1 Pledge of Allegiance to the Flag

Each student in the public schools of the State of Georgia shall be afforded the opportunity to recite the Pledge of Allegiance to the flag of the United States of America during each school day. It shall be the duty of each local board of education to establish a policy setting the time and manner for recitation of the Pledge of Allegiance. Said policy shall be established in writing and shall be distributed to each teacher within the school.

114

State Regulations**

Foreword

As representatives of the citizenry of the State of Georgia, the State Board of Education has as one of its goals the teaching of Americanism as it reflects the heritage of our state and nation. The Board's expectation and intent are that the course in American history and government should be taught so that every Georgian who completes this course should be proud that he is an American and a Georgian and that he is a participating American who knows what his responsibilities are under the American form of government.

The course is organized into three chronological parts—(1) U.S. History and Government in 1865; (2) 1896 to 1932; and (3) 1932 to present—with emphasis on state and local history and government.

In November, 1976, the State Board adopted a pilot program designed to promote "self-reliance" among students. The program emphasizes "contemporary life skills" including those of learner, individual, citizen, consumer, and producer. These skills are related to areas of study (courses) and school terms as follows:

		SEMESTER(S)	QUARTER(S)
Learner:	Communication Skills	6	9
	Mathematics	4	6
Individual:	Health and Safety	1	1
	Physical Education	1	1
Citizen:	Laboratory Science	2	3
	Citizenship/Local, State and National Government	2	3
	Principles of Economics/Business/Free Enterprise	1	1
	U.S. History	1	1
	Social Studies Elective	1	1
Consumer:	Personal Finance	1	1
Producer:	Career Planning and Entry Skills	1	1
Electives:		21	35

This program broadens the scope of social studies directives. Although this linking of life skill, course, and required semesters and quarters strongly suggests course-by-course adoption, the total program is explicitly committed to local autonomy in developing the curriculum, including credit for "subjects in lieu of enrollment" and for "planned off-campus experience."

*SOURCE: *Code of Georgia, Annotated,* title 22 Education.
**SOURCE: *Teaching American History and Government* (Atlanta, Georgia, Department of Education, 1972).

115

TABLE 17 (Continued)

What Georgia Respondents Believed the Mandates Were

COURSES OR TOPICS	TEACHERS* (N = 36)	ADMINISTRATORS* (N = 22)
American history	81%	100%
American government	19	36
American culture	0	0
State history, state government, state studies	47	41
Federal or state constitution	5	0
Citizenship, patriotism	3	0
Law	0	0
Social studies	19	45
World history or culture	5	0
Consumer education	3	0
Free enterprise education	0	0
Minority studies	0	0
Don't know	14	5

*Percentages are based on four responses and add up to more than 100%.

TABLE 20
PENNSYLVANIA SOCIAL STUDIES MANDATES AND WHAT TEACHERS AND SCHOOL ADMINISTRATORS BELIEVED WERE MANDATED

Statutes*

§ 16–1605. Courses of Study

(a) In all public, private or parochial schools, there shall be integrated in the social studies curriculum courses of study as provided in this act. It shall be the duty of the superintendent having supervision over any high school to prepare, and recommend to the board of school directors maintaining the same, suitable courses of study, which shall be adopted by said board of school directors, with such changes as they may deem wise, subject to the provisions of this act. During grades seven through twelve inclusive, there shall be included at least four semesters or equivalent study in the history and government of that portion of America which has become the United States of America, and of the Commonwealth of Pennsylvania, of such nature, kind or quality, as to have for its purpose the developing, teaching

116

and presentation of the principles and ideals of the American republican representative form of government, as portrayed and experienced by the acts and policies of the framers of the Declaration of Independence and framers of the Constitution of the United States and the Bill of Rights. The study of the history of the United States, including the study of the Constitution of the United States and the study of the history and Constitution of this Commonwealth, shall also be such as will emphasize the good, worthwhile and best features and points of the social, economic and cultural development, the growth of the American family life, high standard of living of the United States citizen, the privileges enjoyed by such citizens, their heritage and its derivations of and in our principles of government. Such instruction shall have for its purpose also the instilling into every boy and girl who comes out of our public, private and parochial schools their solemn duty and obligation to exercise intelligently their voting privilege and to understand the advantages of the American republican form of government as compared with various other forms of government.

(Law originally passed in 1911 and last revised in 1961; the four-semester provision dates from 1943.)

§ 15-1545. Bill of Rights Week

The Department of Public Instruction shall designate a week during each year and prescribe a uniform course of exercises to be carried out during that week in the public schools to instill into the minds of the pupils thereof the purpose,[1] meaning and importance of that portion of the Constitutions of the United States and of this Commonwealth known as the "Bill of Rights." Such exercises shall be in addition to the prescribed courses of study in such schools. 1949, March 10, P.L. 30, art. XV, § 1545.

(The act was originally passed in 1941.)

§ 15-1511. Subjects of Instruction; Flag Code

In every elementary public and private school, established and maintained in this Commonwealth, the following subjects shall be taught, in the English language and from English texts: English, including spelling, reading and writing, arithmetic, geography, the history of the United States and of Pennsylvania, civics, including loyalty to the State and National Government, safety education, and the humane treatment of birds and animals, health, including physical education, and physiology, music and art. Other subjects shall be taught in the public elementary schools and also in the public high schools as may be prescribed by the standards of the State Board of Education. All such subjects, except foreign languages, shall be taught in the English language and from English texts; Provided, however, that, at the discretion of the Superintendent of Public Instruction, the teaching of subjects in a language other than English may be permitted as part of a sequence in foreign language study or as part of a bilingual education pro-

117

TABLE 20 (Continued)

Statutes

gram if the teaching personnel are properly certified in the subject fields. Each school district shall provide and distribute to each pupil, enrolled in the eighth grade of the public schools, one illustrated copy of the National Flag Code, and shall, from time to time, make available such copies as are necessary for replacements from year to year. It shall be the duty of each teacher in the public schools to make such use of the code as may, from time to time, seem proper.

(The original act was passed in 1911.)

§ 7–771. Display of United States Flag; Development of Patriotism

All supervising officers and teachers in charge of public, private or parochial schools shall establish and direct the conduct of appropriate daily instruction or ceremonies, or, in lieu thereof, at least one full period per week, for the purpose of affirming and developing allegiance to and respect for the Flag of the United States of America, and for the promoting of a clear understanding of our American way of life, with all of the unparalleled individual opportunities, and our republican form of government, with its responsiveness to majority decisions and demands. Such elements shall be included in this program as instruction in the fundamental principles of our form of government, and understanding of the provisions of the Constitution of the Commonwealth of Pennsylvania and the Constitution of the United States of America, the values to be found in the freedom of speech, of religion and of the press, the values to be found in obedience to the laws of the land and the Commonwealth, the importance of exercising the right of franchise, the obligation of every citizen to stand ready to defend our country at all times from infiltration or aggression by those whose acts and ideologies are contrary to our American philosophy of life. 1949, March 10, P.L. 30, art. VII, § 771; 1952, Jan. 8, P.L. (1951) 1856, § 1.

(This portion of the law was enacted in 1956.)

State Regulations**

7-232 Senior High School Graduation Requirements

Thirteen planned courses for credit in grades 10, 11 and 12 shall be required for graduation for all students and shall include the following:
. . . .
    f. *Social Studies*—Two planned courses in accordance with Section 7–153.
. . . .
    h. *Other Requirements*—Other requirements for graduation may be established at the discretion of the school district so long as such requirements do not conflict with those cited in this section.

7-150 Special Instruction to be Provided in the Curriculum of All Schools

7-151 Racial and Ethnic Group History—In each course in the history of the United States and of Pennsylvania taught in the elementary and secondary schools of the Commonwealth, there shall be included the major contributions made by Negroes and other racial and ethnic groups in the development of the United States and the Commonwealth of Pennsylvania.

7-153 Secondary Social Studies—During grades 7 through 12, six units of social studies shall be offered, of which four units shall be required.

The four required units shall consist of two units of World Cultures and two units of American (U.S.) Culture which shall be interdisciplinary studies taken from the social sciences (anthropology, economics, geography, history, philosophy, political science, psychology and sociology). The two units of electives may be either single-discipline or inter-disciplinary courses.

Of the six units, at least two units shall be taught in grades 10 through 12 and be required for graduation.

*SOURCE: *Purdon's Pennsylvania Statutes Annotated.*

**SOURCE: *Regulations of the State Board of Education of Pennsylvania,* Chapter 7, summary of the regulations in May 1973 which quoted in part Section 1605 of the statutes, "Courses of Study." In addition, in 1971 the department issued a booklet entitled *Social Studies Today, Guidelines for Curriculum Improvement,* which includes the 1969 regulations with a summary and rationale.

What Pennsylvania Respondents Believed the Mandates Were

COURSES OR TOPICS	TEACHERS* (N = 42)	ADMINISTRATORS* (N = 22)
American history	52%	100%
American government	29	18
American culture	26	9
State history, state government, state studies	19	9
Federal or state constitution	0	0
Citizenship, patriotism	2	5
Law	0	0
Social studies	26	55
World history or culture	62	64
Consumer education	14	5
Free enterprise education	0	0
Minority studies	5	0
Don't know	7	9

*Percentages are based on four responses and add up to more than 100%.

TABLE 23
CALIFORNIA SOCIAL STUDIES MANDATES AND WHAT TEACHERS AND SCHOOL ADMINISTRATORS BELIEVED WERE MANDATED

Statutes*

Ch. 3   **REQUIRED COURSES OF STUDY**   § 8571

§ 8571. Areas of Study

The adopted course of study for grades 7 through 12 shall offer courses in the following areas of study:

. . . .

(b) Social sciences, drawing upon the disciplines of anthropology, economics, geography, history, political science, psychology, and sociology, designed to fit the maturity of the pupils. Instruction shall provide a foundation for understanding the history, resources, development, and government of California and the United States of America; instruction in our American legal system, the operation of the juvenile and adult criminal justice systems, and the rights and duties of citizens under the criminal and civil law and the State and Federal Constitutions; the development of the American economic system including the role of the entrepreneur and labor; man's relations to his human and natural environment; eastern and western cultures and civilization; and contemporary issues.**

§ 8574. Requirements for High School Graduation; Alternative Modes for Completion

No pupil shall receive a diploma of graduation from high school who has not completed the course of study prescribed by the governing board. Requirements for graduation shall include:

(a) English.

(b) American history.

(c) American government.

(d) Mathematics.

(e) Science.

(f) Physical education, unless the pupil has been exempted pursuant to the provisions of this code.

(g) Such other subjects as may be prescribed.

The governing board, with the active involvement of parents, administrators, teachers, and students, shall adopt alternative means for students to complete the prescribed course of study which may include practical demonstration of skills and competencies, work experience or other outside school experience, interdisciplinary study, independent study, and credit earned at a postsecondary institution. Requirements for graduation and specified alternative modes for completing the prescribed course of study shall be made available to students, parents, and the public.

(Added by Stats. 1976, c. 856, § 5.)

§ 8553. Instruction in Social Sciences

Instruction in social sciences shall include the early history of California and a study of the role and contributions of American Negroes, American Indians, Mexicans, persons of oriental extraction, and other ethnic groups, and the role and contributions of women, to the economic, political, and social development of California and the United States of America, with particular emphasis on portraying the roles of these groups in contemporary society.

§ 13556.5 Duty Concerning Instruction of Pupils Concerning Morals, Manners, and Citizenship

Each teacher shall endeavor to impress upon the minds of the pupils the principles of morality, truth, justice, patriotism, and a true comprehension of the rights, duties, and dignity of American citizenship, including kindness toward domestic pets and the humane treatment of living creatures, to teach them to avoid idleness, profanity, and falsehood, and to instruct them in manners and morals and the principles of a free government.

§ 8503. Instruction in Personal and Public Health and Safety

The adopted course of study shall provide instruction at the appropriate elementary and secondary grade levels and subject areas in personal and public safety and accident prevention; fire prevention; the protection and conservation of resources, including the necessity for the protection of our environment; and health, including the effects of alcohol, narcotics, drugs, and tobacco upon the human body.

State Regulations***

In recommending this *Social Sciences Education Framework for California Public Schools,* the California State Board of Education intends to provide maximum freedom and flexibility for local school districts to develop their programs in ways that are most effective for their students and communities. However, this freedom and flexibility are to be exercised within the requirements set forth in the Education Code, the administrative regulations of the California State Department of Education, the mandates of the State Board of Education, and the goals and objectives recommended in this framework.

Education Code sections 8501 through 8576 contain certain course requirements affecting social sciences education. According to these requirements, instruction in the social sciences must provide a foundation for understanding the following:

121

TABLE 23 (Continued)

State Regulations

History, resources, development, and government of California and the United States of America

Development of the American economic system

Man's relations to his human and natural environment, including the wise use of natural resources

Eastern and Western clutures and civilizations

Contemporary issues

Role and contributions of women, American Negroes, American Indians, Asian Americans, Mexican Americans, and other ethnic groups to the economic, political, and social development of California and the United States, with particular emphasis to be placed on the roles of these groups in contemporary society

Education Code sections 9240 through 9246 also specify certain content requirements affecting social sciences education. According to these requirements, a school district governing board must adopt only those instructional materials that, in its determination, accurately portray the following:

Contributions of men and women in all types of roles, including professional, vocational, and executive roles

Role and contributions of American Indians, American Negroes, Mexican Americans, Asian Americans, and members of other ethnic and cultural groups to the total development of California and the United States

Role and contributions of the entrepreneur and labor in the total development of California and the United States

Place of human beings in ecological systems and the necessity for the protection of the environment

Effects on the human system of the use of tobacco, alcohol, narcotics, and restricted dangerous drugs

A school district governing board may not adopt instructional materials that, in its determination, contain (1) any matter reflecting adversely upon persons because of their race, color, creed, national origin, ancestry, sex, or occupation; or (2) any sectarian or denominational doctrine or propaganda contrary to law. In addition, the instructional materials must be accurate.

The reader of this publication should be aware that this framework is not a course of study.

*SOURCE: *California Education Code.*

**The 1974 amendment included "instruction in our American legal system, the operation of the juvenile and adult criminal justice systems, and the rights and duties of citizens under the criminal and civil law and the State and Federal Constitutions in subd. (b).

***SOURCE: *Social Studies Education Framework for California Public Schools.*

TABLE 23 (Continued)

What California Respondents
Believed the Mandates Were

COURSES OR TOPICS	TEACHERS* (N = 46)	ADMINISTRATORS* (N = 24)
American history	63%	100%
American government	54	42
American culture	0	0
State history, state government, state studies	19	21
Federal or state constitution	2	0
Citizenship, patriotism	9	0
Law	11	0
Social studies	4	0
World history or culture	6	8
Consumer education	4	4
Free enterprise education	0	0
Minority studies	11	0
Don't know	11	13

*Percentages are based on four responses and add up to more than 100%.

CHAPTER 5

How Law-Related Education Gets into the Curriculum

If mandates are not generally responsible for introducing law-related education into the curriculum, then how do law courses and units enter the course of study? Who are the important actors in the process, what steps do they take, and what factors influence the introduction of law-related education?

It is not easy to trace particular courses, units, or topics back to their origins. Getting them from an idea to the classroom involves differing degrees of inspiration, directives, personal effort, and bureaucratic maneuvering. This is not to say that we have no idea how law-related courses, units, or topics come into the curriculum. This study has provided data on who introduces law-related education, what forms of personal and institutional support are necessary, and what factors influence the way it is carried out.

One key to understanding this process can be found in the ways law-related education differs from innovations of the 1960s, when large, well-financed curricular reform projects tried to make major changes in school programs. The new math, for instance, was a radical new approach to a traditional course of study. The new emphasis in chemistry and physics required expensive new equipment. Advocates of team teaching and open education tried to make fundamental changes in the way schools were structured. These reform efforts differed considerably, but their leaders shared an ambitious, expansive belief that fundamental reform was essential to the rebirth of American education.

The 1970s are obviously very different. Even if they believe fundamental reform is necessary, educators recognize that this is a period of lowered expectations and contraction in education. With enrollments shrinking and money for education in short supply, the climate is more hospitable to curricular reforms such as law-related education, which does not posit a brand new curriculum focus but rather a more intensive look at an area already somewhat familiar to social studies teachers.

Our findings suggest that the present social studies staff and structure of the American secondary school are conducive to this innovation because it does not require expensive equipment and does not require reorganizing the school schedule. The law can be taught one period a day, five day a week, for a quarter, a semester, or a year, with an occasional guest speaker and field trip. All schools have some relevant materials such as library and course books on government, history, the law, and lawyers, and law-related course materials are available for relatively little money, often less than the cost of new textbooks. Although special teacher education programs can improve law-related education, the many teachers who have taken college courses giving them some general understanding of the subject may need only a little assistance to teach effectively. All in all, then, law-related education requires little money, needs no cooperation among various departments, and imposes no awesome new burdens on the schools. Law can be taught without special attention from school administrators or the support of the entire faculty.

This is not to say that there are no obstacles. Any curricular reform faces tough sledding these days. Teachers may not feel competent to teach about law and legal processes. Some teachers may believe that topics like student rights raise volatile issues they are unprepared to deal with. And teachers may not know where to find the institutes, materials, and community resources that will build their confidence and help them teach more effectively.

Moreover, law studies can benefit greatly from flexible schedules, off-campus learning experiences, extensive use of law-related professionals as instructors and advisors, and the involvement of other teachers and administrators. However, law studies do not *require* these major changes. Indeed, they can be—and often are—the result of the interest and commitment of individual teachers.

125

THE TEACHER IS THE ONE[1]

Our research suggests that the classroom teacher is critical to introducing law-related education. Planning, choosing materials, presenting lessons, and evaluating the effects of instruction are teachers' jobs. Unlike several of the ill-fated curricular innovations of the 1960s, law-related education makes no claim to being "teacher proof." Instead, law-related education is teacher-centered.

When the interviewers asked teachers in our five-state sample how law was introduced into the curriculum, the answers ranged from the simple to the complex. At one end of the spectrum were answers emphasizing the autonomy of individual teachers. Some said they could introduce law topics or even a law course on their own, with minimal outside permission or support. At the other end of the spectrum, we found elaborate procedures for planning, polling students, and obtaining approval from several layers of supervisors. *What is notable, however, is that the largest number of responses were some variation of "I wanted to do it."*

Typically, the teachers offering law-related instruction said they chose to teach it because it interested them. Although they did not generally use the words of those who study their profession and did not speak of "psychic rewards,"[2] this phrase does summarize the motivations of teachers presenting law courses, units, or topics. (See Table 30.)

Most often, teachers told us they taught about law because of a "personal interest" in the subject. Sometimes, the interest was in the history of law; sometimes, in its philosophy; sometimes, in current events and

TABLE 30
WHY LAW IS TAUGHT: TEACHERS' MOTIVATIONS

Most important

↑ Teacher's own interest
Student interest
"Tradition"
Curriculum revision in which
   the teacher participated
Other teachers' interest
Contact with a law-oriented group
State requirement
Textbook
↓ Administrative directives

Least important

126

the law. The teacher wanted to say something about the subject, and he gained satisfaction from doing so.

Our teachers felt they played a big role in introducing law-related education. Given the choice of describing their roles as "decisive," "important,' "minor," or "no role," 31 percent said they were "decisive" and 32 percent said they were "important"; only 37 percent said they had played a minor role or no role at all. These self-evaluations of their role fit with their descriptions of what they did. That is, 38 percent said they had "initiated" one or more law offerings; 27 percent said they had "planned" one or more. (Some had participated in both activities.) Another 15 percent stated that they had implemented the decisions of others; 31 percent disclaimed any role.

Since teachers take personal credit for initiating law studies it is not surprising that 44 percent of our respondents said that their own experience, training, world view, and philosophies had the greatest influence on their decisions about what law topics to teach and how to teach them. They said that only after considering their personal resources did they seek information and encouragement from other sources.

Table 31 presents data on teachers' responses to a question asking which group or person had "great influence, some influence, or no influence" on their teaching of law topics. The most frequently mentioned "great influence" was the teacher's college and post-college education. Almost half claimed that a course or teacher education institute "greatly influenced" their teaching about law. Of these, 45 percent credited an undergraduate course; 19 percent, a graduate course; 25 percent, a law-related institute; and 13 percent, other teacher institutes. Of the teachers queried, 6 percent had attended law school. (Some teachers had been influenced by more than one course or institute, so these figures add up to more than 100 percent.)

Data from responses to other questions strongly suggest that these courses and institutes are effective. We discuss these additional findings toward the end of this chapter in conjunction with Table 42.

Law-related institutes have been conducted by a number of groups, many as part of district-wide or state programs. The Constitutional Rights Foundation and Law in a Free Society have offered courses and workshops in California. Law in American Society has offered a summer institute attended by teams from Georgia, Illinois, Texas, and many other states. In Pennsylvania, the state department of education has put on workshops, and the LEAP[3] Temple Law School Project trains teachers in Philadelphia. In Georgia, the Atlanta schools have held summer

TABLE 31
SOURCES REPORTED BY TEACHERS AS HAVING
GREAT INFLUENCE ON TEACHING OF LAW TOPICS

AGENT OF INFLUENCE	CONTEXT FOR TEACHING LAW TOPICS	
	TEACHERS OF COURSES DEVOTED TO LAW* (N = 66)	TEACHERS OF COURSES INCORPORATING LAW TOPICS* (N = 139)
Institute or course	47%	47%
Student	36	35
Department head	27	8
Social studies teacher	25	24
Lawyer	23	20
Justice agency	17	17
Principal	15	6
Bar association	11	11
Superintendent	8	9
State education department	6	8
Civic group	5	6
Other teacher (outside social studies)	4	5
Parent	3	4
PTA	0	1

*Percentages are based on more than one response and will not add up to 100%.

institutes. And in Texas, Law in a Changing Society has offered institutes and courses in many parts of the state.

Every one of these teacher education programs makes heavy use of lawyers and law-enforcement people, and every one has had the cooperation of state and local bar associations and justice agencies.

Lawyers, law enforcement officials, and bar associations were reported to have had a "great influence" on many teachers, and they have had some influence on nearly three-quarters of the teachers we talked to. Fifty-five percent of our teachers said they had been influenced by a lawyer through his lecturing in class, answering questions, and meeting with students. Thirty-nine percent had been influenced by a bar association, and 33 percent by a justice agency. In all, 71 percent of the teachers we interviewed had been influenced by contact with one or more law-related professionals.

Interest in students was another important motivation for teachers.

Studies show that "reaching students" is a critical reward in teaching[4] and that students are a major reference group for teachers.[5] Our teachers told us that in deciding what to teach they frequently attempted to surmise what their students needed.

A Philadelphia teacher told us,

> I ask myself two questions. First, what do the students need to know? Landlord-tenant obligations, divorce laws, and so on. Those are the needs for this community; students at a different school could have different needs. Second, I ask what they want to learn about. Criminal law, civil rights, juvenile law. Those answers define the main points of my course.

Similarly, a teacher from a middle-sized Texas city told us,

> I include the law material I think the kids need most, the material that affects them. Eight of 35 will find themselves in court some day. That's not because they're in a minority group, but because they'll be involved in a divorce or some other civil action.

A teacher from nothern California brought "personal interest" and "student interest" together:

> I always had an interest in the Bill of Rights. And the kids enjoy it. One of the main things in my course is individual rights. We discuss the rights that freshmen have in this school system. I hope I teach them to exercise their rights.

In a sense, teachers who say they are responding to "student interest" may be telling us about their own "personal interest" and how they see the job of teaching. Their personal interest is not so much in subject matter but in the student-teacher relationship.

Most of the time that teachers do not spend with students during the school day is spent with colleagues in the social studies department. In many schools, social studies teachers share a single office—often no bigger than a closet and serving both functions. Before and after school, at lunch and during class breaks, teachers return to this office and talk with their colleagues. Many times, while interviewers in our study waited to speak with someone, they observed teachers comparing methods, experiences, and students.[6] Thus it is not surprising that these teachers were found to credit each other for help in identifying student needs, initiating law studies, suggesting topics, and acquiring materials. Sometimes such help is a result of formal department meetings, but more often it is informal.

129

One colleague of special importance is the department head.[7] Social studies teachers require the support of the department head to institute new courses, and the department head is instrumental in carrying out the department's revision of the curriculum. Many of the teachers we interviewed were quick to acknowledge the support they received from the department head.

Teachers in other departments and administrators outside the school are less important. In general, as Table 32 shows, the farther away officials are from the place of teaching, the less influence they have.

Tables 31 and 32 show the influence of people and groups, but there is one other influence that is important. Thirty-nine percent of the teachers said law-related topics were all over newspapers and television newscasts. For example, a teacher from a small town in Pennsylvania told us "contemporary and controversial issues such as abortion, the right to die, and homosexuality do come up. It just depends on what's current and what students want to cover." Another Pennsylvania teacher said, "I try to organize classes around current issues. . . . I look at major issues and try to work law and order into them." Thus the moral, political, and legal issues swirling about Patty Hearst and Karen Quinlan were intensively discussed in classrooms across the country in 1976, when we were conducting interviews.

Teachers are the central figures in implementing law-related education. *They* choose topics because of their interest or the perceived interest of their students; *they* choose to attend law-related courses and institutes; *they* pick up ideas and assistance from colleagues and lawyers.

TABLE 32
EDUCATORS WITH GREAT OR SOME INFLUENCE
ON LAW-RELATED EDUCATION

EDUCATOR	PERCENTAGE OF TEACHERS REPORTING INFLUENCE* (N = 214)
Social studies teacher	73%
Social studies department head	51
Principal	37
Superintendent	20
State education department	31

*Since respondents often mentioned more than one educator who influenced them, the column adds up to more than 100%.

The overwhelming majority of law-related offerings are in the curriculum because teachers want them there. Less important are external forces that presuppose teachers' passivity—state requirements, textbooks, administrative directives, and, as we shall see in the following section, "tradition." These often have sanctions behind them, but not necessarily rewards.

CONDITIONS THAT AFFECT TEACHERS' ACTION

By examining variations in what teachers do and how successful they are from time to time and place to place, we can get a clearer view of the processes involved in the introduction of new courses, units, and topics. Meaningful differences emerged in our study when we considered two variables: (1) teachers' motivation; and (2) the structure of the offering (course, unit, topic).

Teachers' Motivation

The most vigorous teacher activity, the activity most likely to result in a law-related offering, occurs when teachers are motivated by personal interest in the subject or in students.

As we see in Table 33 teachers define critical decision-making roles for themselves, that is, initiating or planning law studies, when they see law-related offerings growing out of their personal interest or a curriculum design in which they participated. Teachers also assume strong decision-making roles when they act on ideas presented by other teachers or by students. Clearly, they understand that these are circumstances in which they *choose* to act.

TABLE 33
ROLES REPORTED BY TEACHERS,
BY ORIGIN OF LAW STUDIES

	ROLE OF RESPONDENT IN ORIGINATION		
ORIGIN OF LAW-RELATED EDUCATION	NUMBER OF CASES	INITIATING OR PLANNING	ONLY IMPLEMENTING, NO ROLE
Teacher's own interest	58	91%	9%
Curriculum revision	25	92	8
Collectively, other teachers ...	23	65	35
Student interest	29	69	31
Tradition	36	22	78
State requirement	27	22	78
All law-related courses	198	54%	46%

In striking contrast are the passive reactions of teachers who respond to "tradition" and state mandates. When law enters the curriculum because of such factors, teachers say they see their role as "merely implementing." As one might expect, more than half of our respondents who said that the topics had come into the curriculum because of "tradition" or "state requirements" said they played no role in deciding to present law-related offerings.

The content and methods of law-related offerings may be affected by whether the teachers see themselves as planners and movers. Teachers who feel themselves "decisive" in the introduction of law-related topics may teach with more interest and vigor than those who perceive a more passive initial role for themselves. However, we have no evidence on this and suggest it as a subject for further study.

Structure of the Offerings

Teachers report that courses devoted to law originate in a manner somewhat different from that of law units and law topics within broader courses. As we can see again in Table 34, teachers' own interest is the key factor in each type of law-related offering, but in developing a separate law course many teachers apparently need support. Even though a third of the teachers offering a separate course told us that they had introduced the course because of their own interest, 71 percent

TABLE 34
ORIGINS OF LAW STUDIES BY TYPE OF COURSE

ORIGIN OF LAW-RELATED EDUCATION	COURSES DEVOTED TO LAW* (N = 66)	GENERAL COURSES INCLUDING LAW TOPICS* (N = 139)
Teacher's own interest	30%	32%
Curriculum revision	23	9
Collectively, other teachers	18	9
Administration	3	1
Student interest	23	14
Tradition	4	24
State requirement	9	16
Textbook	0	9
Law-related group	18	2
Not ascertained, don't know	9	9

*Percentages are based on three responses and add up to more than 100%.

of them also named other sources of influence or support, such as their colleagues, students, or plans to redesign the curriculum. Redesigning the curriculum may provide a general atmosphere of innovation, specific suggestions for a course, or calendar changes encouraging new courses. Colleagues may share ideas, and students may express enthusiasm and interest. All these made it easier to introduce a new course, according to our respondents.

Bar associations, district attorneys' offices, and law-related education projects are much more important to the development of distinct law courses than to the incorporation of law topics into broader offerings. In many cases, to make contact with these groups is to become part of an information network supplying resources sufficient to build a course, including syllabuses, bibliographies, rosters of guest speakers, and institutes or courses on law-related education. By bringing teachers together with each other and with resources, law-related groups appear to enable them to develop and refine their personal interest in the subject.

Teachers who taught established social studies courses indicated to our interviewers that they needed less outside help for the introduction of law topics. Often, many topics are latent in a lesson plan, a teacher's guide, or a text. They may be covered in a *pro forma* manner or they may be given special emphasis. It is really up to the individual teacher.

ADMINISTRATORS' PERCEPTIONS' OF THEMSELVES AS FACILITATORS[s]

We asked administrators how active they were in initiating, planning, reviewing, or evaluating social studies offerings. As Table 35 shows, 22 percent of the principals and 38 percent of the superintendents simply said they played no role. Although 44 percent of the principals said they played a role in initiating programs, generally administrators claimed only a supporting role.

These responses contrast with some of the findings of other studies of curriculum change,[9] which suggest that superintendents play a large role in educational innovation. However, those studies concerned such fundamental curriculum changes as the introduction of kindergarten or use of the new math, in which one would expect superintendents to be active. Our sample administrators, on the other hand, emphasized that they "worked through channels" and helped others alter the curriculum. As one "moderately active" Chicago administrator told us, "Suggestions are made [by the teacher] to the principal through the assistant principal. I approve them."

TABLE 35
ADMINISTRATORS' INVOLVEMENT IN
DEVELOPMENT OF SOCIAL STUDIES CURRICULUM

Extent of Activity in Social Studies	Principals (N = 72)	Superintendents (N = 42)
Very active	26%	14%
Moderately active	42	36
Slightly active	10	12
Not active	22	38
Total	100%	100%
Role*		
Initiation	44%	26%
Planning	25	24
Review	42	40
No role	22	38

*Percentages are based on more than one response and add up to more than 100%.

Administrators saw three types of facilitative actions as particularly important to the introduction of law-related education. First, principals and superintendents can support changes in the school calendar. As we noted in Chapter 2, creating a quarter system opens the way for law-related courses. Thus a west Georgia principal could describe his role in these terms:

> We were offering a traditional program. I initiated a new curriculum based on a quarter system. We added some new courses.

Similarly, a south Georgia principal told us,

> When we switched to the quarter system six years ago, we completely rewrote our curriculum. All administrators and people in the departments had an input. Since then, the department chairmen and I have worked closely in revision and evaluation.

Second, administrators say they influence the curriculum by hiring teachers who will do things the administrator wants done. Several of our respondents said they put their greatest efforts into selecting faculty. As a principal from a suburban Chicago district said,

> I decided that I'd hire teachers on the basis of their philosophies. I looked for teachers who wanted to individualize materials. Therefore, when the mandate for consumer education came down, I did go down

134

to the department chairman and I did participate in planning, but most of my work had been done when I hired the teachers.

Similarly, an assistant principal in charge of instruction in a California school said, "Teacher selection is much more important than textbook selection. I'm very active in it."

Third, administrators are usually the key actors in establishing the atmosphere of the school in regard to change. They create a climate of innovation or a climate that works against change and new ideas. There is a continuing debate about how administrators develop an atmosphere of innovation—or whether it can be done at all. Our respondents provided some illustrations of how they believe it is being done. A superintendent in western Pennsylvania noted, "I've presented some of my ideas to social studies teachers. I've suggested some simple mini-courses that I think might be interesting." In this way, he kept teachers aware of his interest in and openness to new ideas. A suburban Los Angeles principal described his actions:

> I'm mainly a catalyst and a monitor. Most good ideas come from the staff. I encourage teachers to develop new ideas and then we try them. They're usually successful.

A further illustration of this indirect influence is provided by the answer to another question. When asked directly "If you decided to increase your offerings in the law-related area, how would you go about it? What would you do?" many administrators had trouble formulating an answer. A few thought that such a decision was not really within their power. Many pointed out that their ability to act was limited. In doing so, they often seemed to adopt a perspective that several researchers have noted. That is, each teacher guards his own autonomy and professional independence, and although open to influence, may bristle and resist forceful administrative attempts to change his own style. Thus administrators talked of "preliminary steps," "needs assessments," and "resources." The most frequent answers brought up conversations with faculty members, unofficial memos, or casual statements in meetings. In many cases, administrators said they would try to find "interested teachers," returning responsibility for concrete action to teachers.

Thus administrators are not particularly visible in introducing law-related education. Initiation may be a spark, an idea, a suggestion. It may be as broadly conceived as "evaluate the curriculum" or "discuss program revision." Review is passive and often *pro forma*. Administra-

135

tors make decisions that affect the organization, tone, and style of the school. Teachers make decisions that affect their classroom—what they are going to teach, when, and how. Although administrators' decisions have an effect on teachers' decisions, it is difficult for teachers and administrators to identify direct causal links.

TEACHERS' PREPAREDNESS

Because teachers are key actors in introducing law-related education, we must be concerned with the extent to which they feel well prepared to deal with the subject. It is logical to believe that their understanding of issues is crucial to the quality of law-related education.

Unfortunately, many of our respondents thought they were inadequately prepared to teach about the law. When we asked teachers if they felt any "constraints" in teaching the subject, the largest number who felt constrained mentioned their own lack of knowledge. Here are some sample responses:

> I'm not a lawyer. I can only speak in a general way, not about the intricacies of the law.

> I have feelings of inadequacy with regard to topics and the fine points of law. I do not have information at my fingertips. I could use a lawyer.

> It is difficult to keep up with changes. Decisions are difficult to follow.

> I never feel really comfortable with them (law topics). Discussions are always open-ended, because I'm never able to close a case. It bothers me. I feel inadequate with it. I tell kids, that's why there are juries, because things aren't clear cut.

Teachers generally feel they do not have enough information about legal issues and cases, and they may not know where to get such information.

To find out how teachers evaluate their preparation to teach about law, we had our interviewers ask teachers two questions that tied together information and access to resources:

1. "What has been your source of information on legal developments such as laws or court cases?"
2. "In your experience as a social studies teacher, have there been times when you felt that you did not have a good grasp of laws that affected you as a teacher? (If Yes) Did you do anything?"

Two-thirds of the teachers said they had more than one source of information about the law and court cases, including general reading, courses they had taken, texts and other course material, lawyers, and friends. Table 36 suggests a possible inadequacy in these sources. An overwhelming majority reported using "general reading" as their first or second source of information. A significant minority used it as their *only* source. Such material may indeed give teachers relevant information, but it will usually not provide great detail. Even the *New York Times* prints complete transcripts only of major United States Supreme Court decisions.

Many teachers reported that they relied entirely on textbooks for their information, but most of the texts they named were general history or government texts—volumes that do not provide much law-related information and are not revised often enough to include recent decisions. The contents of the texts did not match the teachers' lists of topics they covered.

Fewer than 40 percent of our teacher respondents named one or more sources that were directly law-related—law journals, lawyers, representatives of justice agencies, court records, briefs, legislative hearings, or legislators.

However, responses to our second question suggest that teachers do

TABLE 36
SOURCES OF INFORMATION ON LAW
AS REPORTED BY TEACHERS

Sources	Percentage of Teachers Reporting Use of Source* (N = 204)
General	
General reading and watching:	
magazines, newspapers, media	63%
(only resource is general reading and watching)..	21
Texts and other teaching materials	21
College and in-service courses	10
Local school professional staff	10
Professional literature, journals	6
Friends	6
Speakers, politicians	4
Law-Related	
Specific law-related material	21
Community legal sources: lawyers, justice agents	12
Other	3

*Percentages are based on two responses and add up to more than 100%.

137

have resources when they seek answers to questions about education law. Sixty-five percent of our teachers said they had sometimes felt they lacked information about laws that affected them as teachers (for example, information about tenure laws). This is not itself evidence of teachers' ignorance—after all, even lawyers have a hard time keeping up with laws and court decisions concerning schools. Indeed, the teachers who never felt they lacked information probably were not so much competent in the law as they were unconcerned about it.

Thus our greater concern is what teachers said they did when they felt they lacked information about education law. When asked what they had done, 31 percent said they had researched the problem or taken a course. Seventeen percent consulted their professional association, 14 percent approached school authorities, 5 percent consulted an attorney. All in all, 74 percent did something. We have no way of gauging the value of these sources, but we think it is impressive that three out of four teachers found some kind of help.[10]

We also approached the question of teachers' preparedness another way, asking them directly what they knew about the law. Obviously, we could not measure all that the teachers knew and still pursue other areas of the study. We could not even measure all they thought they knew about a single area of law, such as landlord/tenant relations or criminal law. Therefore, we decided to ask about two Supreme Court cases that dealt with the schools themselves, *Tinker v. Des Moines Independent School District*[11] and *Goss v. Lopez.*[12] Since *Tinker* and *Goss* affect school people directly by requiring them to make adjustments in the ways they treat students, we thought teachers interested in law might reasonably be expected to be familiar with the cases.

Tinker dealt with a group of students who were forbidden to wear armbands to school in protest against the Vietnam War. The Supreme Court ruled, however, that the Constitution gave students the right to express their political opinions in school, as long as students did not "materially or substantially disrupt" the educational process. The majority wrote,

> It can hardly be argued that either students or teachers shed their constitutional rights to freedom of speech or expression at the schoolhouse gate.

> School officials do not possess absolute authority over their students. Students in school as well as out of school are "persons" under our Consitution. They may not be confined to the expression of those sentiments that are officially approved.

138

In *Goss,* the Court ruled that students could not be suspended without being informed of the reasons for the suspension and the evidence supporting the charge, and without being given an opportunity to tell their side of the story. This landmark case established that public school students are protected by the due process clause of the Fourteenth Amendment, so schools must adhere to "minimum procedures" before students can be deprived of their property right to an education.

What are these "minimum procedures"? The majority explicitly did *not* require formal hearings to "afford the student the opportunity to secure counsel, to confront and cross-examine witnesses supporting the charge or to call his own witnesses to verify his version of the incident." Instead, hearings can take place minutes after the incident and can be quite informal, as long as students learn the charges against them and have the chance to tell their side of it.

The *Tinker* and *Goss* decisions extended certain constitutional protections to students, but they did not give students unlimited power or rights without responsibilities. The disruption proviso in *Tinker* defines a boundary; students may be punished if they cross it. *Goss* does not prohibit suspension as a form of punishment but merely sets up certain minimal standards that must be met before students may be suspended. Both decisions recognize the authority of school officials and teachers and define circumstances under which student action can be controlled.

These decisions raise issues directly relevant to social studies teachers. First, teachers sometimes help develop policies regarding students and often are the key people enforcing school rules. Second, both decisions include clear statements on the importance of schools in citizenship education, noting that young people in school learn the importance of democratic participation, respect for the rights of others, and self-discipline in schools. And both decisions observe that the behavior of teachers and administrators is important in conveying lessons about citizenship, perhaps as important as classroom instruction.

Finally, these cases are directly relevant to three important goals of our teachers. Almost half said that they wanted to promote understanding of school governance and school disciplinary procedures. A third said they wanted to teach students practical skills, and an equal proportion said they wanted to teach students their rights and responsibilities. Not all of these teachers were thinking about the present—problems of authority over students or the rights and responsibilities of student citizens, for instance—but many were.[13] For example, a teacher in Texas emphasized the need to teach students their rights:

Students have to know law to protect themselves so that they can't be suspended from school without a written warning. They should know their rights—police shouldn't treat them poorly simply because they are black. They must know what they can push and what they can't.

To see to what extent school officials and teachers understood *Tinker* and *Goss,* the interviewers asked if they had heard of the cases and recalled what the Court ruled.[14]

Tables 37 and 38 show that our administrators and teachers were not particularly knowledgeable about the two cases. Only 27 percent of the teachers were aware that students had the right to express themselves only if they did not disrupt the educational process. Another 27 percent knew the general direction of the ruling in *Tinker* but either did not mention the disruption proviso or knew only that the Court had found for the students. All in all, then, only a bare majority (54%) could be described as minimally knowledgeable about the case.

TABLE 37
TEACHERS' AND ADMINISTRATORS' UNDERSTANDING OF TINKER CASE

Educators' Perception of Court's Holding in Tinker	Teachers (N = 214)	Administrators (N = 115)
Students have a right to express themselves as long as they don't disrupt	27%	47%
Students have right to express themselves (no mention of disruption)	19	20
Court ruled in favor of students	8	5
Students have no right to wear armbands—Court ruled against students	2	1
Don't know	44	26
Total	100%	100%

Fewer teachers (43%) knew that the *Goss* case established that students must be granted due process (33%) or granted a hearing (10%). When we pursued the question and asked for the elements of due process the Court required, only 4 percent could come up with all three elements.

TABLE 38
TEACHERS' AND ADMINISTRATORS'
UNDERSTANDING OF GOSS CASE

Educators' Perception of Court's Holding in Goss	Teachers (N = 214)	Administrators (N = 115)
Students have to have a hearing	10%	8%
Students have to have due process	33	54
Other	2	0
Don't know	55	38
Total	100%	100%

Educators' Perception of Elements of Due Process Specified in Goss	Teachers* (N = 207)	Administrators* (N = 115)
Student must be told reason for suspension, given chance to explain, and told evidence	4%	17%
Student must be told charges against him	15	17
Student must be given chance to explain his side	6	16
Student must be advised of his rights	1	2
Student must be granted hearing (no further specifications)	26	27
Student must be granted school board hearing	4	2

*Percentages are based on three responses and do not add up to 100%.

We decided that we would accept any correct knowledge of either case as an indication of understanding. Thus our criterion is the weakest possible. Yet Table 39 shows that even given this weak criterion, at best only 32 percent of our teachers had some understanding of both cases.

Administrators are more familiar than teachers are with these decisions, probably because they are responsible for policies affecting students. Even so, fewer than half fully understood either case (Tables 37, 38, and 39), and almost 40 percent had no knowledge of the *Goss* decision (Table 38).

Our analysis has focused on the distinction between some knowledge and no knowledge of the two cases. We should note, however, that educators are frequently misinformed, especially about *Goss*. More than 10 percent incorrectly told us that *Goss* gave students the right to legal counsel. Others incorrectly thought that *Goss* required schools to allow

TABLE 39
TEACHERS' AND ADMINISTRATORS' GENERAL
UNDERSTANDING OF TINKER AND GOSS CASES

At Least Minimal Understanding	Teachers (N = 214)	Administrators (N = 115)
Both cases	32%	52%
One case	32	31
Neither case	36	17
Total	100%	100%

students to bring in witnesses, to cross-examine witnesses, and to appeal suspensions.

When asked about the elements of due process required by the Court, many teachers confused criminal due process with *Goss's* minimal due process, thinking that the careful procedural due process guaranteed to criminal defendants in such landmark cases as *Miranda v. Arizona, Escobido v. Illinois,* and *In re Gault* must now be accorded to school children. Such misunderstanding undermines support for the Court's decisions and reduces respect for the law in general.

A JUSTIFICATION OF OUR MEASURES OF TEACHERS' PREPAREDNESS TO TEACH ABOUT LAW

We readily concede that our measures of teachers' preparedness are limited. Perhaps the teachers who did not understand the *Goss* case were very well informed about *Brown v. Board of Education,* the *Miranda* case, and dozens of others. And it is very difficult to say that one source of information about law is necessarily better than another.

However, we infer that these measures do tell us something about how well prepared teachers are, since the teachers who understand the cases and know how to find resources see themselves as more likely to be active politically and take stands outside the classroom on public issues.[15] (See Tables 40 and 41.) We think that teachers who see themselves as active in the community may really be so, and thereby constitute a valuable model of concerned citizenship for students. Since these teachers also score well on our measures of preparedness, then our measures may well be a part of a general structure of knowledge and commitment.

Table 42 provides further justification of our measures by showing

142

TABLE 40
RELATIONSHIP OF TEACHERS' REPORTED ELECTORAL PARTICIPATION TO UNDERSTANDING OF LEGAL CASES AND SOURCES OF INFORMATION ON LAW

Understanding of Tinker and Goss	Have Worked in an Election	Have Not Worked in an Election	Total	Number of Cases
Has some understanding of both cases	75%	25%	100%	69
Has some understanding of one case	56	44	100	69
Doesn't understand either	46	54	100	76
Sources of Information on Law				
Community legal sources	76%	24%	100%	25
Specific law material	64	36	100	41
Local school professional staff	65	35	100	20
"General" texts, materials, courses	52	48	100	58
Only source is general reading and watching	56	44	100	43
What Teachers Do When They Lack Grasp of Law				
Something	65%	35%	100%	82
Nothing	42	58	100	31

that those who understand one or both of the cases, who do something when they lack a grasp of laws, and who have an explicitly law-related source of information are more likely to teach a course devoted to law and to have attended a law institute or graduate course.

This table also suggests that teacher education programs may be doing their job, since teachers who have attended an institute are far more likely to understand the cases and report a law-related source of information, and they are, according to their self-reports, somewhat more likely to actively seek information when they lack a grasp of the

TABLE 41
RELATIONSHIP OF TEACHERS' TAKING OF PUBLIC STANDS TO UNDERSTANDING OF LEGAL CASES AND SOURCES OF INFORMATION ON LAW

Understanding of Tinker and Goss	Have Not Avoided Public Stands	Have Avoided Public Stands	Total	Number of Cases
Has some understanding of both cases	84%	16%	100%	69%
Has some understanding of one case	82	18	100	69
Doesn't understand either	72	28	100	76
Sources of Information on Law				
Community legal sources	91%	9%	100%	24
Specific law material	83	17	100	40
Local school professional staff	95	5	100	21
"General" texts, materials, courses	78	22	100	55
Only source is general reading and watching	83	17	100	41
What Teachers Do When They Lack Grasp of Law				
Something	84%	16%	100%	79
Nothing	76	24	100	29

laws. Perhaps the most gratifying finding for projects is that those who have attended institutes are three and a half times more likely than those who have not to be part of a network of lawyers, police officials, and other who can serve as law-related sources of information. (The value of the teacher education programs can't be conclusively proved by this table, however, since it is possible that teachers who attend institutes are more interested in law to begin with and may understand these cases and have law-related sources of information before going to the teacher education program.)

TABLE 42
RELATIONSHIP OF TYPE OF COURSE AND OF INFLUENCE ON TEACHING TO KNOWLEDGE OF LEGAL CASES AND SOURCES OF INFORMATION ON LAW

Base N's	Type of Course Respondent Teaching	Know One or Two Court Cases	Do Something When Lack Grasp of Laws	Have a Legal Source of Information	Have Only a General Source of Information
66	Teach a distinct law course	82%	92%	49%	12%
139	Incorporate law in other course	57	64	21	25
	Reported Influence on Respondent's Teaching of Law				
36	Influenced by a law institute	80%	81%	53%	8%
26	Influenced by a graduate course	79	81	25	21
62	Influenced by an undergraduate course	65	67	26	31
89	Not influenced by any course	51	71	15	13

SUMMARY

Law-related education is a "do-able" curricular innovation, which does not require new funding or radical restructuring of school practices. Teachers and students have a great deal of interest in law, and teachers have many law-related resources and information sources. However, teachers think that they don't know enough about law (and their answers to our questions about *Tinker* and *Goss* confirm this belief).

Perhaps the most important finding in this chapter is that classroom teachers are the key actors in introducing law-related education and that their interest is stimulated by undergraduate courses, the needs of their students, current events, reading about legal developments, and informal conversations with friends and colleagues.

These findings suggest that projects will often not have to create an audience but rather be able to build on the already-existing readiness to teach about law and legal process.

The conventional wisdom in the field is that teacher education is the best way to foster programs and build the confidence and skills of teachers. Our findings support this view by showing that teacher education may provide substantive information about law and put teachers in touch with written, audiovisual, and human resources.

The findings discussed in this chapter suggest that school administrators who wish to stimulate more teaching about law should recognize that teachers are the key to successful law programs. Administrators can create a climate encouraging teachers to pursue their own interests in creating new courses or altering present courses. They can call teachers' attention to new materials and to teacher education institutes. Finally, they can provide released time for teachers who attend institutes or underwrite tuition and the expenses of attending institutes.

Law-related projects might try to reach specific teachers believed to be interested or they might tap the general reservoir of interest by opening institutes and workshops to any teacher who wants to attend. This latter self-selection process should weed out those who have no interest in the subject and result in attendance by those who have some interest and previous knowledge and, most importantly, are eager to learn more. Given the importance of student interest, law-related projects would seem to do well to include topics that are important to students. Finally, law-related projects probably should not prepare teachers to offer only one program, because teachers prefer to offer law-related education in a variety of course structures and with a variety of emphases. Moreover, since the success or failure of law-related education ultimately rests with teachers, it would seem far preferable to encourage them to create programs built on their own interests and the interests of their students.

Notes

[1] This section is based on responses to the following questions:

How did (this course, this unit, these topics) come to be introduced into this school's curriculum?

How would you describe your role in introducing these law topics to the curriculum? Would you say that you personally were the decisive factor, and important factor, a minor factor, or unimportant to the introduction of law topics into the school's curriculum?

How did you decide what topics to include and how to teach these topics?

Potentially, there are a large number of people and groups who might take an interest in law-related studies and who might have influenced you in your teaching of law topics. As I mention a group or persons, tell me if you feel that they have exercised great influence, some influence, or no influence on your teaching of law topics.

[2]DAN LORTIE, SCHOOL TEACHER (Chicago: University of Chicago Press, 1975).

[3]The initials stand for Law, Education and Participation, a national project of the Constitutional Rights Foundation.

[4]LORTIE, ch. 5; ERNEST R. HOUSE, THE POLITICS OF EDUCATIONAL INNOVATION (Berkeley, California: McCutchen Pub. Corp., 1974).

[5]JOHN GOODLAD, THE CONVENTIONAL AND THE ALTERNATIVE IN EDUCATION (Berkeley, California: McCutchen Pub. Corp. 1975); HOUSE, THE POLITICS OF EDUCATIONAL INNOVATION.

[6]House contends that although contact among teachers is close they communicate "personal rather than professional concerns." Although we observed professional communication, we could not estimate the amount or proportion. House does not provide any data in support of his statement.

[7]The importance of department heads has been somewhat submerged in the data because of a conceptual decision in the survey design and analysis. We analyzed department heads as teachers because the large majority are primarily teachers and only secondarily administrators. (Most department heads receive only a minor course reduction in their teaching loads.) Furthermore, when the responses of the department heads are analyzed, they are similar to those of other teachers.

[8]This section is based on administrators' responses to the following questions:

What have you done?

Would you say you've been very active, moderately active, slightly active or not active?

At what stage would you say you were the most active: initiation, planning and development, review, evaluation?

If you decided to increase your offerings in the law-related area, how would you go about it? What would you do?

[9]Henry M. Brickell has been one of the principal proponents of the role of administrators in educational change. *See, for example,* his paper in Egon G. Guba *et al., The Role of Educational Research in Educational Change, The United States,* CONFERENCE ON THE ROLE OF EDUCATIONAL RESEARCH IN EDUCATIONAL CHANGE, UNESCO INSTITUTE FOR EDUCATION, Hamburg, Germany, July 19–22, 1967, The National Institute for the Study of Educational Change.

[10]Administrators faced with a legal question have more resources than teachers. Forty-three percent said they would contact the school attorney

147

(only 5% of teachers would consult an attorney), 21% would research the problem, 21% would get help from other administrators, and 11% would seek help from the state education department (no teachers would turn to this source). Only 8% of administrators who sometimes lacked a grasp of the laws said they would do nothing to seek out information.

[11]Tinker v. Des Moines Independent Community School District, 399 U.S. 503 (1969).

[12]Goss v. Lopez, 419 U.S. 565 (1975).

[13]Another YEFC survey also suggests that teachers are interested in student rights and responsibilities. About 1 percent (300) of the readers of YEFC's UPDATE ON LAW-RELATED EDUCATION returned opinion cards on the first issue of the magazine. In response to a question giving them a choice of seven topics that might be emphasized in future issues, half chose "student and teacher rights and responsibilities," and two-thirds chose "practical law/skills that student should know," an option that might include student rights. No other options were as frequently chosen. See page 48 of the Fall 1977 issue of *Update* for the full results.

[14]Educators are familiar with testing and being tested. They and we recognize the limits of our test, and we appreciate their willingness to submit to our inquiry. We think the results reward their efforts.

The exact wording of the questions was:

As you know, there have been a series of Supreme Court cases dealing with student rights, for example, Tinker v. Des Moines Independent School District dealing with students wearing armbands to express political opinion and Goss v. Lopez concerning due process procedures for student suspension. Have you heard of either case?

If Yes to *Tinker*

a. We don't expect you to be a constitutional expert, but do you recall what the Court ruled in the *Tinker* case?

If Yes to *Goss v. Lopez*

a. (Again) we don't expect an expert's answer, but do you recall the ruling of the Court in the *Goss* case?

b. What elements of due process did the Court require?

[15]We asked teachers about their political participation and willingness to take stands outside of the classroom on public issues, because we believe that social studies is more than lesson plans and classroom exercises. It is shaped by the often unconscious attitudes and commitments of teachers and other authorities with whom students come in contact. (See Hess & Torney, pp. 93–94.) Midway through the interview the teacher was asked, "As a teacher in this community have you ever felt you should avoid taking public stands on community, state or national issues outside of class?" Then we asked, "Have you ever worked in an election campaign or run for office yourself?"

148

CHAPTER 6

Laws and Regulations Governing the Preparation of Teachers

We have seen that it is teachers who are for the most part responsible for introducing law into the curriculum and that they credit courses and institutes with helping them teach the subject. In this chapter, we look at state laws governing the undergraduate preparation to teachers and their continuing education and certification, and we suggest how these laws might affect law-related education. Again, we remind readers that our legal research was conducted in 1974–75 and does not reflect developments that may have occurred since then.

UNDERGRADUATE TEACHER EDUCATION

All states require teachers to possess a bachelor's degree to be certified. (See Table 43 on academic requirements at the end of this chapter.)[1] In about a fifth of the states, laws indicate general subject areas in which all teaching candidates are to take courses.[2] For example, in Ohio an applicant must complete a B.A. with 21 semester hours of professional education and 30 semester hours widely distributed over such areas as the sciences, social studies, and humanities.

A number of states go beyond this by requiring that all potential candidates take specific subjects, many of which might help them offer law-related education. Ten states mandate the study of state and federal constitutions for all credential candidates,[3] and one of these,

Nevada, also requires a course in "school law."[4] Four other states make United States history a prerequisite to teacher certification, and Michigan and at least three other states require courses in civics, government, or public administration. In Texas, one cannot get a college degree or teaching certificate without either passing an exam on the state and federal constitutions, or, as a substitute requirement, completing at least six hours in American government or military science.[5]

In addition to laws that set course requirements for all teachers, most states have laws that establish specific requirements for teachers of particular subject areas. (See Table 44 at the end of this chapter.) In the subject area most directly relevant to law-related education, 12 states designate a specialized certificate in social studies,[8] specifying certain required courses and calling for a very heavy emphasis, sometimes as much as 54 semester hours, in the social studies. The other states have no specialized certificate, but holders of a general teaching credential must satisfy certain requirements in order to teach in an academic field like social science or history. These requirements are generally less stringent than those demanded for a specialized certificate. For example, as Table 44 shows, these states tend to specify about 30 hours as the basic requirement for teaching a subject full time and about 20 hours for teaching a subject part time.

College courses in almost all social science areas—American history, American government, political science, sociology, cultural anthropology —could easily include law-related topics, so there is nothing in the laws to prohibit future social studies teachers from gaining a substantial understanding of law, legal processes, and our legal system. However, nothing in these laws requires that law-related education be offered to future teachers.

In conclusion, then, the legal requirements for the undergraduate preparation of teachers are similar to mandates for the teaching of social studies: both provide many opportunities for law-related content, but neither commands that such content be included.

CONTINUING EDUCATION

Many teachers credit institutes and graduate courses with stimulating their interest in law and helping them teach law-related topics. What laws govern continuing education for teachers, and how might they affect the ability of teachers to offer law-related education? This question is difficult to answer since state regulatory schemes differ on so many details and diverse local policies can amplify them in so many ways.

150

(See Table 43, for continuing education provisions in each state.) However, we can say that laws almost universally encourage continuing education for teachers and that nothing in the laws is inimical to law-related courses and institutes.

State Regulation of Advanced Certification

Most beginning teachers do not qualify for a permanent license but rather start teaching on a provisional certificate, and a primary incentive for teachers to continue their education can be found in laws on renewing or extending teaching certificates and laws setting qualifications for more advanced levels of certification. In 33 states, the provisional certificate is of limited duration and validity, and a teacher who wishes to continue teaching must get advanced credits in order to qualify for the standard, professional, or permanent certificate.

The states differ only in detail in providing for advanced certification. State laws in Arizona, Florida, Oklahoma, and other states provide for a provisional certificate but prohibit renewal; teachers in these states must secure the advanced certificate to continue teaching after the term of their provisional license. Pennsylvania permits one renewal of a provisional certificate. Laws in other states indicate the possibility of renewal. The duration of the provisional certification also varies, from 2 years in some states to as much as 10 years in others.

In almost all states, however, continued eligibility and permanent certification require additional schooling and professional growth. Normally, advanced certification calls for a master's degree, usually a fifth year or 30 semester hours beyond the bachelor's degree.[7] Commonly, the requirements for the master's follow the same basic pattern as the requirements for the college degree: The candidate must complete formal education units for the degree, which then qualifies him for permanent certification.

Generally, the code provisions require that to qualify for advanced certification teachers must study at accredited institutions. Several courts have rejected challenges to these requirements, on the assumption that the fact of accreditation indicates a difference in the quality of training.[8] Recent commentary and judicial decisions have cast only a shadow of doubt on these assumptions.[9]

As Table 43 shows, the laws on continued study for certification are largely general, with few specific directives. A few states mandate a certain number of hours in the applicant's teaching fields (Alabama, Georgia, Idaho, Kentucky, Mississippi, Wisconsin) or in professional

151

education related to the teaching fields (Maryland, Ohio). Oklahoma has a unique provision recognizing a J.D. as one of several advanced degrees qualifying for a salary increment, permitting a credentialed teacher to attend law school and then return to teaching at a higher salary.[10] However, we reiterate that these laws are not typical; for the most part, specific areas of study are not prescribed.

State Requirements Governing Local Regulation of Continuing Education

Several provisions in state law deal with professional development programs offered by local districts. State education departments have authority to review and evaluate local in-service programs, to disseminate information about programs, and to furnish resources and financial assistance, but very few states have a well-developed and coordinated plan. For example, only 17 states provide some flexibility for teachers by affording partial credit for training offered under the aegis of a local board of education, or for an independent program approved by a local board. Twelve states have no provisions at all for professional development programs offered by local districts, and many of the others have provisions that apply to teachers in certain subjects only. (See Table 45, "In-Service Training Laws Applicable to Law-Related Education.")

Normally, state statutes and regulations establish a state approval mechanism for professional development programs and merely authorize or require local districts to set up appropriate programs. There are rarely any provisions for state monitoring of the quality of local programs or measuring their relation to curricular needs. The few exceptions require that local programs be based on assessed needs and oriented toward the area for which the teacher is certified,[11] or they permit a wide array of acceptable experiences, including locally designed workshops or planned programs for independent study.[12]

However, the law does often provide incentives for future study. Laws in six states provide for sabbatical leaves, usually for one year, thus giving a financial incentive for teachers who wish to enhance their instructional abilities.[13] Typically, the teacher receives partial compensation, perhaps 50 percent pay, and the year is counted for tenure and retirement purposes. Five states provide for released time for teachers to attend institutes without loss of pay.[14] South Dakota and Montana have legislation giving local boards the authority to require attendance at summer institutes and to discipline those who do not comply.[15]

152

TABLE 45
IN-SERVICE TRAINING LAWS APPLICABLE TO LAW-RELATED EDUCATION

STATES	STATUTORY REQUIREMENTS FOR IN-SERVICE TRAINING	STATE APPROVAL AND ASSISTANCE	LOCAL DISTRICT OPTION TO PROVIDE TRAINING	CREDIT TOWARD ADVANCED CERTIFICATE	SABBATICAL LEAVE, RELEASED TIME	NO PROVISIONS
Alabama	X					
Alaska		X				
Arizona	X					
Arkansas						X
California	X					
Colorado	X			X		
Connecticut				X		
Delaware	X			X		
Florida	X	X				X
Hawaii			X			
Idaho	X					
Illinois						
Indiana					X	
Iowa	X					
Kansas						X
Kentucky	X	X		X		
Louisiana						X
Maine	X					
Maryland	X			X		
Massachusetts						X
Michigan	X	X			X	
Minnesota	X				X	
Mississippi						X
Missouri	X	X			X	
Montana	X					

153

TABLE 45 (Continued)

STATES	STATUTORY REQUIREMENTS FOR IN-SERVICE TRAINING	STATE APPROVAL AND ASSISTANCE	LOCAL DISTRICT OPTION TO PROVIDE TRAINING	CREDIT TOWARD ADVANCED CERTIFICATE	SABBATICAL LEAVE, RELEASED TIME	NO PROVISIONS
Nebraska				X		
Nevada	X					
New Hampshire		X				
New Jersey	X		X			
New Mexico				X	X	
New York				X		
North Carolina	X	X				
North Dakota	X			X		
Ohio					X	
Oklahoma			X	X		
Oregon						X
Pennsylvania				X		
Rhode Island				X		
South Carolina						X
South Dakota				X	X	
Tennessee		X				
Texas		X				
Utah				X		
Vermont				X		
Virginia	X			X		
Washington		X				
West Virginia	X				X	
Wisconsin	X					
Wyoming				X		

Note: Table omits provisions that are limited to particular subject areas unless the provision is somehow related to law studies. For example, the New Jersey provision mandates training in drug education.

154

Another frequent incentive is legislation permitting local boards to set salaries in excess of state minimum requirements for teachers who engage in in-service training[16] or to withhold salary increments from teachers who fail to fulfill local training requirements.[17] Salary scales in local districts are often based on some combination of experience and educational attainments, and courts have uniformly upheld the district's power to reduce salaries or withhold increments as a means of compelling teachers to secure further formal education. In addition, local boards may require further education as a condition of continued tenure of employment. However, once teachers have acquired statutory tenure or permanent status they are entitled to a full panoply of procedural safeguards before they can be removed from their positions.[18]

These varied state and local provisions bear on the continuing education of teachers, but most are not restrictive and offer teachers and local boards many continuing education options. For example, state laws generally specify that continuing education must be undertaken through an accredited institution of higher learning. This may, on the surface, seem to favor colleges and universitites over local in-service programs, but in fact law-related projects report no difficulty in gaining university sponsorship of their in-service efforts, so that teachers can take courses in their own school districts and receive university credit.

All in all, then, law-related projects have ample room under existing law to offer continuing education programs for teachers, and the law provides many incentives for teachers to take such programs.

Notes

[1]*See also* T. M. STINNETT, A MANUAL ON STANDARDS AFFECTING SCHOOL PERSONNEL IN THE UNITED STATES (Washington, D.C.: National Education Association, 1974), Table 1, p. 1, "Increase in Public School Enrollments and Classroom Teachers' Progress in Teacher Preparation 1900 to 1974," and Table 2, p. 2, "Twenty-Three Years of Progress: Minimum Requirements in the States (Bachelor's Degree or Semester Hours) for Beginning Elementary School Teachers 1951 and 1974."

[2]*See* Table 43, "Academic Requirements for Teacher Certification," for initial certification requirements for Delaware, Idaho, Illinois, Kentucky, Nevada, New Mexico, Ohio, Oklahoma, Rhode Island, and Wisconsin.

[3]ARIZONA, STATE DEPARTMENT OF EDUCATION RULES AND REGULATIONS, Art. III, Rule 5; CAL. EDUC. CODE § 44335; FLA. STAT. ANN. § 239.35 (West 1977); GA. CODE ANN. § 32–706 (repealed by Acts 1974); MASS. GEN. ANN. LAWS ch. 73 § 2(A) (1978); NEV. REV. STAT. § 391.090, 394.150, and 394.160 (1973); PA. STAT. ANN. tit. 24 § 16–1605 (Purdon

1962); S.C. CODE § 59–29-120 (1976); TEX. EDUC. CODE ANN. tit. 2 § 13.034 (Vernon 1972); WYO. STAT. § 21–9-102.

[4]NEV. REV. STAT. § 391.090, 394.150, and 394.160 (1973).

[5]TEX. EDUC. CODE ANN. tit. 2 § 13.034 (Vernon 1972) (re § .2663b–1(4) repealed, see n.2).

[6]CAL. EDUC. CODE § 44265, 44282 (1977); Delaware Department of Public Instruction, *Certification of Professional Public School Personnel* (Working Paper to be approved by State Board of Education 1974) pp. 33–35; RULES OF THE STATE BOARD OF EDUCATION OF FLORIDA, ch. 64–4.06; GEORGIA DEPARTMENT OF EDUCATION, TEACHER CERTIFICATION IN GEORGIA (1971), pp. 38–39; IDAHO DEPARTMENT OF EDUCATION, CERTIFICATION OF PROFESSIONAL PERSONNEL (1972), pp. 14–15; INDIANA STATE BOARD OF EDUCATION, BASIC PRINCIPLES FOR CERTIFICATION AND ACCREDITATION (Bulletin 400, revised 1969); KENTUCKY STATE BOARD OF EDUCATION, REGULATIONS OF STATE BOARD OF EDUCATION, R SBE 42.010; STANDARDS FOR CERTIFICATION OF EDUCATIONAL PERSONNEL IN MARYLAND (revised 1971), sec. 617:21; ADMINISTRATIVE RULES AND REGULATIONS OF MINNESOTA STATE BOARD OF EDUCATION (1967), p. 100; MISSISSIPPI STATE DEPARTMENT OF EDUCATION, REGULATIONS FOR TEACHER CERTIFICATION (Bulletin 130, 1970 Revision, p. 22 and Supplement to Bulletin 30); OKLAHOMA STATE DEPARTMENT OF EDUCATION, RULES AND REGULATIONS (1971); RHODE ISLAND STATE DEPARTMENT OF EDUCATION, REQUIREMENTS FOR CERTIFICATION (1964); TEX. EDUC. CODE ANN. tit. 2 sec. 13.039 (Vernon 1972); WASHINGTON ADMINISTRATIVE CODE FOR PUBLIC INSTRUCTION, sec. 3.03 (8c).

[7]For a complete listing of special requirements to teach in an academic field see STINNETT, A MANUAL OF STANDARDS (1974), Table 5, pp. 16–19.

[8]Ahearne v. City of Chelsea 217 N.E.2d 767 (Mass 1967); Aebli v. Bd. of Ed. 62 Cal. 2d 706 (1944); Barnes v. Bd. of Trustees 218 Cal. App. 2d, 881 (1963), *But see,* People *ex rel* Cinquino v. Bd. of Education City of Chicago, 86 Ill. App. 2d 298, 230 N.E.2d 85 (1967) where the board was not permitted to rely on nonaccreditation to retroactively alter salary schedules.

[9]*See* Hunnicutt v. Burge 365 F. Supp. 1227 (MD Ga 1973) where a fully accredited all-Negro state-supported Georgia college was found academically inferior. Since graduates from the college were entitled to teaching certificates, the court held that public school children taught by them were denied equal protection, and it ordered the college desegregated and its educational program upgraded. Another case on parent-teacher interest in the caliber of a school's teaching staff is *in re* Skipworth 14 Misc. 2d 325 Dom. Rel. Ct. N.Y.S. (1968).

[10]OKLA. STAT. ANN. ch. 324 523 (1974) (West).

[11]*See also* COLO. REV. STAT. § 123–17-17 (1974); W. VA. CODE § 18A-3-3.

[12]FLORIDA STATE DEPARTMENT OF EDUCATION, FLORIDA'S STRATEGY FOR

STIMULATING SELF-RENEWAL EDUCATION, 1971: State of Maine, Department of Education and Cultural Services, Administrative Letter No. 56, "In-Service Staff Development and Teacher Re-Certification," August 10, 1973, pp. 3–4; Pennsylvania Department of Education "Guidelines for Approval of In-Service Education Programs," October 1973; Regulations of Board of Education of the Commonwealth of Virginia, "Inservice Training Programs," July 1973; Nevada State Department of Education, "Planning Education for Nevada's Growth, A Master Plan for Education," 1969, pp. 66–78. Vermont State Board of Education Regulations "Certification Through Approval of Local Programs," July 1971.

[13]OHIO REV. CODE ANN. § 3319.131 (1971); W. VA. CODE § 18–2–12 (1977); IND. CODE ANN. § 20–6–12–5 (Burns 1973); MICH. COMP. LAWS ANN. § 340.572 (1976); MINN. STAT. ANN. § 125.18 (West 1968); N.M. STAT. ANN. §§ 77–8–20 to 77–8–24 (Supp. 1975). These provisions are included under local regulation because local districts have ultimate discretion to invoke these statutes for the benefit of particular teachers.

[14]ILL. ANN. STAT. ch. 122, § 24–3 (Smith-Hurd 1962), MICH. COMP. LAWS ANN. § 340.938 (1976); MINN. STAT. ANN. § 121.20 (West 1968); OHIO REV. CODE ANN. § 3313.20 (1971); LA. REV. STAT. ANN. § 17.443 (West 1963).

[15]S.D. COMPLIED LAWS ANN. § 15.902; MONT. REV. CODES ANN. § 75–6111 (1971).

[16]See J. E. Bruno and M. A. Nottingham, *Linking Financial Incentives to Teach Accountability in School Districts*, EDUCATION ADMINISTRATION QUARTERLY (Autumn 1974): 46–62.

[17]E.g., IDAHO CODE § 33–1220 (1963).

[18]States with tenure provisions are indicated in Table 1, in NEA, *Research Report, Teacher Tenure and Contracts* (Washington, D.C.: National Education Association, 1972). *See* LAWYERS' COMMITTEE, A STUDY OF STATE LEGAL STANDARDS FOR THE PROVISION OF PUBLIC EDUCATION, pp. 66–69 for detail on procedural rights accruing with tenure in the various states, and see comment by William R. Hazard, *Tenure Laws in Theory and Practice*, PHI DELTA KAPPAN (March 1975): 451–54.

TABLE 43
ACADEMIC REQUIREMENTS FOR TEACHING CERTIFICATION

State	Initial Certification Requirement I	Number of Years Duration, Renewal II	Continuing Employment, Tenure III	Standard Certification Req. Units* IV	Standard Certification Req. Yrs. Exp. V
ALABAMA	BA (SDE Regs: 1966 *Certification of Alabama Teachers*)	8, can be renewed for additional 8 on proof of 4 yrs. successful experience SDE Regs.	Tenure—After 3 yrs. probation and reemployment for 4th year (tit. 52 ch. 13) (Ala. Code)	BA + MA including 6 SH in teaching field + 6 SH in prof. ed.	
ALASKA	BA (4 Alaska Stat. § 12.020) Type A Cert.	5	Tenure— After 2 yrs. + reemployment by same district for 3rd year (tit. 14 § 14.20.150)	Type A cert. can be renewed if 6 new SH + satisf. service 4 AAC § 12.020	
ARIZONA	BA (1973 SDE *Rules and Regulations Governing the Certification of Teachers & Administrators in Arizona*)	6, nonrenewable (1973 SDE rules)	Tenure—3 yrs. and reemployment for 4th (tit. 15 § 251(2))	MA or 30 SH beyond the BA— valid for 6 yrs. (1973 SDE *Rules*)	
ARKANSAS	BA Exam. (Ark. Rev. Stat. § 80-1201 80-1206)		Local Boards can contract w/teachers for 3-yr. periods. These contracts can be renewed annually.		

State	Requirement		Tenure		
CALIFORNIA	BA (Educ. Code § 13130 Exam.—§ 13130) (Provisional Cert.)	5 (§ 13125.1)	Tenure—After 3 yrs. employment + reemployment for 4th yr. service under Provisional Cert. does not count for tenure	5th yr. college training—(§ 13130)	2 yrs. experience in Cal. schools (§ 13127)
COLORADO	BA (Rev. Stat. § 123-17-14)	5 (§ 123-17-13)	Tenure—After employed for 3 yrs. + reemployment for (4th § 123-18-12 (1971 Supp.))	(§ 123-17-14)	3 yrs. teaching service— § 123-17-14
CONNECTICUT	BA (Gen. Stat. Ann.) (§ 10-146 (1974))	10 (§ 10-146 (1974))	Tenure—After 4 yrs. § 10-151	30 credit hrs. of course work beyond the BA state approved proof or individual proof approved by dist. (§ 10-146 (1974))	From 3 to 10 yrs. teaching experience § 10-146 (1974)
DELAWARE	Provisional Cert. BA including specified SH in gen. & prof. ed. Del *Certification* SBE, 1974 *of . . . Personnel*	3, (Del. Code. Ann. tit. 14 § 1202)	Renewal of Prof. Cert. required every 5 yrs. (tit. 14 § 1203)	Standard Cert. in a subject area good for 10 yrs.; then Professional	3 yrs. exp. req. for Prof. status cert. (SBE Regs.)
DISTRICT OF COLUMBIA	MA (1974 NEA Manual auth. stat. D.C. Code Ann. § 31-102 + 103)		Tenure—After 2 yrs. (tit. 31 § 31-1511, 1512)		

TABLE 43 (continued)

STATE	INITIAL CERTIFICATION REQUIREMENT I	NUMBER OF YEARS DURATION, RENEWAL II	CONTINUING EMPLOYMENT, TENURE III	STANDARD CERTIFICATION REQ. UNITS* IV	STANDARD CERTIFICATION REQ. YRS. EXP. V
FLORIDA	BA (*Rules of SBE of Fla.* ch. 6A-4.04 Supp. #31)	3 (*Rules,* ch. 6A-4.04) Cannot be renewed	Tenure—After 3 yrs. + continuing employment for 4th year. § 231.36	Graduate Cert. good for 5 yrs. must have BA w/major in single subject area. Post-Graduate Cert.—MA, good for 10 yrs. (*Rules,* ch. 64-4.04)	
GEORGIA	BA (*Teacher Cert. in Georgia,* SBE, 1971)	7 yrs.— (SBE Regs.)	Initial cert. renewable on earning credit for 2 additional courses. (SBE 1971 Regs., p. 33) [same renewal for standard cert. req.] No statewide tenure although some local tenure, done by counties.	MA—valid for 7 yrs., including 10 SH in prof. ed. + 25 SH in subject	
HAWAII	BA (authorizing legis. ch. 18 § 296-2)		Tenure—2 yrs. + reemployment for 3rd yr. (Haw. Rev. Stat. § 197-9,10)		

160

State	Certification requirements	Validity (years)	Tenure	Advanced requirement	Experience
IDAHO	BA 24 SH prof. ed. 42 SH gen. ed. (SDE 1972 *Idaho Certification of Professional Personnel*)	5, Renewable (SDE Regs. 1972)	Tenure—2 yrs. + reemployment for 3rd. (Idaho Code § 33- (1212-1215))	MA or approved 5th year program valid for 5 yrs., renewable includes 8 SH prof. ed. 8 SH in teaching field (*SDE '72 Regs.*)	
ILLINOIS	BA 16 SH prof. ed. 42 SH gen. ed. 32 SH area of specialization (Ill. office of Superintendent of Public Instruction, *Certification of Prof. Personnel,* (1972) § 21-5)	4 (§ 21-5)	Tenure—3 yrs. (Ch. 122 § 24-11 to 24-16)		
INDIANA	BA (Ind. SBE 1969 *Bulletin,* "Basic Principles for Certification and Accreditation")	5 (Ind. SBE *Bulletin*)	Tenure—After 5 yrs. + reemployment for 6th. (Ind. Code Ann. §§ 28-4511 to 28-4520)	MA (SBE *Bulletin*)	3 yrs. teaching experience (SBE Bulletin)
IOWA	BA (Iowa SBPI, *Rules & Policies,* Title II ch. 14 § 14.7(2))	10 (§ 14.5(257))	Cert. good for 5 yrs., then must be renewed. (Iowa Code Ann. § 260.12 Renewal for life—after 5 yrs. teaching exp. Iowa Code § 260.13)	30 SH beyond the BA—of graduate credit ((MA) § 14.4(257))	4 yrs. teaching exp. (§ 14.4(257))

161

TABLE 43 (continued)

STATE	INITIAL CERTIFICATION REQUIREMENT I	NUMBER OF YEARS DURATION, RENEWAL II	CONTINUING EMPLOYMENT, TENURE III	STANDARD CERTIFICATION REQ. UNITS* IV	STANDARD CERTIFICATION REQ. YRS. EXP. V
KANSAS	BA (authorized statute —Kan. Stat. Ann. § 72-1388)		Tenure (only in certain cities, no statewide tenure)— after 3 yrs. (72-5401, 5403)		
KENTUCKY	BA includes 45 SH gen. ed. 12-18 SH prof. ed. (SBE Regs. § 42.010)	10 (SBE Regs. § 42.010)	Tenure—After 4 yrs. (§ 161.720)	MA, includes 9 SH in prof. ed. + 12 SH in area of specialization (SBE Regs. § 42.100) [good for 10 yrs., can be extended for life after 3 yrs. successful teaching] (§ 42.100)	
LOUISIANA	BA (La. Standards for State Certification of School Personnel)		Tenure—After 3 yrs. (La. Rev. Stat. Ann. § 17.442)	Type B: BA Type A: MA (La. Standards)	Type B—3 yrs. teaching exp. Type A—5 yrs. teaching exp. (La. Standards)
MAINE	BA (auth. stat. Me. Rev. Stat. Ann. § 20-59)		Tenure—After 3 yrs. (each after 3 yrs.—for at least 2 yrs., automatically renewable) § 20-161(5)	18 SH post BA study (§ 20-1902)	4 yrs. successful teaching (§ 20-1902)

162

State	Certificate (auth.)	Tenure	Advanced	Experience
MARYLAND	BA (*Standards for Certification of Educ. Personnel in Maryland,* 1971, § 612:1) 3 (Md. *Standards* § 613:2)	Tenure—After 2 yrs. + reemployment for 3rd year.	MA, includes 15 SH relevant + anticipated prof. respons. + up to 15 SH in-service training (Md. *Standards* § 612:2)	3 yrs. teaching + 6 SH *or* 5 yrs. teaching (Md. *Standards* § 612:2)
MASSACHU-SETTS	BA (Mass. Title 71 § 38 G) 2 (Mass. Title 71 § 38 G)	Tenure—After 3 yrs. (Mass. ch. 71 § 38 H)		
MICHIGAN	BA (R 390.1125— *Administrative Rules Governing the Certification of Michigan Teachers,* Mich. Dept. of Ed. 1973) 6 (R 390.1127— *Admin. Rules*)	Tenure—After 2 yrs. + reemployment for 3rd year (Mich. Comp. Laws § 38.71 et seq.)	18 sem. hrs. beyond the BA (R 390.1132— *Admin. Rules*)	3 years successful teaching (R 390.1132— *Admin. Rules*)
MINNESOTA	BA (auth. stat.: Minn. Stat. § 125.05)	Tenure—After 3 yrs. + reemployment for 4th yr. (§ 125.17)		
MISSISSIPPI	BA (Class A) (Miss. *Regulation for Teacher Certification,* SDE 1970, Bulletin #130) 5 (Miss. *Regs.*)	No tenure—code permits long-term contracts. (Miss. Code Ann. § 6282-13 et seq.)	Class AA—MA and 15 SH in subject of desired endorsement Class AAA—MA+ 30 SH, (*Regs.—1970 Supp.*)	Class AAA—3 yrs. teaching exp. (1970 *Regs., Supp.*)
MISSOURI	BA (auth. stat.: § 168.021)	Tenure—After 5 yrs. + reemployment for 6th yr. (Mo. Rev. Stat. § 168.102-168.130)		

TABLE 43 (continued)

STATE	INITIAL CERTIFICATION REQUIREMENT I	NUMBER OF YEARS DURATION, RENEWAL II	CONTINUING EMPLOYMENT, TENURE III	STANDARD CERTIFICATION REQ. UNITS* IV	STANDARD CERTIFICATION REQ. YRS. EXP. V
MONTANA	BA (*Certification of Teachers & School Administrators in Montana*, 6th ed. 1973)	Initial Cert. renewable on completion of 4 SH credits (*Cert. of Teachers*)	Tenure—After 3 yrs. and reemployment for 4th. (Mont. Rev. Code Ann. § 75-6101 et seq.)	1 yr. study beyond BA (*Cert. of Teachers*, 1973)	3 yrs. successful teaching (*Cert. of Teachers*, 1973)
NEBRASKA	BA (Neb. Rev. Stat. § 79.1247.06)	3 (§ 79.1247.06)	No tenure— teacher must give evidence of professional growth every 6 yrs. (§§ 79-1255 to 79-1262)		
NEVADA	BA teaching field major + 20 SH prof. ed.	5 yrs. (renewable w/6 new SH credit) (SDE *Regs.* 1972)	Tenure—After 3 yrs. (Nev. Rev. Stat. § 391.3197)	MA (good for 6 yrs., renewable w/3 SH credit (SDE *Regs.* 1972)	3 yrs. teaching experience (SDE *Regs.* 1972)
NEW HAMPSHIRE	BA (auth. stat.: N.H. Rev. Stat. Ann. § 186:11)		Tenure—After 3 yrs. (ch. 189 § 14a		
NEW JERSEY	BA (N.J. Rev. Stat. § 6:11-5.1) (N.J. *Regulations & Standards for Certification*, 1973)	lifetime validity	Tenure—After 3 yrs. (§ 18A:28-5)		

164

NORTH DAKOTA	BA (auth. stat.: D.C. § 15-36-01)		Tenure—no mention of probationary period (§§ 15-47-26, 15-47-27)	*Professional Cert.* 27 mos. successful teaching
OHIO	BA 21 SH prof. ed. + 30 SH gen. ed. (Ohio Rev. Code Ann. § 3319.24) (Provisional Cert.)	4 (§ 3319.24)	Tenure—After 3 yrs. (§ 3319.07-3319.18)	*Professional Cert.* 18 SH beyond BA in prof. ed. + related disciplines (*Laws & Regulations Governing Teacher Education & Cert.*, Ohio SBE (1972) § EDb-301-10-04) *Permanent Cert.*— MA + 45 mos. teaching (*Laws & Regs.* § EDb-301-10-04)
OKLAHOMA	BA includes 15 SH prof. ed. (Okla. SDE, *Rules and Regulations* 1971)	3, non-renewable (SDE *Rules*)	Tenure—After 3 yrs. (Okla. Stat. Ann. tit. 70 §§ 6-101, 6-103)	Standard Cert.— good for 5 yrs. Professional Cert. good for 7 yrs. Req.: "approved program," incl. Okla. history (Okla. *Rules*)

TABLE 43 (continued)

STATE	INITIAL CERTIFICATION REQUIREMENT\n\nI	NUMBER OF YEARS DURATION, RENEWAL\n\nII	CONTINUING EMPLOYMENT, TENURE\n\nIII	STANDARD CERTIFICATION REQ. UNITS*\n\nIV	STANDARD CERTIFICATION REQ. YRS. EXP.\n\nV
NEW MEXICO	BA including 42 SH gen. ed. + 18 SH prof. ed. + specified units in subject area	4 (can be renewed w/8 SH graduate credit) (SBE *Regs.* 1973)	Tenure—After 3 yrs. + reemployment for 4th. (N.M. Stat. Ann. §§ 77-8-8 to 77-8-18)	8 SH beyond MA— good for 5 yrs. and can be renewed with 8 additional SH grad. work (SBE *Regs.* 1973)	
NEW YORK	BA (auth. stat.: N.Y. Educ. Law § 101)	5 (§ 101)	Tenure—After 3 yrs. (§ 2573)	5th yr., beyond BA (§ 101)	
NORTH CAROLINA	BA + NTE (exam) now being challenged) (auth. stat.: N.C. Gen. Stat. § 115-2)		Tenure—After 3 yrs. (N.C. § 115-142)		
OREGON	BA (Or. Admin. Rules § 31.060)	3 (OAR § 31.060)	No state-wide tenure, renewal every 3 yrs. in areas covered by *Fair Dismissal Law*—tenure after 3 yrs. (applies to districts with/ADA —4,500) (Or. Rev. Stat. §§ 342.805 to 342.955)	5th yr. beyond BA + 2 yrs. teaching experience (good for 5 yrs.) Renewal on evidence of 9 quarter hrs. instruction (§ 342.135 and OAR §§ 31-065, 31-075)	

PENNSYLVANIA	BA (Pa. Stat. Ann. tit. 24 § 12-1204)	3, renewable once (auth. stat.: tit. 24 § 12-1252)	Tenure—After 2 yrs. (tit. 24 § 11-1101 et seq.)	24 SH post BA, for Perm. cert. (auth. stat.: tit. 24 § 12-1252)	Permanent Cert. 3 yrs. teaching exp. (tit. 24 § 12-1205)
RHODE ISLAND	BA (SDE *Requirements for Cert.* (1964)) includes 18 SH prof. ed. + specific subjects	6 (*SDE Requirements* 1964)	Tenure—After 3 yrs. (R.I. Gen. Laws §§ 16-13-1 to 16-13-8)	MA or 36 SH beyond the BA (SDE, *Requirements for Cert.* 1964)	3 yrs. teaching
SOUTH CAROLINA	BA (auth. stat.: S.C. Code § 21-45)		No tenure law	18 SH beyond the BA (1962 *Rules & Regulations*) (§ 21-45)	
SOUTH DAKOTA	BA (auth. stat.: S.D. Comp. Laws Ann. § 13-1-32)		Tenure—After 2 yrs. (§§ 13-43-9 to 13-43-15)		
TENNESSEE	BA (auth. stat.: Tenn. Code Ann. § 49-1201)				
TEXAS	BA (Tex. Educ. Code Ann. § 13.036)	no duration limit— shall be valid for life unless cancelled (§ 13.038)	Tenure—After 3 yrs. + reemployment for 4th. This can be extended to 4 yrs. + reemployment for 5th. (§§ 13.101 to 13.116)	30 semester units beyond the BA § 13.037)	3 yrs. experience

TABLE 43 (continued)

State	Initial Certification Requirement I	Number of Years Duration, Renewal II	Continuing Employment, Tenure III	Standard Certification Req. Units* IV	Standard Certification Req. Yrs. Exp. V
UTAH	BA (auth. stat.: Utah Code Ann. § 53-2-15)	5 (§ 53-2-17)	No statewide tenure law. Code allows long-term contracts (for no longer than 5 yrs.) (§ 53-4-14)		
VERMONT	BA (auth. stat.: Vt. Stat. Ann. tit. 14 § 164)	3, (tit. 16 § 1792)	No statewide tenure—certs. must be renewed by SDE every 3 or 5 yrs., depending on type of cert. (tit. 16 § 1751, 1752)	MA or 5th yr. and 5 yrs. successful teaching (Vermont *SDE Certification Regulations* (1971) (must be reviewed every 5 years)	
VIRGINIA	BA (1968 Virginia SDE *Regulations*)		Tenure—After 3 yrs. + reemployment for 4th (Va. Code § 22-217.3 + § 22-217.4)		
WASHINGTON	BA (Wash. Admin. Code § 180-80-210)	3, renewable once (Wash. Admin. Code § 180-80-705), renewal conditions on completing 12 additional quarter hr. units (W.A.C. § 180-80-210)	Statewide tenure— no probationary period—Title 28A § 28A.258.100 et seq.)	5th yr. beyond BA (Wash. Admin. Code. § 180-80-215)	2 yrs. teaching exp.

168

State				
WEST VIRGINIA	BA (W. Va. Code § 18A-3-2)	3 (§ 18A-3-2)	Code goes into *continuing contracts*, after 3 yrs. teaching (same as tenure) (§ 18A-3-2)	18 SH credit and 5 yrs. teaching (§ 18A-3-3)—this is done in 3 stages, or renewals, presenting evidence of 6 SH units for each renewal. After 3 renewals, cert. becomes permanent. (§ 18A-3-3)
WISCONSIN	BA W.A.L. (Public Instruction Code § 118.19)	3, (Wis. Admin. Code P.I. 3.03(5))	Tenure, only in Milwaukee, after 3 yrs. probation. Rest of state has *continuing contracts* (Wis. Stat. Ann. chs. 37.31, 118.23, 119.42)	Life certificate granted after teaching 3 yrs. No additional units necessary. W.A.C. Public Instruction § 3.04(3)
WYOMING	BA (Wyo. Stat. § 21.1-14(c)(i))		Tenure—After 3 yrs. teaching (§ 21.1-152(b))	

*SH means semester hours.

169

TABLE 44*

BASIC AND MINIMUM REQUIREMENTS FOR AUTHORIZATION TO TEACH AN ACADEMIC FIELD OR SUBJECT

State	Social Science		History		Geography		Sociology		Anthropology		Economics		Civics		Pol. Sci. & Government	
	BR	MR	BR	MR	BR	MR	BR	MR	BR	MR	BR	MR	BR	MR	BR	MR
12	14		15		16		18		19		20		21		22	
Alabama	30[b]	18	24	18	24	18	24	18	–	18	24	18	–	–	24	18
Alaska	AC	AC	AC	AC	AC	AC	AC	AC	AC	AC	AC	AC	AC	AC	AC	AC
Arizona	30	24	30	18	30	18	30	18	30	18	30	18	30	18	30	18
Arkansas	24	24	24[b]	24	24[b]	24	24[b]	24	24[b]	24	24[b]	24	24[b]	24	24[b]	24
California	AC	AC	AC	AC	AC	AC	AC	AC	AC	AC	AC	AC	AC	AC	AC	AC
Colorado	M	20[a]	–	20[a]	–	20[a]	–	20[a]	–	20[a]	–	20[a]	–	20[a]	–	20[a]
Connecticut	30	–	18	–	–	–	18	–	–	–	18	–	–	–	–	–
Delaware	30[l]	18[m]	–	–	–	–	–	–	–	–	–	–	–	–	–	–
District	30	–	–	–	–	–	–	–	–	–	–	–	–	–	–	–
Florida	30	–	24	–	18	–	18	–	–	–	18	–	–	–	18	–
Georgia	36	–	24	6	24	6	27	6	27	6	24	6	–	–	24	6
Hawaii	M	M	M	M	M	M	–	–	–	–	–	–	M	M	M	M
Idaho	30	20	30	20	30	20	30	20	30	20	30	20	–	–	30	20
Illinois	24	24[c]	–	–	–	–	–	–	–	–	–	–	–	–	–	–
Indiana	40	24	40	24	40	24	40	24	40	24	40	24	40	24	40	24
Iowa[a]	30[d]	20	30	20	30	20	30	20	30	–	30	20	–	–	30	20
Kansas[a]	36	–	36/12[l]	–	36/6	–	36/6	–	36/6	–	36/6	–	–	–	36/12	–
Kentucky	48[g]	–	30	21	30	21	30	21	–	–	30	21	–	–	30	21
Louisiana	24	24	–	–	–	–	–	–	–	–	–	–	–	–	–	–
Maine[a]	50	50	–	–	–	–	–	–	–	–	–	–	–	–	–	–
Maryland	36[d]	36[d]	24[e]	24[e]	24	24	30	30	24	24	30	30	–	–	30	30
Massachusetts	18	–	18	–	18	–	24	24	–	–	24	24	–	–	24	24
Michigan[a]	36	24	30	20	30	20	18	20	24	20	30	20	30	20	30	20
Minnesota[a]	M	m	M	m	M	m	M	m	M	m	M	m	M	m	M	m

170

State												
Mississippi	30	30	—	—	—	—	—	—	—	—	—[d]	—[d]
Missouri	40	40	—	—	—	—	—	—	—	—	—[d]	—[d]
Montana	30	20	18	18	18	18	18	18	18	18	30	18
Nebraska	45	18	30	18	30	18	30	18	30	18	30	18
Nevada	M	—	M	—	M	—	M	—	M	—	M	—
New Hampshire[a]	AC	AC	AC	AC	AC	AC	AC	AC	AC	AC	AC	AC
New Jersey	30[a]	—[a]	24[d]	—[a]	24[d]	—[a]	24[d]	—[a]	24[d]	—[a]	24[d]	—[a]
New Mexico	24	24	24	24	24	24	24	24	24	24	24[f]	24
New York	36	36	—	—	—	—	—	—	—	—	—	—
North Carolina	35%	—[c]	—[c]	—[c]	—[c]	—[c]	—[c]	—[c]	—[c]	—[c]	—[c]	—[c]
North Dakota	M	16	M	16	M	16	M	16	M	16	M	16
Ohio	—	60	30	20	30	20	16	20	16	20	16	20
Oklahoma	36	18	36[b]	18	36[b]	18	36[b]	18	36[b]	18	36[b]	18
Oregon	36	—	AC	AC	AC	AC	AC	AC	AC	AC	AC	AC
Pennsylvania	AC	AC	AC	AC	AC	AC	AC	AC	AC	AC	AC	AC
Rhode Island	36[d]	18	18	18	12	12	12	12	12	12	12	12
South Carolina	30	18	18	—	—[b]	—[b]	—[b]	—[b]	—[b]	—[b]	—[b]	—[b]
South Dakota	24[b]	—[b]	—[b]	18	12	12	12	12	12	12	12	12
Tennessee	36[d]	18	18	18	12	12	12	12	12	12	12	12
Texas	48[c]	48	36[d]	24	24	24	24	24	24	24	24	24
Utah	42	42	27	15	27	15	27	15	27	15	27	15
Vermont[a]	M	15	M	15	M	15	M	15	M	15	M	15
Virginia	42[e]	24	18	18	18	18	18	18	18	18	18	18
Washington[a]	R	R	R	R	R	R	R	R	R	R	R	R
West Virginia[a]	48[d]	—	—	22[e]	22	22	22	22	22	22	22	22
Wisconsin	54[d]	22	22	22	22	22	22	22	22	22	22	22
Wyoming[a]	36	12	36	12	36	12	36	12	36	12	36	12

*Adapted from T. M. Stinnett, A Manual on Standards Affecting School Personnel in the United States (Washington, D.C.: National Education Association, 1974), pp. 16-19.

LEGEND: Requirements stated in figures are semester hour requirements. BR means the basic requirement for teaching a subject full time, for a major fraction of the school day, or in the highest classification of schools. MR means the minimum requirement for teaching a subject part time, for a minor fraction of the school day, or in the lowest classification of schools. — means not reported. M means a major, m means a minor. AC means approved curriculum. R means institutional recommendation.

TABLE 44 (Footnotes)

Alabama

b A major in social science must include at least two fields.

Arkansas

b Certification in social studies, including 6 s.h. (semester hours)in the specific subject and 3 in state history.

California

a BR—upper division, 24; MR—upper division, 18 or 9.

Colorado

a Including 5 s.h. in the specific subject taught.

Delaware

l Thirty s.h. in specified areas.

m Minimum requirement, including two semester courses in U.S. history, for permission to teach up to three sections or classes along with certificated area.

Illinois

c May be a minor of 16 s.h. in history, provided the applicant has a total of 24 in social science.

Iowa

a Iowa actually issues two authorizations: a general certificate and an approval statement. Institutions are authorized to file programs of teacher education specifying higher than minimum standards. When such programs are approved, students attending such institutions must meet the institutional standards, even though they exceed the minimum state standards, in order to secure "regular approval." Teachers devoting a major portion of time to a subject area are urged to have 30 s.h. of preparation in it.

d Standards require a teaching major (30) or minor (20) in the specific subject or 24 s.h. in social studies, including 12 in the specific subject.

Kansas

a Where two numbers appear, the first is in the field, the second in the subject.

i American history and government or world history.

Kentucky

g Area in social studies includes 18 s.h. in history and 6 each in political science, economics, sociology, and geography; remainder in electives.

Maine

a Maine requires a 30 s.h. major and an 18 s.h. minor, or an area of 50 s.h. Applicants are not limited to subject matter in the major or minor.

Maryland

d Including 18 s.h. in history (6 in U.S. history), 6 in economics, and one course each in sociology, political science, and geography.

e Including 6 s.h. in U.S. history.

Michigan

a The s.h. listed are for majors (BR) and minors (MR). Michigan teachers may teach full time in minor fields.

Minnesota

a College minors must be upgraded to majors within seven years for continued teaching in the subject or field.

Missouri

d Assigned by superintendent.

New Hampshire

a Persons not prepared in a program approved by the New Hampshire State Board of Education, or experienced educators who wish employment in an area for which they are not certificated, may be issued a provisional conversion license, renewable annually on prescribed growth toward standard certification.

New Jersey

a Social studies certification only. Applicants with individual social science specialities receive a temporary certificate.

New Mexico

d Twenty-four s.h. in social science, including 10 in the specific subject.

e Twenty-four s.h. in social science, including 10 in government.

f In social science.

North Carolina
c History and social science.

Oklahoma
b Social studies certification.

Rhode Island
d Must include at least 18 s.h. in history.

South Dakota
b At least 8 s.h. in the subject taught.

Tennessee
d Must include 12 s.h. of history and 6 each of sociology, geography, economics, and government.

Texas
c Must include at least 3-6 s.h. in government, economics, geography, sociology, and history.

Vermont
a Guidelines recommend that all professional certificates must carry one or more endorsements indicating the subject, specialty, instructional level, or range. Applicants shall possess the following academic qualifications or equivalent: (a) In departmentalized schools—an academic concentration or major directly related to the teaching field and taken at an accredited college; at least 15 s.h. in any subject to be taught, even as a minor assignment. (b) In nondepartmentalized schools—75 s.h. of general education distributed with reasonable balance through at least four academic areas.

Virginia
e Including history, 18; government, 12; geography, 6; and economics, 6.

Washington
a Washington issues initial provisional teaching certificates valid for teaching K-9, K-12, or 7-12. Beginning teacher assignments are limited to levels and subjects recommended by the approved institution.

1971 Guidelines and Standards now provide alternate, concurrent standards, including certificate endorsements: "Initial and continuing certificates will be endorsed to indicate grade level(s), content area(s), and/or specialization(s) for which the professional is or has been prepared."

West Virginia
a BR—minimum for grades 7-12 certification; MR—minimums for grades 7-9 certification.
d Must include 24 s.h. of history and 6 each in government, sociology, and geography.

Wisconsin
d Thirty-four s.h. in one subject and 20 distributed among at least two others; or 22 s.h. in one subject and 32 distributed among at least three others. Social studies teachers must complete the legislative requirements of instruction in conservation of natural resources and in consumer cooperatives/cooperative marketing.
e Economics teachers must complete the legislative requirement of instruction in consumer cooperatives/cooperative marketing.

Wyoming
a BR applies to the field, MR to a specific subject.

CHAPTER 7

The Effect of State Law
on Selection of Materials

An extensive body of state law governs the selection of curricular materials and might well affect law-related education. In this chapter, we try to determine that effect by briefly examining the law in the 50 states. We then turn to an examination of the law in the five states we selected for intensive scrutiny. We also look at the processes by which educators in those states select materials.

LAW IN THE FIFTY STATES
Who Has Authority to Select Textbooks?

Textbook selection laws run the gamut from absolute local discretion in choosing materials to complete state control. (See Table 46, "Local Selection of Textbooks.")[1] At one end of the spectrum, Colorado's constitution prohibits both the legislature and the state board of education from playing any role in selecting books for the public schools.[2] Nine other states (those marked with an "x" in column 1) follow a decentralized model exemplified by Connecticut statutes:

> The board of education of each school district shall purchase such books, either as regular texts, as supplementary books or as library books, and such supplies, material and equipment, as it deems necessary to meet the needs of instruction in the schools of the district.[3]

174

In another six states, (those marked with a "P" in column 1) the local district may select some of its textbooks without state approval.[4]

In the 11 states marked in column 2 of Table 46, local choice of texts is extensive but must conform to state guidelines. Often the state educational agency will supply a recommended list even though it does not directly oversee local selection.[5]

In the remaining states, those marked in column 3 of Table 46, the

TABLE 46
LOCAL SELECTION OF TEXTBOOKS

STATES	WITHOUT STATE APPROVAL*	WITHIN STATE STANDARDS**	FROM STATE-APPROVED LIST***
Alabama			X
Alaska			X
Arizona	P		P
Arkansas			X
California			X
Colorado	X		
Connecticut	X		
Delaware		P	
Florida		P	P
Georgia			X
Hawaii			
Idaho			X
Illinois			X
Indiana			X
Iowa	X		
Kansas			X
Kentucky		P	P
Louisiana			X
Maine	X		
Maryland	X		
Massachusetts	X		
Michigan		P	P
Minnesota	P	P	
Mississippi			X

TABLE 46 (Continued)

STATES	WITHOUT STATE APPROVAL*	WITHIN STATE STANDARDS**	FROM STATE-APPROVED LIST***
Missouri			X
Montana			X
Nebraska	X		
Nevada			X
New Hampshire			
New Jersey		P	
New Mexico	P	P	P
New York	X		
North Carolina			X
North Dakota	P		P
Ohio	P		P
Oklahoma	P		P
Oregon		P	P
Pennsylvania	X		
Rhode Island			X
South Carolina			X
South Dakota		X	
Tennessee			X
Texas			X
Utah			X
Vermont			
Virginia		P	P
Washington		P	P
West Virginia			X
Wisconsin			X
Wyoming	X		

SOURCE: Lawyers' Committee for Civil Rights Under Law, *A Study of State Legal Standards for the Provision of Public Education* (Washington, D.C., 1974), p. 73.

*The district may select all (X) or part (P) of its textbooks.

**The district board must select all (X) or part (P) of its textbooks in accordance with certain state standards (i.e., with approval of specific textbooks).

***The district board may select all (X) or part (P) of its textbooks from the state's list of approved textbooks.

176

state selects a list of approved basic texts, leaving the local agency to choose from the materials on the list.[6] Typically, the laws provide sanctions for use of unapproved texts[7] but permit some exemptions. In California (where the state selects materials only for the elementary level), if local school officials demonstrate that state choices do not promote "maximum efficiency," they may, with state approval, purchase alternative materials out of the instructional fund. In some states, districts over a certain size may use their own texts in lieu of state selections.[8] Just as in the area of curriculum control, the state's authority has uniformly been upheld against claims that it infringed on local discretion.[9]

A study of the law alone cannot indicate its effect on curricular innovation. For example, even when local districts are required to select texts from a state list, state regulation may be less extensive than it first appears. The state list normally includes only "basic" texts, with local boards remaining free to select any "supplementary" materials.[10]

On the other hand, state regulation may sometimes be more extensive than it first appears. For example, once a textbook is selected in a New York school district, it may not be superseded for five years except by a three-fourths vote of the local board of education.[11] A recently repealed California law that textbooks must be hard-covered could have impeded the use of more diversified and often more current paperback materials.[12] Requirements of this sort, while a reasonable means of guaranteeing durable texts, might prevent the use of current materials.

Frequently, the law gives local school systems the opportunity to select books not on the approved list, but this option may be rarely exercised. In Georgia, for example, local school districts can spend state funds only for books on the approved list, and additional books must be purchased at the district's own expense. Since many financially strapped local districts may not be able to afford other materials, the approved list has far-reaching influence throughout the state.[13] Similarly, a Florida provision permits only 25 percent of the state instructional fund to be expended on supplementary materials, thus encouraging local systems to prefer texts.[14] Even states that empower local districts to choose their own materials sometimes require that they be paid for entirely out of local funds[15] (although presumably the general education allocation from the state might take this into account).

State Law Regarding the Content of Materials

Statutes on the content of teaching materials tend to further the same goals as statutes on the curriculum. Indeed, very often a single statute covers both the curriculum and teaching materials. (See the discussion of legislative goals for curriculum mandates in Chapter 3.)

Statutes dealing specifically with materials include a New York law excluding books that contain disloyal or seditious matter or are "favorable to the cause of any foreign country with which the United States may be at war" and a Louisiana law requiring that all books be thoroughly "screened" so that all "unwholesome, offensive and unacceptable books" are excluded. Alabama prohibits the use of any written material (except newspapers, magazines and legal opinions by courts of record) which does not contain a statement by the publisher or author indicating that the author "is or is not a known advocate of communist or Marxist socialism, is or is not a member or ex-member of the communist party, and is or is not a member or ex-member of a communist-front organization. . . ." An Oregon provision excludes any textbook "which speaks slightingly of the founders of the republic or of the men who preserved the union or which belittles or undervalues their work." And Nevada will not permit use of any book whose influence on children is "not in harmony with truth and morality or the American way of life, or not in harmony with the Constitution and laws of the United States or . . . Nevada."[16]

Obviously, many of these proscriptions are so indefinite as to be susceptible to countless interpretations, giving school authorities and state officials the power to exclude materials on the basis of vaguely articulated standards or even without any standards. But any attempt to use these provisions to curtail student publications or to discipline teachers who allegedly do not comply would encounter serious constitutional objections because the language is not sufficiently precise to permit restrictions on First Amendment rights.[17]

STATUTES ON CURRICULUM MATERIALS IN THE FIVE-STATE SAMPLE

Statutes dealing with curricular materials differ considerably among the five states we studied. Statutes in Texas and Georgia call for the state to provide a list of acceptable textbooks, in effect limiting the discretion of local school districts. In contrast, the education codes in Pennsylvania, Illinois, and California allow local school districts to choose high school textbooks from the full field of available material.

Texas

Texas law specifies that statewide textbook adoption lists be created

178

"at the various grade levels and in the various school subjects" (2:12.11e). For high schools, the lists must include from three to five textbooks in each of 29 specified subjects, including civil government and American history (2:12.15). In each subject area, a textbook committee of 15 members, at least half of whom must be classroom teachers, chooses a preliminary list (2:12.11). These lists are submitted first to the commissioner of education and then to the state board of education.[18] The final adopted lists are usually maintained for five years. The state board purchases books on the lists directly from publishers, and local school districts requisition the books they want from the state.

These lists "are adoptions for every public school in this state and no public school in the state shall use any textbook unless it has previously been approved and adopted by the State Board of Education" (2:12.16). Fines are also levied for disobedience. School trustees who prevent the use of adopted books and teachers who "wilfully fail or refuse to use the books adopted" are guilty of a misdemeanor and subject to a fine of between $5 and $50 per day for each offense.

A statute deals directly with the content of materials. This section (2:12.28) enables the state board to order "changes, amendments and additions to" adopted books which "in the discretion of the board shall keep them up-to-date and abreast of the times."

The state board has prescribed five textbooks each for the high school civil government and American history courses.[19] From what our interviewers could determine, the lists effectively limit textbook selection. One respondent said he used a text whose title did not appear on the list, but the incompleteness of his citation suggests that he had mistaken the title. Every other Texas history and government teacher our interviewers talked to said he used a book on the list.

On its face, limiting Texas history and government teachers to ten of the hundreds of textbooks published in these subject areas is restrictive. However, our study cannot fully evaluate the effect of Texas policies.[20] Without more extensive data, we can make only a few limited observations.

Our data suggest that the limited selection available to Texas teachers sets them apart from teachers in the four other states we examined, but by no means entirely so. Three books[21] that 16 Texas teachers reported using were used by only three other teachers in the five state sample. On the other hand, three texts reported used by Texas teachers were used extensively outside Texas. The most frequently mentioned book by respondents in Texas was *Magruder's*

179

American Government. This book was frequently mentioned by respondents in other states and may be the most widely adopted high school American government text in the nation.

Georgia

The only content reference in Georgia education law is a restriction on textbooks that "contain anything of a partisan or sectarian nature" (32.708). Like Texas, Georgia law sets up statewide textbook lists; however, the Georgia lists include many more titles, and Georgia law gives local districts the option of selecting texts not included on the lists.

Georgia law provides for the state board of education to prescribe approved textbooks for all grades in the public schools (32–707). The lists may contain many texts or may specify the book to be adopted in a given subject or grade. Unlike Texas, there is no specified number of books that can appear on the lists.

Georgia law calls upon the state board to select a committee or committees of educators actually engaged in public school work in the state to examine textbooks and make recommendations to the board (32. 709). These textbook advisory committees usually deal with a specific curricular area and are limited to five members. A social studies advisory committee is convened every five years to prepare a new list. However, the state board has provided a procedure for including new texts on the list between meetings of the social studies committee and the other advisory committees. The state board has ultimate authority over the lists; its policies provide for it to "approve, add to or delete materials from" the recommendations of the Advisory Committee(s).

The policies of the state board require school systems to select from these lists if they propose to spend state funds for the materials. Although local schools can spend their own money on basal texts not included in the lists, this is financially impractical since about 80 percent of textbook expenditures come from state funds.[22] However, the law does give local districts some choice, since state funds can be used to purchase supplementary books not included on lists, such as paperbacks and library books.

Our data suggest that schools do choose from these lists. All the history and government texts used in the schools we visited were included on the social studies lists.

The 1976 high school social studies listing contains 93 textbooks.[23] These are subdivided into seven areas: American history and government (44); world history and geography (13); Georgia history (4);

180

behavioral sciences (anthropology, sociology, psychology) (8); economics (9); problems of democracy and social problems (5); and sets of books designed to supplement regular texts (10). Although board policies broadly define textbooks to include "basic material essential to instruction . . . including but not limited to hardbound books, softbound books and basic instructional multi-media programs," the list consists largely of hardbound texts.

How much choice does the list provide? Clearly, it provides more choice than the Texas list does. Just as clearly, there are books that are not included. Indeed four of the ten books on the Texas history and government lists are not on the Georgia list.

Many observers alleged that a Georgia text selection controversy in 1971 shows that the lists are available as a device for circumscribing local discretion.[24] The controversy peaked when the state board overrode a decision of an advisory committee and removed from the list 10 books edited by Edwin Fenton. His books, which emphasize the teaching of inquiry skills, had aroused criticism from traditionalist quarters, including a private group called the Georgia Basic Education Council.

A month after it removed the Fenton books, the state board prescribed a year course in history and government. In addition to designing an explicitly chronological course of study, the board limited text selection to four traditional history texts. This decision aroused many protests, and the Board later postponed implementation of the textbook limitation but said the postponement was mainly to avoid the expense of a new adoption.[25]

California, Illinois, and Pennsylvania

These three states do not maintain secondary textbook adoption lists comparable to those of Georgia and Texas. Pennsylvania has no list, and Illinois has only a list including information on book prices. It is based on reports every publisher wishing to sell books in the state must supply to the state superintendent of public instruction. The language of the statutes, enacted in the School Code of 1961 (28–1–3), makes it clear that these lists are intended to provide pricing information to local schools, and are not designed to create approved lists such as those of Georgia and Texas.

California does not have approved textbook lists for secondary schools (it does for elementary schools), but California statutes do provide local school systems with specific content guidelines for teaching materials. For the most part the guidelines relate to sexual, racial, ethnic, and religious considerations. Some guidelines apply to all courses; others are applicable only to courses in designated subject areas.

Two sections of the law are broadly applicable to all materials. The first (9240: 1972) instructs governing boards to include only teaching materials that, in their determination, accurately portray the cultural and social diversity of our society including:

1. the contributions of both men and women in all types of roles, including professional, vocational, and executive roles;

2. the role and contributions of American Indians, American Negroes, Mexican Americans, Asian Americans, European Americans and members of other ethnic and cultural groups in the total development of California and the United States; and

3. the role and contributions of the entrepreneur and labor in the total development of California and the United States.

These provisions parallel statutes governing social science and citizenship education. (See Table 23, Chapter 4.)

A second section of California law (9243) prohibits a school board from adopting material "which, in its determination," contains:

1. any matter reflecting adversely upon persons because of their race, color, creed, national origin, ancestry, sex or occupation; or

2. any sectarian or denominational doctrine or propaganda contrary to law.

Additional statutes instruct governing boards to see that certain topics and values are included in materials for specific courses and subjects. One section (9242:1972) instructs boards to adopt textbooks containing the Declaration of Independence and the Constitution for courses in social science, history, or civics "when appropriate to the comprehension of pupils."

Though these requirements of California law are fairly specific, they give school boards great discretion. School boards are left to decide what is racist or sexist and which materials incorporate the prescribed values.

HOW EDUCATORS PERCEIVE STATE LAW DEALING WITH CURRICULAR MATERIALS

Educators' perceptions of the importance of state laws on materials tend to reflect the law in their state.[26] (See Table 47.) In Texas and

TABLE 47
TEACHERS' AND ADMINISTRATORS' PERCEPTIONS OF THE IMPORTANCE OF LAWS, BY STATE

TEACHERS

IMPORTANCE OF TEXT ADOPTION LAWS	CALIFORNIA (N = 45)	GEORGIA (N = 36)	ILLINOIS (N = 23)	PENNSYLVANIA (N = 43)	TEXAS (N = 43)	ALL (N = 190)
Very important	18%	47%	13%	7%	30%	23%
Moderately important	24	33	22	7	37	25
Of minor importance	18	3	17	23	28	18
Not important	40	17	48	63	5	34
Total	100%	100%	100%	100%	100%	100%

ADMINISTRATORS

	(N = 21)	(N = 21)	(N = 14)	(N = 21)	(N = 22)	(N = 99)
Very important	24%	48%	21%	14%	64%	35%
Moderately important	9	33	7	24	18	19
Of minor importance	33	19	29	29	14	25
Not important	34	0	43	33	4	21
Total	100%	100%	100%	100%	100%	100%

Georgia, where schools must by law choose from a state-approved list, teachers, principals, and superintendents in our sample were more likely to say that laws on materials were very important. In Pennsylvania and Illinois, where there are no comparable laws, respondents were more likely to say that such laws were not important.

Many California respondents thought the laws were important, but many did not. These responses may well reflect the numerous California laws that seek to influence the content of materials. Additionally, they may reflect the fact that until recently California did have state-wide materials lists for secondary schools and still has such lists for elementary schools.

In general, these findings suggest that educators are more likely to be influenced by laws on teaching materials if these laws directly affect the selection process, as they do in Texas and Georgia. If (as in California) the laws are specific about the content and values in materials but do not touch directly on the selection process, they are less likely to influence educators. This underscores our findings about curriculum mandates—educators are more likely to be influenced by mandates directly affecting the curriculum (for instance, requiring a course) or directly affecting teachers (for instance, requiring them to give a constitution test) than by mandates merely indicating that certain values and subjects be included somewhere in the curriculum.

HOW MATERIALS ARE SELECTED IN THE FIVE STATES

In the five sample states, some statutes on materials selection allow much more flexibility than others, but even the more restrictive statutes give local school districts some choice. How do teachers and administrators in the sample use this choice? What did they tell our interviewers about how materials are actually selected in these five states?

First of all, who selects curricular materials? The interviewers asked teachers in the sample to describe how the materials they used "came to be selected." When necessary the interviewers employed a series of probes such as "Who identified the materials initially?" "Who participated in selection?" "Did any guidelines apply to selection?" "Did anyone review the selection?" Using the information developed in response to these questions, we attempted to determine who chose the most important material used in the course.

The Teacher Is the One Again

As Table 48 shows, 40 percent of the teachers said they took complete responsibility for the selection of the most important classroom

TABLE 48
SELECTED PROCEDURE FOR MOST IMPORTANT CLASS
MATERIAL, BY TYPE OF COURSE

SELECTION PROCEDURE	TEACHERS OF COURSES DEVOTED TO LAW (N = 62)	TEACHERS OF GENERAL COURSES INCLUDING LAW TOPICS (N = 121)	ALL (N = 183)
Respondent says he has complete responsibility for selection	47%	35%	40%
Respondent says he identified materials and chose with review	21	15	17
Respondent says teachers collectively, department chose (respondent participated)	22	24	23
Respondent says committee or other person chose or provided materials (respondent did not participate)	10	26	20
Total	100%	100%	100%

material, and another 17 percent said they identified and selected the most important materials but that their selection had been reviewed. But since half of this latter group indicated that the review was *pro forma,* it seems reasonable to combine the two categories and conclude that if these self-reports are accurate, a majority of the teachers in the sample are primarily responsible for the most important materials in their law-related courses. Another 23 percent said that they made the decision with their department head or that the teachers collectively had decided. With only a few exceptions, when respondents told us that teachers collectively had chosen, they indicated that they had participated in the process. Only 20 percent of our respondents told us that the choice had been made by a committee of which they were not a member or by some other person. Therefore, in materials selection, as in course design, teachers indicated that they were the most important figures.

As Table 48 shows, teachers of courses devoted to law apparently had a larger role in materials selection than that of teachers of general courses incorporating law topics. The difference is easily explained. Some of the courses devoted to law are experimental, many are new, and most involve only one teacher. In such circumstances, teachers tend to have maximum discretion. By contrast, broader courses that deal in part with law are more likely to be a traditional part of the curriculum and to involve greater numbers of students and teachers. These circumstances tend to reduce the discretion available to individual teachers.

Teachers of courses devoted to law also have a large role in selecting materials because such courses are newer. Teachers are still experimenting with topics and approaches, and there are few basal texts in the area. Teachers said they select a variety of materials, including paperbacks, pamphlets, magazine articles, and other teaching aids, further enhancing their personal responsibility.

An examination of the role claimed by teachers in selecting materials and the type of materials teachers rely on shows that those who claimed a greater role did indeed rely on different materials. As Table 49 shows, respondents who said they had sole responsibility for choosing materials were less likely to use texts than were teachers who said the decision had been made collectively and teachers who said they took no part in the process. Furthermore, teachers who had sole responsibility for choosing materials were more likely to use materials they had developed themselves or pamphlets and handouts they had managed to accumulate.

There is, additionally, a strong positive relationship between respondents' roles in course origination and their roles in materials selection. Table 50 shows that teachers who claimed to have been decisive in introducing law into the curriculum were most likely to also take complete responsibility for the selection of the most important material they used. Those who claimed a minor role in introducing law were most likely to select the most important material collectively or have no role in the process.

The Role of Department Heads and School Administrators

Teachers view the administrator's role in selecting materials as minor and limited to review and approval. In our sample, only one teacher credited an administrator as initially identifying materials, only three credited curriculum coordinators, and only ten the department head. None of our teacher respondents suggested that an administrator or curriculum coordinator had chosen materials, and only two said that the department head had chosen them. The administrators we interviewed tended to confirm their own limited role.

186

TABLE 49
MOST IMPORTANT CLASS MATERIAL, BY
MATERIALS SELECTION PROCEDURE

		SELECTION PROCEDURE		
MOST IMPORTANT CLASS MATERIAL	COMPLETE RESPONSIBILITY FOR SELECTION (N = 72)	IDENTIFICATION AND CHOICE WITH REVIEW (N = 32)	COLLECTIVE CHOICE BY TEACHERS OR DEPARTMENT (N = 44)	CHOICE OR PROVISION BY COMMITTEE OR OTHER PERSON (N = 37)
Textbook	44%	38%	64%	70%
Paperback or supplementary book	21	29	27	16
Teacher-prepared materials, learning packages	14	9	5	3
Documents, pamphlets, freebies	15	9	0	8
Audiovisual	4	6	2	3
Other	2	9	2	0
Total	100%	100%	100%	100%

187

TABLE 50
IMPORTANCE OF RESPONDENT'S ROLE IN INTRODUCING LAW, BY MATERIALS SELECTION PROCEDURE

SELECTION PROCEDURE

IMPORTANCE OF RESPONDENT'S ROLE IN INTRODUCING LAW	COMPLETE RESPONSIBILITY FOR SELECTION (N = 72)	IDENTIFICATION AND CHOICE WITH REVIEW (N = 32)	COLLECTIVE CHOICE BY TEACHERS OR DEPARTMENT (N = 44)	CHOICE OR PROVISION BY COMMITTEE OR OTHER PERSON (N = 37)
Decisive	50%	27%	18%	17%
Important	24	46	41	33
Minor or unimportant	26	27	41	50
Total	100%	100%	100%	100%

The curriculum coordinators with whom our interviewers spoke did not claim significant roles in materials selection.[27] They appear to operate on the peripheries of the decision, mainly facilitating the work of others and reviewing and approving the materials they choose.

Curriculum coordinators said they acted primarily as facilitators. They provide teachers with information about new materials, they organize committees to study materials, they act as conduits between the teachers and the district administration. They do not, however, seem to play much part in deciding what materials are selected. The comments of four curriculum coordinators are illuminating.

When I run across material I think would be relevant, I pass it along to the teachers. Teachers have to be interested in your idea or forget it.

The curriculum consultant works with the department chairman. Our role is not one of development but review.

I organize teacher groups, which decide on curricula and write the curriculum guide. I provide texts and materials to teachers who evaluate them for courses.

I set up committees of teachers, and act as moderator. The teachers decide.

Principals and supervisors appear to be less active than curriculum coordinators. When we asked if they played any role in textbook selection, 57 percent of the principals and 42 percent of the superintendents surveyed in our study said they played no role. Those who did claim a role tended to say they participated in the final stages and limited their activities to review and approval (principals, 30 percent; superintendents, 40 percent). The following comments are typical for principals and superintendents who claimed a role in text selection:

Principal: The only role I play is that final approval goes through me. Book samples may or may not go through me. The teachers make their own decisions.

Superintendent: The principal approves or disapproves teacher selections. I try to sustain the final choices to the Board of Education, which has final approval.

Superintendent: I do not play a direct role in textbook selection. The board of education has to approve all texts. I recommend books to the board.

Administrators in California, Illinois, and Pennsylvania largely restricted themselves to this sort of review and approval. Eleven percent of the administrators, almost all of them from Georgia and Texas, said they were active in appointing teachers to textbook committees.

A handful of administrators maintained that they were catalysts for change and that they passed along materials to teachers. The few administrators who pass on materials and actively encourage teachers to seek out new materials may be frustrated in their efforts. One principal from a town north of Los Angeles expressed exasperation about his attempts to stimulate the use of new materials. He said,

> Have you seen the materials in the library? Sometimes the librarian will come to me and tell me the teachers are not interested. I go to the teachers. There is always more money for materials than teachers are willing to spend. The materials specialists are forced to go out and spend without teacher advice. Sometimes the media people buy materials beyond the need of teachers.

The principal's comments offer several perspectives on materials selection. First he was suggesting that teachers were sometimes lax in seeking out and using new materials, that they did not take advantage of opportunities provided by specialists. But he was also saying that providing materials without teacher participation could be wasteful. Interestingly, our interviewers spoke with several teachers who said they discovered relevant materials gathering dust when they checked out the school library and departmental storeroom after deciding to teach law topics. Somebody, sometime had ordered the materials, but they sat unused until a teacher discovered them.

The Role of Guidelines for Materials Selection

One could argue that administrators and school board members need not take an active role in selecting materials if they formulate detailed guidelines for their selection. However, other than the state lists in Texas and Georgia, we found few guidelines governing the choice of materials. Only one school system among those our interviewers visited had itself developed an approved list of materials. Teachers generally mentioned only such obvious criteria for selection as materials appropriate to the grade level and reading ability of students. A few mentioned budgetary constraints.

Although there are few formal guidelines for selecting materials, good taste and community mores provide important informal parameters

190

in text selection. Several schools our interviewers visited had experienced textbook controversies,[28] and several teachers said that they had rejected materials for fear of offending students or parents and thereby provoking community conflict. Furthermore, several administrators suggested that it was precisely this problem they had in mind in reviewing materials and deciding whether to grant approval.

CONCLUSION

The data developed in this chapter suggest two main conclusions on materials selection: first, teachers are the most important actors in the process; second, while laws on materials selection vary greatly in their influence, even the most restrictive laws leave teachers and administrators with significant choice—which they exercise.

In Texas and Georgia, for example, local districts choose among the books on the state textbook adoption lists. It is noteworthy that in Texas, the state that most limits choice, the administrators were also most likely to claim an active role in text selection. A number of administrators in Texas said they both appointed teachers to text committees and reviewed and and approved selections. Whereas one might expect the elaborate decision process at the state level and the radical reduction of alternatives to lessen the need or desire for elaborate procedures on the local level, the effect in Texas appears to be the opposite. Our interviewer's description of the text selection procedure at one Texas school district is a fascinating testament:

> The respondent was one of 20 members of the school district textbook committee that was to advise the superintendent on a text. All social studies teachers in the district filled out reports on their evaluation of the books. The respondent viewed each school as a subcommittee in this process and was particularly attentive to evaluations from teachers at this school. The committee evaluations were passed along to the superintendent. A public hearing was held before the decision was made. The text selected by the district was *Magruder's American Government.*

This is an example of a highly elaborate selection process within a highly constrained set of alternatives. The school could select one of only five books on the state adoption list, but teachers, administrators, and the community all actively participated in selecting among the five books. In the end they adopted perhaps the most widely adopted government textbook in the nation.

About 40 percent of the states have no approved lists of texts, and those that do have lists clearly leave room for choice among texts and generally do not restrict choice at all among paperbacks and other supplementary materials. The existence of the lists suggests that while it would be advantageous to law-related education if the kind of standard history and government texts often included on the lists had more emphasis on law and the legal process, the existence of the lists is not a serious obstacle to law-related education. The laws of every state provide plenty of opportunity for selecting nontext materials that are specifically law-related, and teachers and administrators agree that teachers themselves—individually or as a team—already have much latitude to select materials.

Therefore, changes in materials selection laws probably are not essential to bring about wide use of law-related units; what is needed are effective campaigns by curriculum developers to call their law-related materials to the attention of social studies teachers and other decision makers.

Notes

[1]We have not here considered in any systematic way numerous provisions regarding other teaching materials. *See, e.g.,* CAL. EDUC. CODE § 51870–71; MASS. GEN. LAWS ANN. ch. 71 § 13 (1978); S.C. CODE 59–9–80; ARK. STAT. ANN. §§ 80–3901, 80 3905; W. VA. CODE §§ 10–5–1 and 10–5–2 (1977) authorizing the use of television for educational purposes; FLA. STAT. ANN. § 233.50 (West 1977) (repealed by Laws 1974 ch. 74–337, § 22) empowering local boards to purchase paperbacks, slides, films, and other material related to required textbooks, as long as they are approved by the state textbook council.

[2]COLO. CONST. art IX § 16.

[3]CONN. GEN. STAT. ANN. § 10–228 West 1977). *See also* WYO. STATE. ch. 10, art. 2 § 181 and ME. REV. STAT. tit. 20 § 161(7) (1965) conferring similar authority on the local district superintendent.

[4]*See* Table 46, and *see* note 10 below.

[5]*See* LAWYERS' COMMITTEE FOR CIVIL RIGHTS UNDER LAW, A STUDY OF STATE LEGAL STANDARDS, p. 71; *see also, e.g.,* S. D. COMP. LAWS ANN. § 13–34–1.

[6]The state education agency prepares the list in the few states in which an independent textbook committee performs that function. *See, e.g.,* ARIZ. REV. STAT. ANN. § 15–442 (2) (1974).

[7]*E.q.,* UTAH CODE ANN. § 53–13–10 (1974) ($100 fine and removal from office); CAL. EDUC. CODE § 9255 and N.D. CENT. CODE § 15–43–12 (1960)

(misdemeanor); NEV. REV. STAT. § 390.230 (1973) ($100 fine); S.C. CODE § 59–31–30 (denied of all state aid).

[8]OR. REV. STAT. § 337.141 (1971) (districts of more than 20,000); S.C. CODE § 59–31–260 (more than 5,000 people).

[9]Wagner v. Royal-Westland Publ. Co. 78 P. 1096, 36 Wash. 399 (1904); Smith v. State Bd. of Control 10 P.2d 736 (Cal 1932).; Leeper v. State 103 Tenn. 500, 53 S.W. 962 (1899); Clark v. Haworth 122 Ind. 642, 23 N.E. 946 (1890).

[10]*E.g.*, N.D. CENT. CODE § 15–43–04 (1960). *See also* CAL. EDUC. CODE § 10002 and 5 CAL. ADM. CODE 9582 distinguishing and defining basic and supplementary texts. *E.g.*, TEX. EDUC. CODE ANN. tit. 2 § 12.62 (Vernon 1972) (for a five-year period); OR. REV. STAT. § 337.050 (for a six-year period).

[11]N.Y. EDUC. LAW § 702 (McKinney 1969).

[12]This provision was superseded in 1970 by Assembly Bill 531. Conversation with Donald Nelson, Director of Instruction, Orange County Educational Research Center, May 13, 1975.

[13]GA. CODE ANN. § 32–721. *See* Mary A. Hepburn's comments on the impact of this law in *A Case Study of Creeping Censorship, Georgia Style,* PHI DELTA KAPPAN (May 1974): 611–14.

[14]FLA. STAT. ANN. § 233.34 (West 1977).

[15]*E.q.*, ILL. ANN. STAT. ch. 122 § 10–20.13 (Smith-Hurd 1962); IOWA CODE ANN. § 301.1 (West 1949).

[16]N.Y. EDUC. LAW § 704 (McKinney 1968); LA. REV. STAT. ANN. § 17–352 (West 1963); ALA. CODE tit. 52 § 433(6a) (1960); OR. REV. STAT. § 337.260 (1971); NEV. REV. STAT. § 385.240 (1973). *See also* S.D. COMP. LAWS ANN. § 13–34–11 (1975) permitting the state board to withdraw from use books that are "undesirable in nature."

[17]*See* Cintron v. State Board Ed. 384 F. Supp. 674 (D.P.R. 1974) striking down as vague, overbroad, and contrary to First Amendment rights a regulation prohibiting circulation of materials "alien to school purposes" and precluding recruitment from the school population of followers for "any organization of political-partisan and/or religious-sectarian character" within the school. *See also* Heady v. James 408 U.S. 169 (1972) regarding campus recognition of Students for a Democratic Society (SDS).

[18]The commissioner of education, an appointee of the state board, can remove books from the list but cannot add any. The state board can remove books from the list submitted by the commissioner, but it too cannot add any. Neither the commissioner nor the state board can reduce this list to one book and thereby eliminate local choice.

[19]Civil Government, High School. BALL AND ROSCH, CIVICS: *rev. ed.;* EBENSTEIN AND MILL, AMERICAN GOVERNMENT IN THE TWENTIETH CENTURY: A PROCESS APPROACH; MCCLENAGHAN, MAGRUDER'S AMERICAN GOV-

ERNMENT; MEHLINGER AND PATRICK, AMERICAN POLITICAL BEHAVIOR; SCHICK AND PFISTER, AMERICAN GOVERNMENT: CONTINUITY AND CHANGE. American History, High School: EIBLING, CHALLENGE AND CHANGE, UNITED STATES HISTORY: THE SECOND CENTURY; GANDY, *et al.*, PERSPECTIVES IN UNITED STATES HISTORY: GRAFF AND KROUT, THE ADVENTURE OF THE AMERICAN PEOPLE; SANDLER, *et al.*, THE PEOPLE MAKE A NATION, VOLUME II; TODD AND CURTI, RISE OF THE AMERICAN NATION: 1865 TO THE PRESENT.

[20]We think a full evaluation of the effect of Texas textbook law would include:

1. A complete picture of the actual distribution of listed texts to see which ones local districts have adopted. (Two books on the American History list, Gandy *et al.* and Sandler *et al.*, were not mentioned by any Texas respondents. Ball and Rosch, on the Government list, was not mentioned by any Texas respondent.)

2. A content analysis of the listed texts compared with other texts to see the extent to which listed texts (and the most frequently used texts) represent the range of other texts.

3. A study of Texas teachers designed to show what books they would select given the full range of available texts.

[21]GRAFF AND KROUT, EBENSTEIN AND MILL, and EIBLING *et al.*

[22]"Many country school districts do not have any other funds for textbook purchase. Thus the recommended list, by what it includes or excludes, has far reaching influence...."*See* Hepburn, *A Case of Creeping Censorship*, PHI DELTA KAPPAN 611.

[23]GEORGIA DEPARTMENT OF EDUCATION, THE GEORGIA TEXTBOOK LIST 1976.

[24]See, for example, Hepburn, A Case Study of Creeping Censorship, PHI DELTA KAPPAN 611, 612.

[25]The textbook limitation was never implemented.

[26]This section is based on responses to a question asking educators whether textbook adoption laws were "very important, moderately important, of minor importance, or not important at all."

[27]Our sample of curriculum coordinators is small and not systematic. The data we collected are suggestive only. Our confidence is increased by the uniformity of the coordinators' responses and the corroboration of their accounts by what teachers told us.

[28]Academic freedom issues are taken up in Part III of the study.

CHAPTER 8

The Effect of State Law on Use of Community Resources

Many contemporary educational innovators assert that the community is a source of experts for the classroom and a laboratory for learning, and most directors of law-related projects believe that the legal system is an especially good resource for the schools. For example, almost every project director who contributed to YEFC's *Teaching Teachers About Law*[1] noted the contribution that lawyers and law-enforcement people have made to the classroom, and they extolled the educational value of studying the legal system in action through courtroom observation, visits to correctional facilities, police ride-alongs, and many other techniques that get students out of the classroom and into the real world. Several of law-related projects, including two of nationwide importance—the Institute for Political/Legal Education and the Constitutional Rights Foundation—have made community involvement the cornerstone of their programs.

Since the community offers a particularly good opportunity for law-related education, we were naturally interested in how teachers make use of the community and how laws and regulations affect what they do.

In general, two kinds of statutes may affect the schools' use of the community. First, there are state laws governing who may teach. To what extent do the laws permit noncertified experts to instruct students in their specialty? Social studies teachers often invite guest speakers from the community into their classrooms. This is an approved educational method for taking advantage of community resources and would seem to raise few legal problems. Less common and more controversial is turning over the class to a community resource person for an extended period, so that the guest replaces the teacher for a set time and purpose.

Second, there are laws governing off-campus activities. To what extent do the laws affect students' ability to leave the school building for alternative educational experiences? Field trips are pretty much like guest lectures. They are well-accepted methods that would seem to raise few problems under the statutes. But there is more uncertainty about longer off-campus experiences, such as for a week, a month, or a semester, or about periodic off-campus jaunts, such as one day a week during a semester. What legally constitutes pupil attendance, and how is the school day defined legally?

STATE LAWS ON THE USE OF COMMUNITY RESOURCES
The Use of Noncertified Persons

Since certification is normally a prerequisite for teachers, it is important to discover which provisions of state law afford additional flexibility in diversifying teaching personnel. What roles may lawfully be undertaken by noncertified individuals who have special familiarity with the law? Under what circumstances may they assist in the teaching program?

Fewer than half the states have any laws on the status and functions of teacher aides and paraprofessionals. But where there is such legislation, it is clear that it is not designed to diversify or expand the personnel resources available for instruction but rather to afford the opportunity for persons without a college education to participate in the educational process. The few statutes that specify anticipated activities in detail talk about hall supervision, lunchroom duty, and help in after school activities or in vocational projects.[2] These stipulations in the education codes are found not among instructional provisions but among those covering noncertified clerical personnel, vocational aides, or janitorial personnel.

There are, then, basically three means of access to classroom teaching for persons who can demonstrate subject-matter competence but who do not satisfy the standard credentialing criteria because they have not completed professional training requirements. One applies to nonaca-

196

demic fields like driver education, vocational education, home economics, and agricultural training, for which until recently there was no approved teacher preparation program.[3] Individuals in these fields can obtain a special subject certification and then are governed by the same personnel and tenure regulations as are regularly credentialed teachers in academic areas. It seems, however, that diversification of curriculum in teacher training institutions may soon make available fully "qualified" teachers even in these areas and thereby curtail use of these provisions.[4] Furthermore, there is no precedent for creating a special subject certificate in an area like law.

A second access route is found in statutes permitting issuance of temporary certificates on a showing of subject-matter knowledge and experience. These are usually of limited duration and are designed to permit a district or school to meet special needs while the teacher completes requirements for regular certification. However, such provisions are usually applicable only when no qualified certified teacher is available,[5] and fully certified social studies teachers are available in abundance.[6]

Thus, for the present, the access of noncredentialed personnel to responsible teaching roles in law studies programs must be authorized by statutes dealing with "experimental" or "special" programs. Such laws permit local boards to employ people who have specialized subject matter skills that teachers with the standard teaching certificate lack. These special projects invariably require approval from the state education department, which must determine whether the proposal will "enhance the level of instruction" in the local district.[7] The lack of provisions institutionalizing such appointments permits the conclusion that "resources specialists" are hired from year to year and do not enjoy the benefits of tenure or job security offered to regular teachers. Laws indicating the duration of such employment limit the position to one year.[8] The statutes speak of persons with "unusual qualifications" or "recognized expertise" in a "specialized limited course of study" or one "not ordinarily coming within the prescribed curriculum of the public schools."[9] The Washington law permits employment of "special instructors" from local institutions (presumably including law schools) or from the community to conduct classes for students showing exceptional academic promise.[10]

All these exceptions to certification requirements are limited in scope and do not seem conducive to establishing long-term arrangements. Moreover, in a period of serious surplus and unemployment, teachers are understandably concerned about any development that might limit

197

job opportunities. While teachers have not opposed the advent of para-professionals and noncredentialed personnel in schools, they have sought with considerable success to control their status and functions,[11] and labor-management negotiations frequently deal with policies regarding teachers' qualifications.[12]

As we stated at the beginning of this discussion, certification laws present no problems for outside speakers, lawyers who help out in mock trial decisions, or others who volunteer to help a certified teacher. Nor is there any legal prohibition against law student volunteers conducting law-related courses in schools and receiving academic credit in law school. However, the laws generally are not hospitable to programs in which noncredentialed persons receive full-time remuneration and are charged with the primary responsibility for educating students.

Fortunately, large numbers of lawyers, law students, and judges have volunteered their time to work with students and teachers, and there is clearly nothing magical about lawyers which automatically imbues them with teaching skills or qualifies them to replace teachers. Law-related projects are virtually unanimous in emphasizing the central role of teachers in law-related education. Nonetheless, state certification laws might pose an obstacle to a few instructional possibilities.

Laws Affecting Off-Campus Learning

Do laws regulating the educational process prohibit or facilitate non-traditional, participatory learning experiences that might enhance students' appreciation for the legal-political process? To paraphrase Mark Twain, do the laws "let going to school get in the way of getting an education?"

Contact and Calendar Laws and Regulations

We look first to laws and regulations that specify the ways of meeting compulsory attendance requirements. Of major concern to school districts because state financing is usually linked to computations of "average daily attendance," they include, for example, school calendar regulations defining the minimum number of days in a school term and contact-hour specifications prescribing the length of a school day and of a classroom session. (See Table 51.)

Reflecting the prevailing view in the early twentieth century that performance should be measured in terms of time spent in the classroom, the Carnegie Foundation for the Advancement of Teaching defined one unit of credit earned as a year's study in a particular subject for 120

TABLE 51

STATE LEGAL STANDARDS CONTROLLING SCHOOL CALENDAR

States	Pupil-Instruction Days — Statute	Pupil-Instruction Days — Regulation	Pupil-Instruction Days — Minimum	Pupil-Instruction Days — Maximum	Sanction for Violation	Length of Day (in hours) by Grade Level	Minimum Class Length — Daily (Min.)	Minimum Class Length — Annual (Hrs.)	Minimum Lab Course Length — Daily (Min.)	Minimum Lab Course Length — Annual (Hrs.)	Calendar Prohibitions — Year Round School	Calendar Prohibitions — Saturday School
Alabama	X		175			K-12:8	50					
Alaska	X		180			K-3:4 4-12:5						
Arizona	X					1-3:4 4-6:5 7-8:6						
Arkansas						K-12:5						
California	X		175		A	K:4 1-3:5½ 4-8:6						
Colorado	X		172			1-12:5½						
Connecticut	X		180			K:2½ 1-12:4						
Delaware	X		180			K:2½ 1-2:5 3-12:6		120				
Florida	X		180			K:3 1-3:4 4-12:5						
Georgia	X					1-3:4½ 4-12:6						
Hawaii	X		180				40					
Idaho	X		180[a]			Primary:4½ above:5	120		145			
Illinois	X		180	185		K:2 1:4 2-12:5						
Indiana		X	175		b	1-2:4½ 3-4:5 5-6:5½ 7-12:6	50		55			
Iowa	X		180			K-3:4 4-12:5½	55					
Kansas		X	180			9-12:6	40		55		X[c]	
Kentucky	X		185			K:3 1-12:6	45					
Louisiana	X		180			K-12:5	55					X
Maine	X		180[e]		A							
Maryland	X		180			K-12:6						X
Massachusetts		X	f		A	Ele:5 Sec:5½						
Michigan	X		180									X

TABLE 51 (Continued)

STATES	PUPIL-INSTRUCTION DAYS Stat-ute	Regu-lation	Mini-mum	Maxi-mum	SANCTION FOR VIOLATION	LENGTH OF DAY (in hours) BY GRADE LEVEL	MINIMUM CLASS LENGTH Daily (Min.)	Annual (Hrs.)	MINIMUM LAB COURSE LENGTH Daily (Min.)	Annual (Hrs.)	CALENDAR PROHIBITIONS Year Round School	Satur-day School
Minnesota	X		175		A	K:2½ 1-3:5 4-8:5½ 9-12:6	50		55			
Mississippi	X		155			K-12:5					X^c	
Missouri	X		174		A	K-12:6						
Montana	X		180		A	K:2	g	116		145		
Nebraska	X		175			K:2 1-3:4 4-12:6	45		55			
Nevada		X	180		A		40	120				
New Hampshire	X		180			1:4½ 2-8:5¼ 7-12:5						
New Jersey		X	180									
New Mexico		X				1-3:4½ 4-6:5 7-12:5½	h					
New York	X		180		A		40	120		165		X
North Carolina	X		180			K-12:6						X
North Dakota	X		180			K-12:6						X^i
Ohio	X		180			K-2½ 1-6:5 7-12:6	40		55			
Oklahoma	X	X	180			K:2½ 1-12:6						X
Oregon	X	X	175			1-2:3½ 4-6:5 7-8:5½ 9-12:6	55					X
Pennsylvania	X		180		A	K:2½ 1-6:5 7-12:5½	j					X
Rhode Island	X		170	k		K:2½ 1-6:5 7-12:5½						X
South Carolina	X		180		A	K:2½ 1:5 2-12:6	50					
South Dakota	X		180	190		K-12:5		120				
Tennessee	X		175			K-12:7						
Texas	X		180			K-12:7					X^c	
Utah	X		180			K-12:7					X^c	
Vermont	X		175^f			1-12:5½						

200

Virginia	X	180		A	K-8:5	9-12:6	55		
Washington	X	180			K:2½	1-3:5		120	X
West Virginia	X	180	185						
Wisconsin	X	180		A					
Wyoming	X	175							

A-Loss of State Aid

SOURCE: Lawyer's Committee for Civil Rights Under Law, *A Study of State Legal Standards for the Provision of Public Education*, pp. 64-65.

NOTE: *Pupil-Instruction Days*—By statute or regulation the state sets the maximum and/or minimum days that a school must be in session. If a school does not meet the state requirements for a calendar year, the state may have some sanction for this violation such as cutting off or reducing state aid (A).

Length of Day—A school must be in session a certain number of hours at each grade level.

Minimum Class Length—The state requires that each regular class period meet for a certain number of minutes each day or a certain number of hours each year.

Minimum Lab Course Length—The state sets separate class length requirements for laboratory courses.

Calendar Prohibitions
1) *Year-Round School*—A state's school calendar directly or indirectly prohibits the introduction of year-round schools.
2) *Saturday School*—The state prohibits any school from having classes on Saturdays.

FOOTNOTES

a) Idaho—minimum of 177 days in elementary schools.
b) Indiana—loss of accreditation.
c) No state aid to districts possible without enabling legislation.
d) Kentucky—without approval of State Board.
e) Maine—not less than 175 school days, no more than 5 days for in-service training.
f) Massachusetts—local board establishes minimum.
g) Missouri—length of class shall conform to one of the following plans:
  1) 6 periods of 55 minutes
  2) 7 periods of 50-55 minutes
  3) 8 periods of 40-45 minutes
  4) combination of 7 periods which are 40-60 minutes
  5) a weekly schedule providing 250 minutes for library classes and 200 minutes for other classes
h) New Jersey—no limitation on class length.
i) North Carolina—Saturday school prohibited unless the needs of agriculture or other conditions make it desirable.
j) Oregon—class length shall conform to one of the following plans:
  1) 6 periods of 55 minutes
  2) 7 periods of 50 minutes
  3) 8 periods of 45 minutes
k) Rhode Island—no teacher required to teach more than 190 days.
l) Vermont—school can petition to State Board for a waiver of this requirement.

60-minute hours or their equivalent. This became known as the "Carnegie unit," was widely accepted as the predominant measure of college preparatory work, and was incorporated into many state codes or regulatory provisions regarding accreditation of schools by the state educational agency.[13] For example, North Dakota requires all courses to be taught a minimum of 40 minutes a day for 180 days, and Kansas specifies 30 units of instruction in separate classes.[14]

Although the vast majority of state codes are silent about where a student must put in the required time, two states expressly demand that it be spent in the classroom. The Massachusetts school calendar is 180 to 185 days "in which both pupils and teachers shall be present and engaged in regular teaching and learning activities." A school day will not be counted for purposes of computing average daily attendance unless a student is physically present for the required number of hours.[15] Arizona law stipulates that high school students be physically present and carry as least four subjects.[16]

Most states recognize time equivalency or permit students to obtain course credit by taking an examination without class attendance.[17] New Mexico has a provision designed to facilitate greater flexibility:

> Credit may be granted for work completion in a period of time that is either longer or shorter than the time normally required. Criteria for successful completion should be developed by the schools as a guide to both students and teachers in assuring quantity and quality of performance regardless of time involved.[18]

In a similar provision, Pennsylvania in addition stipulates that students may earn course credit by independent study, correspondence study, attendance at summer school, Saturday classes, study at summer camps, or any other means approved by the education department.[19]

Even without such exceptions to normal school calendar rules, the authority of local districts may be broadly construed. In the face of a provision of the Illinois education law requiring that days "of attendance by pupils shall be counted only for sessions of not less than five clock hours of school work per day under direct supervision of teachers," the legal adviser to the state superintendent upheld a school's "open campus" scheduling plan. As long as there was an *average* of five hours per day students could do independent work off campus, he wrote, and direct supervision by a certified teacher did not necessitate the teacher's constant presence, nor would a student's absence from the campus result

202

in the loss of an attendance day for the school district for state aid purposes.[20]

To keep apace of educational developments,[21] schools generally are accorded broad discretion in class scheduling and in methods of instruction. Moreover, while legal provisions create some difficulty for off-campus learning, the law does not prevent a school or district from expanding the notion of "campus" to accommodate different types of facilities.[22] And the local agency has similar discretion regarding uses of school property, as long as there is no interference with the proper maintenance and operation of the school.[23]

Laws on Field Experience

State laws regarding field trips and other off-campus experiences are virtually nonexistent, although the frequent use of these educational devices leads one to suspect that there is a vast nebulous realm of unwritten or local rules in this area. Illinois and New York have statutes expressly encouraging released time for field experience,[24] and California law requires that first-aid kits be available.[25] The New Jersey provision, which is frequently used in law-related studies in that state, has been construed by the state commissioner to be such an integral part of a child's educational experience that expenses are met through general instructional funds and not charged to parents of participating students.[26] Hawaii has a rather extensive provision noting that "field trips shall be considered a valid part of the instructional program supplementing and enriching classroom learning experiences." Objectives must be clearly defined and related to the planned itinerary, and arrangements must be made for guides at the visitation site, and for transportation, parental permission, and adequate supervision.[27]

Many laws dealing with school transportation are applicable to field experiences. States have extensive rules about transportation of students to and from school or school activities. There are mandatory provisions that schools furnish bus transportation, precatory rules merely authorizing districts to do so, and laws regarding inspection and minimum standards for buses and the training and licensing of drivers.[28] Districts are either required or authorized to procure liability insurance on vehicles used.[29] Usually, transportation may be provided at public expense to any officially designated school activity either within or without the territorial limits of the district and either during or after school hours.[30] Districts often provide reimbursement for travel on public conveyances

203

or in private vehicles that are adequately covered by insurance. When transportation is in school buses, health and safety requirements usually require buses to be driven by certified operators only.[31]

The issue of liability for injury has sometimes been so seriously distorted as to constitute a substantial impediment to worthwhile educational functions requiring transportation to and from school. David Schimmel points out how educational journals tend to portray the law as "a ubiquitous monster hiding in every education shadow and ready to ensnare any innocent teacher who takes a chance."[32] Although parental permission for field experience cannot relieve a teacher or school district from liability for negligence, the law of liability is no different for injuries sustained on field trips than for injuries occurring in a conventional classroom context.[33] School officials are liable for injury arising out of *any* educational activity if they fail to provide adequate supervision or to otherwise exercise ordinary reasonable care. Decisions regarding innovative programs or field trips should be made on educational grounds and not out of consideration of unknown legal hazards or fear of lawsuits. The law is simply not the problem in this area.

There is, however, one potential obstacle to field experience for public school children. Some state laws require that identical transportation services be made available to parochial school students wherever furnished for public schools. Given the limited amount of funds available for these purposes, school officials constrained by such laws might become very selective in furnishing transportation for off-campus learning. The Pennsylvania provision is exemplary:

> When provision is made by a board of school directors for the transportation of public school pupils to and from such schools or to and from any points in the Commonwealth in order to provide field trips . . . the board of school directors shall also make identical provision for the free transportation of pupils who regularly attend non-public kindergarten, elementary and high schools not operated for profit to and from such schools or to and from any points in the Commonwealth in order to provide field trips. . . .[34]

This statute and a similar one in Illinois have been sustained against judicial challenge.[35] However, it should be noted that state legislatures may refuse to furnish transportation funds to private school children. They have the prerogative to enact laws making money available only to the public schools.[36]

Internships in a lawyer's office, judge's chamber, or law enforcement agency offer another kind of off-campus learning experience. Educators considering such programs might fear that they would be liable for injuries suffered by student interns. However, the same principles concerning negligence for liability on field trips apply to work-study programs. School officials are liable to no greater extent than they are for injuries in the classroom: their responsibility, whether inside the classroom or for outside training experiences, is to provide adequate supervision or to exercise reasonable care.

Notwithstanding these principles, the lack of accident insurance and the fear of liability may discourage work-study programs. Hence, adequate insurance protection should be arranged so that appropriate decisions may be made on educational grounds rather than in response to confusion about the law.

Work-study is further complicated by another type of insurance coverage, workman's compensation. Many employers might want the protection offered by workman's compensation, but it is normally not available for unpaid trainees. Under relevant decisions regarding the scope and coverage of workman's compensation, the student who is working for his own benefit in what is primarily a learning experience and of no great value to the employer is not considered an "employee."[37] Hence he need not be paid the minimum wage and he is not subject to the insurance program and its requirements. A West Virginia policy may offer a way around this problem. In order to induce employers to make available high quality nonpaid work experience programs for public school students, the West Virginia State Education Department has extended workman's compensation coverage to employers and school districts, which may pay a premium based on a hypothetical rate of pay. Since students receive no remuneration for services, they are deemed to be receiving the equivalent of the state minimum wage.

Another potential obstacle to work-study is the type of law found in every state restricting child labor. These follow a common pattern, shaped by the Uniform Child Labor Law first recommended by the National Conference of Commissioners on Uniform State Laws in 1911 and by the federal Fair Labor Standards Act of 1938.[38] The minimum age for work during school hours corresponds in most states to the compulsory schooling requirement.[39] Some states require completion of a certain grade level before a work certificate may be issued.[40] Although at least nine state legislatures have recently reconsidered statutory prohibitions on work during school hours, none have substantially altered the laws.[41] The minimum age for work outside of school hours or for children not attending school is 16 in approximately half the states and 14 in the other half.[42]

It appears that many of these laws need revision to facilitate the expansion of both traditional and experimental work programs and to better reflect the relationship between employment and education. The original rationale of these laws was to protect children against hazardous conditions, unsavory work, excessive hours, or work that would interfere with schooling. Few state laws now expressly recognize constructive work experience as a legitimate part of the educational process, and these are often limited to students engaged in vocational training. An Oregon statute typifies the potential broader exceptions:

> In addition to regular courses of study, any district school board may make available to its students extended educational experiences through public and private community agencies when such experiences can be provided by the agencies more appropriately or at a lesser cost than by the school district. Programs under this section may include but are not limited to work experience programs conducted on a contractual basis with individual employers or employer groups.[43]

Another example is found in the preamble to a recently reformulated Utah law, which encourages "the growth and development of young people through providing work opportunities while at the same time adopting reasonable safeguards to protect them from certain working hazards."[44] We recommend that part-time employment for minors be authorized by statute, at least where it serves as an integral part of or support to the school's education program. One such facilitative law is the 1974 Minnesota act that recognizes employment as an "aid in the economic, social and educational development of young people. . . ."[45]

However, though explicit statutory language of this sort resolves potential problems, a recent court decision may serve as a precedent for excluding student internships from the prohibitions of child labor laws. In this case students challenged a Hawaii state regulation requiring everyone enrolled in public school through twelfth grade to serve on cafeteria duty seven days a year, on pain of one-day suspension for each violation. A federal judge rejected the contention that this amounted to involuntary servitude, because the imposition on the children seemed minimal compared to military conscription or serving as a conscientious objector in a labor camp, which the courts had condoned in the past. Similarly, the court ruled that the Fair Labor Standards Act had not been violated. Comparing the duties to such tasks as dusting erasers,

206

erasing blackboards, putting chairs on tables, and serving as crosswalk monitors, the court deemed this work as "education activity" in the public interest: "These experiences teach not only neatness and responsibility but also civic attitudes fundamental in a collective society where a citizen is often called upon to do his share without economic compensation."[46] If the kind of compulsory labor compelled in Hawaii schools violates neither constitutional nor statutory rights, then student internships with attorneys, law-enforcement agencies, or courts would surely be found to be outside the scope and design of child labor laws and to have substantial educational benefit.

LAWS ON THE USE OF COMMUNITY RESOURCES IN THE FIVE SAMPLE STATES

Exceptions to Certification Requirements

An examination of teacher certification in our five sample states shows that the states can be groups on a familiar continuum. Once again, the two southern states (Texas and Georgia) seem to take a different approach from the northern states in our sample.

Our staff could find no statutes or regulations in Texas that would permit exceptions to normal certification for community representatives who might wish to offer instruction in law-related education. The Texas Education Agency encourages teachers to use the community as a learning resource and suggests that each school maintain a current community resource file, but apparently the agency is seeking to encourage guest speakers and others who will supplement the work of teachers.

One of Georgia's four categories of certification—"permitted personnel"—allows people who qualify on the basis of experience rather than formal education to function as certified personnel. This category is probably intended for people who will offer vocational or technical courses.

Another provision of Georgia law (32–6090a) may permit opportunities for noncertified persons to teach in other courses. It states that the state board of education may "provide for implemention of . . . educational programs not ordinarily within the prescribed curricula . . . which may or may not require use by local units of . . . specially qualifield personnel." The statute authorizes the board to establish "priorities, standards, and criteria" for such programs. This might permit exceptions to certification requirements, but the language of the statute is not clear on this point.

The other three states do have provisions explicitly authorizing teaching opportunities for noncertified persons. Illinois law allows such persons to offer "specialized instruction related to a course assigned to the certified teacher on a regular basis, not otherwise readily available in the immediate school environment." Such instruction must be offered "under the direction of a certified teacher," who is to determine its function "in view of the educational need to be satisfied." Before using the noncertified person the school board must secure the written approval of the county superintendent of schools.

Since the statute points out that the provision is not intended to apply to guest lecturers or resource persons under the "direct supervision" of a certified teacher, it seems likely that what is envisioned is a noncertified teacher actually taking over a course for a period of time, under the general direction of a teacher who probably will not often be present in the classroom.

A Pennsylvania regulation provides that the state department of education may issue, at the request of a local school board, a letter of certification enabling a "competent" person to teach up to 300 hours a year under the supervision of a certified teacher. According to Russell Sutton, Superintendent of Teacher Certification for the Pennsylvania Department of Education, "direct supervision" requires the teacher to be in the classroom while the noncertified person is teaching. Mr. Sutton adds that the provision is designed to enable schools to bring experts from the community into the classroom. He says that the local district has the option of reimbursing the noncertified person. (Interview with Mr. Sutton conducted on May 9, 1978.)

California encourages using community resource persons both inside and outside the formal classroom. A recent report of the Commission on the Reform of Intermediate and Secondary Education in May, 1975, commonly referred to as the "RISE Report," has called for "inclusion of resource people and experts from the community on the instructional staff [and] broad and effective use of human and physical resources in the community and the use of incentives to promote such community participation."

California already has an exception to certification that could facilitate adoption of the RISE program. Section 13133 of the California Education Code provides that on recommendation of local school boards, the Commission for Teacher Preparation and Licensing can issue an "eminence credential to any person who has achieved eminence in a field of endeavor commonly taught ... in the public schools of

208

California." This provision, added to the code in 1970, states that the credential has a one-year duration. It can be renewed three times, after which the holder is eligible for a permanent eminence credential "which may be issued by the Commission."

USING COMMUNITY RESOURCES IN THE
FIVE SAMPLE STATES

The interviewers asked teachers and administrators many questions about their use of the community as an educational resource in order to find out what resources are available and why teachers may or may not have used them. We were especially interested in the effect of law.

Asked if they had tried to use the community as a resource, 85 percent of teachers and all but a few administrators said they had.[47] There was one small difference among teachers from different states. In Texas 75 percent said they used people from the community, compared with 84 to 88 percent in the other four states.

Guest Speakers

Generally, representatives from the community serve as guest speakers, but for 21 percent of the teachers they provided materials or served as curriculum consultants. In addition, a few teachers said that outsiders supervised interns or came to class periodically to teach their specialty. In several programs, teachers said lawyers or law students taught a series of classes.

Teachers reported that the guests in the classroom were almost always lawyers, law enforcement personnel, police, district attorneys, probation officers, judges, elected officials, or business people. Very few teachers invited the clientele of the justice system—prisoners, ex-convicts, ex-addicts, or alcoholics.

The teachers in our sample also appeared unlikely to have had speakers from universities. Only a few teachers mentioned bringing in professional historians or political scientists, perhaps because many towns do not have a college nearby and scholars are less visible than other potential guests in large communities.

Here is how some representative teachers in the sample made use of resource persons. A teacher in a mid-sized Pennsylvania city reported bringing in psychologists, members of a council on drug and alcohol abuse, and the school principal (if students were concerned with a school policy). The teacher said, "I use them as resource people. It's important to learn the interest of students beforehand and help the resource person prepare for questions that are likely. I like discussions with kids getting time to ask what they want to know."

Another teacher in that district reported bringing in lawyers, the D.A., a magistrate, and law enforcement officers such as state police and detectives. They were used mostly as speakers, but they also served as consultants on curriculum and materials. The teacher asked them for suggestions for materials to use and ideas for elective courses, such as one suggested by the D.A. in consumer protection.

A teacher in a Los Angeles suburb reported bringing in political candidates, bar association speakers, and representatives of the League of Women Voters. She used them as guest speakers, informal consultants on course planning, and sponsors for independent study. A Texas teacher reported bringing in local businessmen and county commissioners to talk to classes. An Atlanta teacher had such guest speakers as police, parents, city planners, drug experts, and representatives of the major political parties. An Illinois teacher brought in his congressman to discuss specific problems. He reported that the congressman liked it—after all, kids "are going to be voters."

However, some teachers and administrators told our interviewers that there were problems with using guest speakers. For example, a south Georgia superintendent said: "I've never known a school system that did a real good job at this. It takes motivation and it's time-consuming. You're going to get a nut in eventually, and that discourages us." A second Georgia superintendent told us: "My major disappointment is the hesitancy of teachers and principals. They don't like outsiders in their rooms and in the school; they're afraid they'll find out what they don't know. I did it when I was teaching social studies. It's very important." A central Illinois principal responded: "The thought's been there (but) the faculty is opposed, they feel threatened. The community is afraid too. It's hard to talk to kids. It's a small community."

Teachers who did not bring in community representatives gave several reasons. The largest number said the community did not support the idea of guest speakers. These teachers reported that community people had no time or had been unreliable. A teacher from a mid-sized Pennsylvania city said, "I've tried. They don't like to do it. I'd like to have some into work with students on an extended basis of study." And a teacher in central Illinois said, "It's hard to get their time. I teach three classes. It's hard to get them to come for a whole day."

A less frequent reason was "red tape." Many schools have elaborate procedures for administrative approval of guest speakers. Some even require approval by the school board. These policies often came about because controversial speakers had gotten communities up in arms. A Texas superintendent said:

> We have people in the social science area in the community, but they have biases and present controversial aspects that make them a problem. The true community and state leaders that would give balanced views are too busy to come. We have radicals at both ends, the John Birch Society and the ACLU. These people would be out here every week if I let them.

And a Los Angeles area superintendent said,

> I wouldn't dare let people in without controls. We have to protect our students. It would lead to chaos on campus and insecurity of teachers.

In fairness to school administrators, we should note that most teachers said the requirements to notify administrators were simple and approval was usually routine. Although some teachers were unwilling to go through the procedures, a large majority were not deterred.

A handful of teachers said that outsiders would add nothing to the education of their students. A history teacher from central Texas said: "There are not many people who can speak on history. The good ones are dead." Another teacher from the same county said that he was concerned about bringing in guests because he could not be sure of the quality of their presentation:

> Sometimes speakers say what I want, but I can't be sure, so I don't use people. For instance, if a policeman comes to talk on drugs, I'm not sure what he will say. I do not like to give up control of the subject matter in my courses.

A teacher in a small town in rural Illinois said:

> A lawyer from here has come in a few times, usually around Law Day. Nothing beyond that. Don't see what I'd gain by the mayor or county people coming in. They're not educated people.

Finally, a few teachers told us that their own lack of interest in the community was a reason for not inviting local resource people to be guest speakers. They had not given it sufficient thought and did not know who was available.

So teachers who do not use outsiders as guest speakers offer a wide variety of reasons. We must reiterate, however, that the vast majority of the sample's teachers do use outside speakers in the classroom.

Getting Students Out of the Classroom and Into the Community

Teachers in the sample generally said they saw the community as a place for additional learning experiences. Our interviewers asked, "Have you or any of your colleagues tried projects which take students off the school campus?" Again the number who responded affirmatively—84 percent—was high.

There were some state differences that again suggest that Texas teachers differed somewhat from the rest of the sample. In Texas only 62 percent of teachers said they or their colleagues used off-campus activities. More teachers in Georgia (78%) and Pennsylvania (86%) reported that they or their colleagues took students off campus, and in California and Illinois almost all sample teachers responded affirmatively.

Deterrents to outside projects are transportation and money. Some respondents in all states mentioned one or the other as a problem. For example, a Georgia superintendent shared his transportation problems with an interviewer:

> When a student leaves the campus, transportation is involved. Private vehicles lead to danger. That was the only thing available to us until this year. We took the state to court and for the first time the state is now financing buses. But bus drivers have to be trained. . . . If we were not negative about this, we would have 12 to 24 bus loads daily going hither and yon. Last time they went to Atlanta the bus broke down and they had to be towed.

Some respondents in each state told our interviewers that trips put a strain on school budgets, and two teachers in Pennsylvania mentioned recent rulings that provide for equal transportation for private and public school students. If public school students go on a trip, the district must supply equivalent opportunities to private school students.

There are other problems, according to the responses of our sample. Seven teachers said that there were too many students to take out and supervise adequately. Another seven said that their fear of liability for accidents kept them from planning outside trips.

There were 15, including 9 Texans, simply opposed to leaving the classroom. A few said they did not have time for trips. However, most said that learning belonged in the classroom and leaving it was a waste of time. As a Texas teacher put it,

> I think it is a bad theory. It's a negative approach to education. Trips are not used well. The former principal made us stay in the classroom. Ninety students are too much to take.

212

These teachers, however, were in the minority. Here are some comments from more representative teachers whose students get out of the classroom to learn in the community.

> Every year for three or four weeks students go into the community every day and come back to report to class. Last year the students went to court every morning for a week for a criminal trial. A convict accused of assulting a guard was on trial. (Illinois teacher)

> We look at the legal process in three stages. First students visit a police station, then the courthouse, then the jail—to see what it's like. (Pennsylvania teacher)

> We visit courts, the general assembly of the Georgia legislature, and campaign headquarters. Students also go to a social studies fair, when projects they've made are displayed for regional competition. (Georgia teacher)

> We put kids out in agencies for a day or two. I think there should be more of this. But it should be a learning experience. Some municipal offices get a kid in and have him shuffle papers. A meaningful thing might be for a lawyer to take a kid for a week to watch preparation of a case from start to finish, or get kids riding with cops. (California teacher)

While a few students have become involved in political campaigns, taken public opinion polls, or done independent study off campus, most of the sample teachers said they did not put students into internships. Off-campus projects consisted primarily of class trips to local government-related settings. Courts and city halls were favorites, with jails and police stations visited less frequently. Teachers in all states told us of trips to the state capital, and a few said they have taken students to Washington, D.C.

THE EFFECT OF LAW ON THE USE OF COMMUNITY RESOURCES

As we have seen, most teachers said they invited outsiders into the classroom and got students out into the community. How does law affect these activities?

We asked teachers and administrators:

> Do you know of any laws, rules or regulations which facilitate or deter community involvement in teaching or projects which take students off campus?

> If yes: What effect have they had on education programs here?

213

Larger numbers of administrators (75%) than teachers (60%) said they were aware of such laws and regulations. There were also large differences among the states in the percentage of those aware of such laws and regulations. Teachers and administrators in Texas and Georgia were less aware of laws and regulations than teachers and administrators in other states. Our study found that 49 percent of Texas educators and 57 percent of Georgia educators felt they knew of relevant laws and regulations, contrasted with 67 percent in the other three states. Comparing awareness of laws and regulations in each state with reported use of community resources shows that in those states with greatest awareness there is most use of the community.

Three areas of law or administrative policy stand out in educators' minds: liability for accidents and injury, certification, and school procedures. As Table 52 shows, majorities of both teachers and administrators said fear of being held liable for accidents or injuries was a factor in their thinking about taking students off campus.

A teacher in the Houston area told us his concerns about liability for accidents or injury.

> I get a lot of students who are suit happy. It comes out in classroom discussion that they think if you sue it's a get-rich scheme. The AFT uses the liability issue very heavily to get you to join, at a great cost.

He then showed us a union brochure dramatically illustrating negligence cases that have been brought against teachers. A suburban Chicago area teacher told us:

> If you do take students off campus during school hours you are responsible for them and what they do.

> If you drive students in your car, especially if it's a girl, and she says you did something, oooo! I'd rather take one step back than two steps forward.

A number of teachers are brought face to face with the negligence problem in the form of parental approval of trips. For example, in California parents must fill out "trip slips" before students can go on a class trip.

For many teachers it was not as much a knowledge of negligence law as ignorance of that area of law that deterred them. A comment by a teacher from southern Illinois illustrates the uncertainty many educators feel:

> I would like the law to clarify whether students can or cannot go off campus. It may just be an administrator somewhere who decides against

it. I'd like a law I could show the superintendent who is very in favor of trips but himself under pressure.

What is the effect of these widespread fears? Our interview schedule did not include a question directed specifically at the consequences of fears about liability negligence, but our interviewers estimated on the basis of respondents' informal remarks and their answers to other questions that over half of those who mentioned fear of liability were dissuaded from fully using community resources. The rest lived with their fear and apparently eliminated no trips. However, the respondent who said "I worry a lot" probably spoke for them.

As Table 52 shows, many more administrators than teachers mentioned certification laws as a factor that might affect the use of community resources. They tended to say such laws inhibited their doing more with community representatives in the classroom.

A principal from western Illinois said:

We wanted to use retired people, but we couldn't get them paid for it because they weren't certified teachers. We wanted to use an engineer but he was not allowed to teach physics. We wanted to bring a lawyer into the school but couldn't. A teacher's degree is needed to teach. This

TABLE 52
TEACHERS' AND ADMINISTRATORS' AWARENESS OF LAWS AND REGULATIONS AFFECTING THE USE OF COMMUNITY RESOURCES

LAWS AND REGULATIONS	TEACHERS* (N = 120)	ADMINISTRATORS* (N = 93)
Liability for accidents	54%	58%
Laws and regulations governing parental approval of trips	13	3
Laws governing certification of teachers	9	55
Administrative regulations	36	16
Laws and regulations governing scheduling	9	1
Court rulings requiring equal transportation for public and parochial school children	4	4
Other	5	12

*Since respondents were often aware of more than one law or regulation, columns add up to more than 100%.

has good and bad effects. The good effects are that it makes sure that the teachers have filled some basic requirements. The bad effects are that it is restrictive. The law should allow for some community experts to teach, subjects to review by a certification board.

A California superintendent told us:

Certification is so screwed up in California that nobody knows what it is. We need more of getting community people in the classroom, often in the area of art or music rather than law. Eminence credentials exist now but create tremendous red tape. The procedure should be simplified.

A teacher in a district in the California wine country saw changes in certification as part of an extensive reorganization of the school:

Teachers' certification and tenure laws should be totally eliminated. That would allow the local carpenter to teach kids in the school. There is a monopoly element that allows only certified teachers to teach students right now.

High schools should be opened up to all ages of people, all days of the week, at all times of the day. Schools should be allowed to rent out space to commercial enterprises in order to make a community out of a school. Adults could wander in and take courses.

Discipline problems would be treated in the same manner as they are in society. One would call in the police. Now, children are expected to behave better than they are in the real world. All community services would be available there. It is natural for high schools to involve adults and it makes it become a more natural environment for the kids.

Whereas more administrators than teachers think certification is an important factor, more teachers than administrators note the importance of administrative regulations. Many teachers told us of the need to get approval for off-campus activities and requirements to formally request transportation. An additional group of teachers told us of the need to get approval for speakers. Although administrators found these procedures easy to justify, many teachers felt these requirements limited use of the community.

These findings disclose a puzzling situation. Although certification laws are designed to protect the professionalism of teaching, and although they serve to limit competition for teaching jobs, less than one teacher in ten in our sample considered them a factor affecting the use of community resources. On the other hand, more than half the administrators did find these laws a factor. Perhaps this was because admin-

216

istrators must be familiar with education law if they are to perform their job effectively, but it may also be that the existence of certification laws provided administrators with a way of pointing a finger at teachers to explain the school's inability to take full advantage of community resources. Conversely, the fact that teachers were more than twice as likely as administrators to say that administrative regulations were a factor may have been a way for teachers to point a finger at administrators.

What can we say in summary about the effect of these various laws and regulations regarding use of the community? As we noted earlier, the wide range of responses made it impossible to link each law or regulation with a specific result. However, Table 53 does enable us to draw some conclusions about the general effect of laws and regulations in this area. We found 34 percent of the teachers and 44 percent of the administrators said they thought the laws and regulations had no effect on whether teachers used community resources. In reply to a follow-up question about why the laws and regulations had no effect, most of these educators said they went through the procedures anyway or thought the laws and regulations were just conveying common sense guidelines. Thus the law had consequences for these educators but did not encourage or deter.

However, except for a handful who thought the laws and regulations encouraged use of the community or thought they protected the licens-

TABLE 53
TEACHERS' AND ADMINISTRATORS' PERCEPTIONS OF
THE EFFECT OF LAWS CONCERNING THE
USE OF COMMUNITY RESOURCES

PERCEPTIONS OF EFFECT	TEACHERS* (N = 114)	ADMINISTRATORS* (N = 85)
Limiting effect, slow things down, restrictive	43%	45%
No effect	34	44
Made teachers more careful	9	14
Ensure that only licensed persons teach	1	8
Eliminate programs, opportunities	7	6
Encourage programs	3	1
Other	7	7

*Since respondents often named more than one effect, columns add up to more than 100%.

217

ing of teachers, the rest of the sample said these provisions limited opportunities to make educational use of the community. In contrast to this study's findings on the generally small impact of curriculum mandates and laws regarding materials, this suggests that laws and regulations dealing with the educational use of the community do have a deterrent effect. The problem, however, may have to do with how educators perceive the law, rather than with the law itself. In this report's final chapter, we recommend programs to more adequately inform teachers of guiding legal principles.

Notes

[1]Chicago: ABA Special Committee on Youth Education for Citizenship, 1976.

[2]*E.g.*, OKLA. STAT. ANN. § 6–127.

[3]*E.g.*, CAL. EDUC. CODE § 13128; OR. REV. STAT.. § 343.045–065 (1971); MONT. REV. CODES ANN. §§ 75–6004 and 75–6006 (1971); GEORGIA DEPARTMENT OF EDUCATION, TEACHER CERTIFICATION IN GEORGIA (1971).

[4]American Association of Colleges of Teacher Education, Pamphlet on VOCATIONAL EDUCATION IN TEACHER'S COLLEGES, 1974.

[5]*E.g.*, MONT. REV. CODES ANN. § 75–6011 (1971); PA. STAT. ANN. tit. 24 § 12–1201(8) (Purdon 1962); WASH. REV. CODE sec. 180.80.060.

[6]EVELYN ZERKEES AND LEO J. SHAPIRO, THE SUPPLY AND DEMAND OF TEACHERS AND TEACHING. Study Commission on Undergraduate Education and the Education of Teachers (SCUEET), Lincoln, Nebraska, 1972; Shapiro, *Manpower: Supply and Demand for Teaching Personnel,* THE UNIVERSITY CAN'T TRAIN TEACHERS, pp. 18–26, Lincoln, Neb. 1972; U.S. COMMISSION OF EDUCATION, THE EDUCATION PROFESSION, Washington, D.C. 1972.

[7]*E.g.*, N.C. GEN. STAT. § 115–35(h) (1978) (Educational Research Proposal); WIS. STAT. ANN. § 115.29 (West 1973).

[8]ALASKA ADM. CODE § 12.070; MASS. GEN. LAWS ANN. ch. 71 § 38(G) (1978).

[9]*Id.;* NEV. REV. STAT. § 391.010 (1973) (special teaching certificate); GA. CODE ANN. § 32–609a (1976); WIS. STAT. ANN. § 115.29 (West 1973); KAN. STAT. ANN. § 72–1381 (1977); IOWA CODE ANN. § 260.17 (West 1949); N.Y. EDUC. LAW § 3006.4 (McKinney 1969); Comsr. New York State Regulations § 80.33(c) makes specific reference to use under this provision of guest lecturers, although it is doubtful that teachers need authorization to invite volunteers into their classrooms to participate in instruction. Perhaps the statutory authorization would permit payment to guest speakers.

[10]WASH. REV. CODE § 16.010.030.

[11]Paul T. Tractenberg, Testing the Teacher: How Urban School Districts Select Their Teachers and Supervisors (N.Y.: Agathon Press, 1973), pp. 146–51. *Cf.* Council of Supervisory Associations of Public Schools of New York City v. Bd. of Educ. of City of New York 24 N.Y.2d 1029, 250 N.E.2d 251, 295 N.Y.S.2d 88 (1969), where school administrators unsuccessfully sought to prevent the Board from making temporary appointments in experimental school without adhering to normal selection priorities and procedures. *See also* Porcelli v. Titus 431 F.2d. 1254 (3d Cir. 1970).

[12]National Education Association of Shawnee Mission v. Bd. of Educ. 215 N.W.2d 837, 85 LRRM 2801 (use of teachers aides nonbargainable); Matter of West Irondequit Teachers Association 4 PERB 4511 (New York 1971); but see Danville Sch. Dist. v. Fifield, 315 A2d 473 (Vt. Supr. Ct. 1974). Laws in most states permit public sector bargaining over "terms and conditions of employment" but not on matters of public policy. The courts are faced with the formidable duty of perceiving the separation.

[13]This standard is reflected in the rules of the six private regional accrediting associations which review secondary school offerings in terms of regular daily classroom work and defined semester hours.

[14]N.D. Cent. Code § 15–41–06; Kansas State Dept. of Education Certification Regs. § 91–2–9, Standard IX (1968); Vermont SRE Regs. (1967); Wash. Rev. Code § 180–56–330 (1976).

[15]Mass State Board of Education Reg. No. 7–15.

[16]Ariz. Rev. Stat. § 15–1212(C) (4) (b) (1975).

[17]*E.g., Tennessee,* SBE Rules, Regulations and Minimum Standards (1973) p. 97; Minimum Requirements for Schools in New York State (1973); Policies of Texas State Board of Education § 3712 VI–25.

[18]Minimum Standards for New Mexico Schools, State Department of Education, 1974 p. 20.

[19]State Department of Pennsylvania Regulations § 5.15.

[20]Allen D. Schwartz, Legal Adviser to Illinois SSPI, formal opinion No. 8 May 15, 1973.

[21]*E.g.,* Schwan v. Bd. of Educ. Lansing School Dist. 183 N.W.2d 594, 27 Mich. App. 391 (1970) (authority to operate nongraded elementary schools).

[22]*E.g., In re* Bd. Publ. Instr. Alachua County 160 Fla. 490, 35 S.2d 579 (1948) (school authority to buy a campsite to diversify its program by creating an experimental farm, and to facilitate the acquisition of necessary skills); Woodson v. Sch. Dist. 274 Pac. 728, 127 Kan. 651 (1929) (power to build a gymnasium for athletics and dramatics); Dodge v. Jefferson Cnty. Bd. of Educ. 298 Ky. 1, 181 S.W.2d. 406 (1944); Dilday v. Beaufort Cnty. Bd. of Educ. 148 S.E.2d 513, 267 N.C. 438 (1966) (authority to enlarge the school building).

[23]*See generally* Erica F. Wood, *An Identification and Analysis of the*

219

Legal Environment for Community Education, JOURNAL OF LAW AND EDU-
CATION 3 (January 1974): 1–32, and especially 5–6, and typical statutory
provisions conferring authority to open the school building for community
activities. FLA. STAT. ANN. § 235.02 (West 1977); PA. REV. 24 § 7–775
(Purdon 1963); ALA. CODE tit. 52 § 147 (1960); COLO. REV. STAT. § 22–32–
110 (1974).

[24]ILL. ANN. STAT. ch. 122 § 10–22.29 (Smith-Hurd 1962); N.Y. EDUC.
LAW § 3210(2) (b) (McKinney 1969); Board of Regents Reg. § 109.1(e).

[25]CAL. EDUC. CODE § 32040 (West 1977).

[26]New Jersey Ed. Comsr., School Law Decision 202 (1966) affirmed by
State Board of Education SLD 276 (1968). The ILPE contract with school
districts provides for released time at least twice a month. *See* LAW-RELATED
EDUCATION IN AMERICA, pp. 208–211.

[27]Policies and regulations of instruction, Dept. Ed., State of Hawaii §§
2320.2, 2320.3 (1970). In all other states field experience is governed primarily by local districts, which may have policies similar to the Hawaii
provision.

[28]LAWYERS' COMMITTEE, pp. 57–59.

[29]*Compare* DEL. CODE tit. 14 § 2901 (1975) and FLA. STAT. ANN. §
234.03 (West 1977) with COLO. REV. STAT. § 22–23–110 (1974).

[30]*E.g.,* WASH. REV. CODE § 28A.24055 (1971).

[31]*E.g.,* ARK. STAT. ANN. § 80–1824 (Cum. Supp. 1977); PA. REV. STAT.
tit. 24 § 13–1362 (Purdon Cum. Supp. 1978).

[32]David Schimmel, *When a Child Is Injured,* CHANGING EDUCATION, supplement to THE AMERICAN TEACHER, November 1972, P.C.E. 6.

[33]*Id.; see also* Reynolds C. Seitz, *Legal Responsibility Under Tort Law of
School Personnel and School Districts as Regards Negligent Conduct Toward
Pupils,* HASTINGS LAW JOURNAL, 519 (1964); Richard S. Varca, *Teacher
Malpractice,* RICH. U. LAW REV. 447 (1974); Paul O. Prochl, *Tort Liability
of Teachers,* VAND. LAW REV. 12 (1959) 723.

[34]PA. REV. STAT. tit. 24 § 13–1361 (Purdon Cum. Supp. 1978).

[35]Rhoades v. Sch. Dist. of Abington Township 424 Pa. 202, 226, A.2d 53
(1967), *cert. den.* 389 U.S. 846; Bd. of Educ. School Dist. No. 142, Cook
County v. Bakalis 299 N.E.2d 737 (Ill. 1973).

[36]Luetkemeyer v. Kaufman 364 F. Supp. 376 (W.D. Mo. 1973).

[37]*E.g.,* IOWA CODE ANN. § 92.4 (West 1949); FLA. STAT. ANN. § 450.161
(West 1977); N.M. STAT. ANN. § 59–6–5 (Supp. 1975). *See generally* IN-
EQUALITY IN EDUCATION, (No. 16, March 1974), special issue on legal prob-
lems related to vocational and career education.

[38]*See* Note, *Child Labor Laws—Time to Grow Up,* MINN. LAW REV. 59
(1975): 375 describing state and federal child labor laws and including an
appendix of all such laws.

[39]*Id.,* 583–86.

[40]*E.g.*, KAN. STAT. ANN. § 38–606 (1977).

[41]ALA. CODE tit. 26 § 354 (Cum. Supp. 1973); COLO. REV. STAT. ANN. § 80–6–5(2) (Cum. Supp. 1971); IOWA CODE ANN. § 92.4 (West Cum. Supp. 1978); KAN. STAT. ANN. § 38–601 (1977); NEB. REV. STAT. § 48–304 (Supp. 1978); NEV. REV. STAT. § 609.250 (Ann. 1974); N.H. REV. STAT. ANN. § 276-A: 4(IV) (1978); TENN. CODE ANN. § 50–709 (1977); UTAH CODE ANN. §§ 34–23–1 to 34–23–3 (1974).

[42]The federal Fair Labor Standards Act sets 16 as the basic minimum age for employment, but provides so many exceptions that the rule for non-hazardous work is effectively 14 years. 29 U.S.C. §§ 201 *et. seq.*

[43]OR. REV. STAT. § 336.175 (1971), *See also* N.Y. EDUC. LAW § 4606 (McKinney 1969); N.M. STAT. ANN. § 77–11–73(E) (Supp. 1975).

[44]UTAH CODE ANN. § 34–23–1 (1974).

[45]MINN. STAT. ANN. § 181A.02 (West Cum. Supp. 1977).

[46]Bobilin v. Hawaii St. Bd. Ed. 403 F. Supp. 1095 (D. Haw. 1975).

[47]The exact wording for our question to teachers was, "People in education, and social studies in particular, have heard a lot about using the local community as a classroom resource, yet few have discussed exactly what this involves. Have you tried to use community people as a resource for your students?" The question to administrators was indentical except that it asked if they encouraged teachers to make use of community people.

Part III

CHAPTER 9
Rationale for Examining the Informal Curriculum

Many observers have likened the public school to a miniature society. Both the school and the larger society have their own rules, their own rewards, their own punishments, and their own authority relationships.

It seems likely that students will learn much about citizenship through the thousands of days they spend as citizens of the school. How do schools create and administer rules? How is punishment determined? What values are fostered—obedience? diversity? participation? creativity? What is the school's concept of a "good" student citizen? How schools perform as a society—in the classroom, in the principal's office, and in student government, sports, and extracurricular clubs—may well shape students' sense of the obligations and possibilities of citizenship.

Certainly many educators have argued that school experiences are an important part of the political socialization of the young. Many believe with Sarason that in each classroom there is a constitution, "verbalized or unverbalized," that governs the behavior of students.[1] What students learn from the school constitution they then apply to new contexts in the larger society. And Ehman and Gillespie argue, "Students first form attitudes toward school and other institutions of which they are an active part, and then generalize these attitudes outward to the general society."[2]

223

The courts have often agreed that what happens in the school outside the explicit curriculum context constitutes important lessons for students. Chief Justice Earl Warren made this point in speaking for the Court in *Brown v. Board of Education*.[3] He wrote, "Does segregation of children in public schools solely on the basis of race, even though physical facilites and other 'tangible' factors may be equal, deprive the children of the minority group of equal educational opportunity?" The Court concluded that segregation generated feelings of inferiority and could affect the hearts and minds of minority children independent of any equality of facilities, resources, or curricula.

As we pointed out in Chapter 5, both the majority and the minority in the *Tinker* and *Goss* cases were concerned about what school policy taught students about citizenship. In *Tinker* the majority argued that the informal "intercommunication" among students caused by the Tinker children's demonstration was an important part of the educational process. In Justice Fortas' words, "In our system, students may not be regarded as closed-circuit recipients of only that which the State chooses to communicate." Justice Black responded that the decision would teach students that they could disrupt the school with relative impunity. "School discipline, like parental discipline," he wrote," is an integral and important part of training our children to be good citizens."[4] In *Goss* the majority opinion stated that it would be a "strange disciplinary system in an educational institution" if there were no communication between the disciplinarian and the student. The minority again argued that the decision would undermine the school's ability to teach the "lesson of discipline. Education includes the inculcation of an understanding in each pupil of the necessity of rules and obedience thereto. This understanding is no less important than learning to read and write."[5]

Teacher behavior is also said to be important in shaping student citizens. Several court cases have noted that teachers' rights have implications for lessons in democratic citizenship. An example is *Russo v. Central School District*,[6] in which a teacher refused to salute the flag or recite the Pledge of Allegiance during the school's daily morning exercises. The court noted that Mrs. Russo's students were tenth graders and said:

Young men and women at this stage of development are approaching an age when they form their own judgments. They readily perceive the existence of conflicts in the world around them, nor is this knowledge something to be dreaded. As we said in *James*, "schools must play a central role in preparing their students to think and analyze and recognize the demagogue."[7]

Assumptions on the impact of school policy are widespread and also, at this stage, unproven. As Willis Hawley notes in a recent study, "Despite considerable speculation that teacher behavior and classroom structure comprise important lessens for political learning, there is . . . limited research on the topic. . . ."[8]

Generally, this research suggests that school policy and teacher behavior have some effect on students. Almond and Verba found that adults who recalled participating in school were more confident of their ability to influence government decisions.[9] In a national study of high school seniors, Jennings and Niemi found a small positive relationship between students' perceptions of school fairness and their political trust.[10] In a study of 13 high schools, Ehman and Gillespie found that students attending those schools which permitted the greatest student participation had the highest levels of trust and confidence.[11] Finally, in a study of 79 fifth-grade classrooms, Willis Hawley found that teachers who were perceived by independent observers as provoking respect for the opinions of others teach their students to believe in this type of diversity.[12]

Although the effect of school policy and teacher behavior on students needs study, we believe that the research conducted to date, as well as the widespread belief that the school environment shapes students' attitudes, justifies looking into this area as part of our study. Unlike the studies mentioned above, we did not attempt to correlate school policy and teacher behavior with students' attitudes. To do so would have involved extensive interviews with students which would have been far beyond the resources of the study. Rather, we used our interviews with teachers and administrators to paint a picture of current school policies and educators' attitudes which may shape students' perceptions of citizenship. This picture should help us understand how other aspects of law—court decisions affecting teachers' rights and students' rights, school rules, and the resolution of conflicts within the school—affect citizenship participation.

Chapter 10 focuses on how teachers and administrators have reacted to changes in the school brought about by numerous decisions and changes in education law, which have altered both the relationship of the schools to other institutions and the relationships among administrators, teachers, and students. In general, school administrators and teachers have responded by developing new attitudes and policies that potentially affect the attitudes of students toward law and authority.

Chapter 11 examines how teachers react to authority or embody authority in three settings: the community, the classroom, and the school. In each of these three settings, teachers have traditionally felt restraints, limiting their ability to participate and to express themselves. In this chapter we examine the extent to which teachers in our sample exercise their rights and experience restraints in the three settings. Their experience is important educationally because it affects how social studies teachers perceive citizens' rights and responsibilities and what sorts of citizenship models they present.

Chapter 12 deals with students and authority. We begin with an examination of student-related controversies to see what types of policies are practiced in schools and how controversies are resolved, then we probe what school authorities would do when faced with a demonstration such as that in the *Tinker* case. The chapter continues with a discussion of our respondents' conceptions of appropriate citizen roles for students and ends with some hypotheses which we think are suggested by our findings in this part of the study. We hope that readers of these three chapters will join us in speculating on how students' learning about citizenship may be affected by the policies and attitudes of school people.

Notes

[1]SEYMOUR B. SARASON, THE CULTURE OF THE SCHOOL AND THE PROBLEM OF CHANGE (Boston: Allyn and Bacon, 1971), p. 175.

[2]Lee H. Ehman and Judith A. Gillespie, *Political Life in the Hidden Curriculum: Does It Make a Difference?* paper presented to the National Council for the Social Studies, Chicago, November 1974, p. 45.

[3]347 U.S. 483 (1954).

[4]399 U.S. 503 (1969).

[5]419 U.S. 565 (1975).

[6]469 F.2d 623 (2d Cir. 1972).

[7]The reference is to James v. Board of Education (461 F.2d 566 [2d Cir. 1972]), a case involving a teacher suspended for wearing a black armband in protest against the Vietnam War.

[8]Willis D. Hawley, *Reforming the Civics Curriculum Through the Restructuring of Teacher Behavior,* paper presented to the Midwestern Political Science Association, Chicago, April 1977, p. 11. Hawley provides a useful summary of existing research on pages 8–15.

[9]GABRIEL A. ALMOND AND SIDNEY VERBA, THE CIVIC CULTURE (Prince-

ton, N.J.: Princeton University Press, 1963), chapter 12: "Political Socialization and Civic Competence," pp. 323–74.

[10]M. Kent Jennings and Richard G. Niemi, The Political Character of Adolescence (Princeton, N.J.: Princeton University Press, 1974), pp. 223–25.

[11]Ehman and Gillespie, p. 47.

[12]Hawley, p. 19.

CHAPTER 10

How Educators Respond to New Developments in Education Law

Over the last 20 years many changes in education law have altered fundamental relations between the schools and other government institutions and among administrators, teachers, and students within the school. In response, school officials have altered policies and developed new perspectives on the law. Since they affect day-to-day workings of the school and are communicated to students, these policies and perspectives potentially have a strong influence on students and their developing sense of citizenship.

This chapter focuses on recent changes in state and federal law which have reduced the autonomy of the schools, and on court decisions that have altered relationships between educators and students. Both teachers and administrators in the sample were aware of these changes and felt that the schools had been affected by them

The Growing Importance of Education Law

School districts have a long tradition of relative autonomy.[1] Since at least as early as the beginning of this century, educators have made a concerted effort to keep politics out of the school. They have tried to keep public education separate from other governmental services and provide education with its own government and administration. This separation has produced independent school boards with taxing and governing powers.

In recent years, however, local districts have begun to lose some of this autonomy. There has been an increase in the amount of state aid to local districts,[2] and states appear to be making more concerted efforts to influence the curriculum.[3] These efforts are perhaps most visible in the nationwide efforts to develop competency-based instruction programs.[4]

In addition, the federal education role has increased greatly in recent years. Tyll van Geel has provided an excellent description of how the federal government's role in education has grown.[5] He points out that the Elementary and Secondary Education Act of 1965 (ESEA) dramatically increased the amount of federal money for schools, and Title I of ESEA authorized the U.S. Office of Education to "demand from local school boards significant changes in their educational program." Aid to districts was linked to compliance with federal regulations.

The federal regulations that have had the most impact on local districts are those that prohibit discrimination on the basis of race or sex.[6] Under the Civil Rights Act of 1964 the federal government is prohibited from giving financial assistance to programs that discriminate on the grounds of race, color, or national origin. To this list, Title IX of the Education Amendments of 1972 adds discrimination by sex. These provisions are enforced by the Department of Health, Education, and Welfare and the Office of Civil Rights, and these agencies have been responsible for developing regulations and guidelines for local districts receiving federal funds.

There can be little question that federal efforts aimed at increasing school integration and reducing sex discrimination in the schools have had a great impact.[7] Almost every school in the country with a racially diverse student body has had to develop an integration plan, and many school districts have been involved in litigation over racial integration. Similarly, almost every school district in the country has revised or is now revising policies in response to Title IX guidelines against sex discrimination.

At the same time that state and federal governments have been increasing their regulation of local school systems, the courts have become more and more involved in school questions. The courts have traditionally expressed a loathing to become enmeshed in school policy. In 1948 Supreme Court Justice Robert Jackson warned against the Supreme Court becoming a "super board of education" decreeing uniform and rigid standards for districts with localized interests and needs.[8] In 1971 Justice Black repeated the warning in commenting on *Karr v. Schmidt,*[9] a hair-length case. He said, "Surely few policies can be thought of that States are more capable of deciding than the length of hair of school-boys. . . . It would be difficult to prove by reason, logic or common sense that the federal judiciary is more competent to deal with hair length than are the local school authorities and state legislatures of all our 50 states." And members of the Court have repeatedly recognized the broad discretionary authority of school authorities in the daily operation of the schools.[10]

However, despite these admonitions, the federal courts have vastly increased their review of school policies. Between 1946 and 1956, the federal courts heard 112 school cases; in 1956 to 1966 they heard 729 cases; in 1967 to 1971 they heard 1,273 cases.[11]

The Supreme Court has been active on a variety of education fronts. *Brown v. Board of Education*[12] and subsequent lower court rulings have made the courts active partners with the schools in developing school integration plans. In *Abington School District v. Schempp*[13] and *Engel v. Vitale,*[14] the Supreme Court struck down school prayers and Bible reading in the schools. In such decisions as *Board of Education of Central School District v. Allen*[15] and *Everson v. Board of Education,*[16] the Court has dealt with church-state separation. As we have seen, in *Tinker* the Supreme Court ruled that schools could not deny students the exercise of their free speech and assembly rights without reasonable justification, and in *Goss* the Court ruled that students had a right to minimal due process when faced with suspension. And in *Pickering v. Board of Education*[17] the Court dealt with the First Amendment rights of teachers.

State and lower federal courts have been involved in all of these issues and in a number of others, such as dress codes and school searches and seizures, which have not yet reached the Supreme Court.

Judicial decisions in the past two decades have had broad effects on immediate policy and more importantly on the autonomy of the schools. The decisions have tended to open the schools to judicial scrutiny and to decrease somewhat schools' autonomy in handling teacher and student expression, assignment of teachers and students, school discipline, and a host of other areas. For example, courts are beginning to downplay such doctrines as *in loco parentis,* which gave school officials wide powers to protect the safety and welfare of students. Instead, courts are beginning to accord students who are accused or suspected of misbehavior some of the rights they would have in a police station or courtroom. While courts have stopped far short of applying the same due process guidelines to students accused of misbehavior as to adults accused of crime, the general effect of decisions has been to reduce the discretion of school officials and to grant more rights to students.

Our findings show that these legal developments have had great consequences for the schools.[18] Not only have they led to new policies and procedures and new relationships within the schools, but they have also produced hostility in about 25 percent of teachers and administrators. These respondents tended to view the law and courts as failing to provide appropriate support and as frustrating the schools' educational goals.[19]

Respondents' Reactions to New Developments in Education Law

Educators in the sample told our interviewers that new developments in education law made them aware of their own lack of legal knowledge. In response to the question, "In your experience as a social studies teacher (school administrator) have there been times when you felt you did not have a good grasp of laws which affected you as a teacher (school administrator)," 65 percent of teachers and 70 percent of administrators said there had been times when they lacked a grasp of legal issues that affected them professionally. These issues were divided between student-related concerns and problems relating to employment.

Table 54 displays the types of legal issues of which teachers and administrators had indicated they lacked adequate understanding. (Because both groups were allowed to identify more than one legal issue the columns will add up to more than 100%.) The law dealing with three student-related issues—educators' liability for accidents occurring to students, student discipline, and student rights—seemed particularly elusive to respondents.

Table 54 supports a finding we reported in Chapter 8—teachers are very concerned about their legal liability for accidents occurring to students. Teachers in the sample wanted to know more about the law governing such situations. Far fewer administrators felt that they lacked knowledge about the law on liability for accidents to students. This parallels the limited interest they showed in the liability issue when asked about student activities outside the classroom. Perhaps administrators feel that teachers have the primary responsibility in this area.

TABLE 54
ISSUES OF LAW ABOUT WHICH TEACHERS AND ADMINISTRATORS FELT THEY HAD INADEQUATE COMPREHENSION

ISSUES	TEACHERS* (N = 95)	ADMINISTRATORS* (N = 54)
Liability, responsibility for students in/out classroom	29%	13%
Student discipline	27	30
Other student-related issues (rights and responsibilities, search and seizure, student records)	14	41
Teacher tenure	9	2
Other working rights issues	19	13
Political and expressive rights in/out of school	13	5
Plant or maintenance	8	7
Other	8	7

*Percentages are based on two responses and add up to more than 100%.

They may think that their responsibility is to hire teachers with good judgment whose decisions are educationally defensible. Thus, in the administrators' view, it may be up to the teacher to decide whether or not to conduct field trips or engage in any other activity that might result in liability for a student accident.

In contrast to the difference in concern about liability, teachers and administrators showed similar levels of concern about laws affecting student discipline. About 30 percent of both teachers and administrators wanted to know more about laws affecting such disciplinary matters as suspensions, expulsions, transfers, and corporal punishment.

As for the third student-related concern, a large number of administrators felt they needed to know more about laws governing such student rights issues as search and seizure in the schools, access to student records, and equal treatment of boys and girls. Although some teachers mentioned these student rights issues, teachers were much less likely than administrators to say they needed to know more about such laws, perhaps because student rights issues concern administrators more directly than teachers.

Problems relating to employment constitute a second broad category about which educators indicated they felt ignorant. This category includes such topics as tenure, firing and hiring, maternity leave, and educators' rights of expression. Teachers were slightly more likely than administrators to identify these topics as areas of law that had troubled them.

Almost all observers of the education scene agree that court decisions and changes in the law have had pronounced consequences for the schools. They have affected both formal school procedures and the more general atmosphere of the school—that is, the day-to-day relationships among students, teachers, and administrators. To find out what these consequences were in the sample schools, we asked teachers and administrators a series of questions.

Respondents were asked if they were familiar with the *Tinker* and *Goss* cases, and all respondents, including those who did not know about *Goss* and *Tinker,* were then asked, "Have these or other court cases affected the actions of local school people?" Sixty-four percent of teachers and 70 percent of principals and superintendents said yes. The respondents who said yes were then asked: "What case is that? What effect has it had?"

The cases mentioned most often as affecting local schools involved student suspension procedures (teachers 50%, administrators 58%), student expression such as demonstrations and school newspapers (teachers 18%, administrators 23%), and the breakdown of discipline (teachers 14%, administrators 13%). The specific areas mentioned were no doubt strongly influenced by our having drawn respondents' attention to *Tinker* and *Goss,* but it is noteworthy that about two-thirds of the respondents did say that one or more court cases affected what educators did in local schools. And half the respondents who said their schools were not affected by court decisions said that the schools already had procedures required by the courts. Perhaps these schools had anticipated the court decisions, or perhaps the policies were a response to the general increase in judicial activism.

As Table 55 shows, teachers and administrators see three general effects of recent court cases. One effect has been for the schools to create explicit guidelines and more formalized procedures; another effect has been to limit the options of teachers and administrators; and a third effect has generally been to loosen up the school atmosphere and provide more rights for students.

Twenty-one percent of teachers and 43 percent of administrators said that in response to court decisions schools have worked to develop written policies that educators are encouraged to follow in appropriate

TABLE 55
REPORTED EFFECTS OF COURT CASES ON
TEACHERS AND ADMINISTRATORS

EFFECTS OF COURT CASES	TEACHERS (N = 214)	ADMINISTRATORS* (N = 54)
Tighten up, more attention to procedures, develop written rules	21%	43%
Tie hands of administrators or teachers, reduce their effectiveness to control situation or maintain learning atmosphere	10	26
Loosen up, eliminate rules, more permissive, more options	13	12
Reduce discipline	7	13
Listen to students before acting, more respect for students	5	9
Other	4	9
No effect ascertained	40	23
Total	100%	—

*Percentages are based on two responses and add up to more than 100%.

situations. For instance, a teacher in Illinois said of his school's response to the *Goss* decision, "We had to definitely outline our procedure and it had to be followed." A teacher in California told us, "A number of old-time regulations were rescinded and replaced with new regulations." A Pennsylvania principal said the decisions "have given consistency to administrative decisions. We used to have many different ways of handling a particular situation—now we have a definite direction." And a Texas superintendent told us, "We follow guidelines, and put everything on paper." Although this may seem like a typical bureaucratic response, it is in keeping with the decisions in *Tinker* and *Goss*. The main purpose of these rules is to reduce what the Court has found to be arbitrary, capricious, inconsistent, and unconstitutional actions by teachers and school administrators.

The second major effect, a corollary to the first effect, is that school officials have less latitude. Ten percent of teachers and 26 percent of administrators said the decisions reduced educators' effectiveness and ability to maintain a good atmospeher for learning. One school administrator complained,

Everyone is so skittish. They won't take action, because they are afraid of suits and hearings. The court cases have had a very adverse effect. They have interfered with discipline and made teachers and administrators afraid to take action.

And another administrator noted that increases in "red tape" had made teachers "nebulous" about the law. As a result, he said, "teachers are reluctant to do things."

Seven percent of teachers and 13 percent of administrators said that the changes reduced discipline. A teacher said, "We're really aware of student power. *In loco parentis* is very weak, if not dead. We were told in a faculty meeting that it's a new era and we'll have to adjust to student rights." Hear are three other typical responses:

The disciplinary procedure has certainly changed since I first taught here. In many cases discipline has broken down.

The students have more rights, and they know it. There's a "I don't give a damn" attitude.

I sense that the administration and faculty may be backing off in some sense on discipline.

A California principal told an interviewer, "I sometimes feel that we are getting boxed in more and more in what we can do." And a principal at a small school in southern Illinois discussed the problems he had with new rules.

More and more my freedom to act according to situations is being restricted. A new state law says you have to write up a handbook with specific penalties for infractions. This is a bad idea in my opinion because it provides no flexibility. There is also a new law against corporal punishment. It would make suspension the only recourse.

We will get predictable responses. For example, [under the old system] when a girl said, "why don't you just throw me out of school," I said, "no way, that's a cop-out." With rules and regulations I would have to throw her out. Also, with a few kids, they'd love to be sent out to go fishing for three days. If I can tell them I'll set them on fire they'll behave.

There are a lot of problems with the bigness and overorganization of large schools. Teachers should be allowed to handle students on a personal basis here.

The third major effect—that students now have more latitude—follows logically from the other two. The previous paragraph shows that many respondents were distressed by the trend, but to many respondents it seemed like a good thing. As Table 55 shows, 13 percent of teachers and 12 percent of administrators saw a loosening up of the school atmosphere, and a smaller percentage of each group said that students were now listened to and accorded more respect. For example, a superintendent said that as a result of *Goss* and *Tinker* the school was more conscious of student rights. "The school in essence is less dictatorial. Due process is involved in most things we do to students today." And a teacher noted with approval, "teachers seem less concerned with dress, hair, and student expression."

As the comments we've quoted show, many teachers and administrators made explicit value judgments of the effects of court decisions on student rights. In coding responses, we attempted to pick up their judgmental comments and distinguish these who thought conditions in the schools were better as a result of court decisions from those who thought conditions were worse. Table 56 shows the results of the coding. Most administrators and teachers said they saw no effect or that the effect was neither good nor bad. Teachers and administrators who thought the decisions had worsened the situation in the schools had a slight edge over those who thought the decisions had improved things.

About a quarter of the teachers and administrators in the sample thought the courts' involvement in education had been detrimental. These respondents felt that in general the courts had tied their hands and reduced their control in the schools. A California superintendent told us: "Law and lawyers are trying to put the schools out of business. If they wouldn't meet for about five years, we might be able to

TABLE 56
FEELINGS ABOUT THE PERCEIVED EFFECTS
OF COURT CASES

EFFECTS ON RESPONDENT'S SCHOOL	TEACHERS (N = 214)	ADMINISTRATORS (N = 132)
Improve	18%	21%
No effect	4	14
Worse	23	28
No feeling ascertained	55	37
Total	100%	100%

implement the changes they've ordered." A superintendent from a Texas city had a similar complaint: "I'm so busy reading court cases on the running of the schools, I don't see how I survived prior to the time a lawyer told us how to do it." A south Georgia principal pinpointed a particular area of interference: "All social ills wind up in the schools to solve. I doubt where the law is heading in education, always emphasizing students' rights but never their responsibilities."

However, a slightly smaller percentage of respondents (20%) thought court decisions had improved conditions in the schools. For example, a teacher in Pennsylvania was very positive about court decisions:

They provide definite procedure. There is security because both students and teachers know the procedure. They're not groping in the dark. It brought order out of chaos. You might think it's terrible, but then you should go back and check your philosophy of justice. If you try to control a class with strong arm tactics you will find yourself in difficulty when the club is taken away. Kids have the same rights to dignity [as adults]. Their feelings about themselves are as important as ours.

The courts have done teachers a service because teachers must now dig deeper into their resources. They must try to motivate kids more.

Similarly, a Texas school administrator said that court decisions had a "humanizing effect."

We're treating students as individuals. They have rights now. Teachers and administrators can't act arbitrarily. The student has rights and is more a personality now.

Since much of the response to recent court decisions is characterized by confusion, it occurred to us that there might be some relationship between lack of understanding of the decisions and negative assessments. Table 57 shows that this is indeed the case. Those teachers and administrators who had the best understanding of the *Goss* and *Tinker* decisions were more likely to feel that the court action had improved conditions and less likely to think it had worsened conditions. (See Chapter 5 for a discussion of how we measured understanding of the cases.) This suggests that there is a strong element of legal ignorance and misunderstanding underlying negative assessment of court actions. Thus, the challenge for supporters of these decisions and advocates of student rights is to find a way of explaining the decisions clearly and fully to administrators and teachers.

TABLE 57
RELATIONSHIP BETWEEN UNDERSTANDING GOSS AND TINKER AND FEELINGS ABOUT THE GENERAL EFFECTS OF COURT DECISIONS

TEACHERS

	DECISIONS HAVE IMPROVED THE SCHOOL	DECISIONS HAVE NEUTRAL EFFECT, NO EFFECT	DECISIONS HAVE MADE SCHOOL WORSE	TOTAL	NUMBER OF CASES
Understands both cases	78%	0%	22%	100%	23
Understands one case	33	13	54	100	24
Does not understand either case	25	12	63	100	51

ADMINISTRATORS

	DECISIONS HAVE IMPROVED THE SCHOOL	DECISIONS HAVE NEUTRAL EFFECT, NO EFFECT	DECISIONS HAVE MADE SCHOOL WORSE	TOTAL	NUMBER OF CASES
Understands both cases	34%	28%	38%	100%	29
Understands one case	38	14	48	100	21
Does not understand either case	28	22	50	100	32

238

Summary

This chapter has reported on areas of law that respondents would like to know more about and has looked into the effect of recent court cases on respondents and their schools.

In general, respondents either did not voice opinions on court decisions or said that their effect was neutral. This suggests that, contrary to what some observers have feared, educators as a group may not be bitterly opposed to the courts' involvement in education or to some specific decisions. However, about 25 percent of our respondents did complain about what the courts have wrought.

Respondents differed in what they saw as the practical consequences of court decisions. Some discussed procedural changes and new guidelines within their school. Others said the general atmosphere of the school had greatly changed, usually in the direction of greater freedom for students.

What can we conclude from these varying opinions of our respondents? What result might these opinions have on the formal social studies/citizenship curriculum or on the informal curriculum, the lessons students learn by being exposed to the way the school creates and administers rules, disciplinary procedures, and punishments?

Trying to systematically trace these many strands through to their ultimate result—what students learn—clearly is not possible within the scope and resources of our study. However, there are some hypotheses we can advance that might suggest some directions for future inquiry. But first, it is necessary to look at two other important components of the informal curriculum—teachers as citizenship role models (Chapter 11) and students and the school authority structure (Chapter 12).

Notes

[1] A number of scholars and researchers in the field of education have discussed the tradition of the autonomy of educators and local school districts. *See* FRED WIRT AND MICHAEL KIRST, THE POLITICAL WEB OF THE AMERICAN SCHOOL (Boston: Little, Brown and Company, 1972), pp. 4–11, 111–12.

[2] NATIONAL EDUCATION ASSOCIATION, FINANCIAL STATUS OF THE PUBLIC SCHOOLS, 1974.

[3] Looking to see if an increase in state contributions to education is related to an increase in state control, Fred Wirt found no relationship between the number of a state's mandates and the state's education expenditures. (Frederick Wirt, *The State of Politics of Education*, draft chapter for HERBERT JACOBS AND KENNETH VINES, POLITICS IN THE AMERICAN STATES [Boston: Little, Brown and Company, 1976].)

[4]The January 1974 issue of PHI DELTA KAPPAN is devoted to articles describing competency-based teacher education. *See also* Alfred P. Wilson and William W. Curtis, *The States Mandate Performance-Based Teacher Education,* PHI DELTA KAPPAN (Sept. 1973): 76. And Ben Brodinsky reports, "Educators predicted that by 1984 (Orwell, can you hear?) nearly all the states will have incorporated minimal competency testing into promotion and graduation requirements. And then, what then?" *See* Brodinsky's *Back to Basics: The Movement and Its Meaning,* PHI DELTA KAPPAN (March 1977): 527.

[5]VAN GEEL, AUTHORITY TO CONTROL THE SCHOOL PROGRAM, chapter 3, pp. 43–71. *See also* L. Harmon Zeigler, Harvey L. Tucker, and L. A. Wilson, *How the School Was Wrested from the People,* PHI DELTA KAPPAN (March 1977): 537.

[6]Zeigler, Tucker, and Wilson have written, "The intervention of the federal government in education has had a consistent pattern, whether the source of the intervention is the courts, the Congress, or the Department of Health, Education, and Welfare. The national government has intervened to increase the educational, and by inference economic, opportunity of deprived populations."

[7]"Schools and Their Insurers Keep Uneasy Eye on Lawsuits," Education Daily (July 21, 1976): 5–6. "Title IX of the 1972 Education Amendments bans sex discrimination in federally assisted educational institutions. Although final regulations governing Title IX weren't published until June, 1975, some 20 Title IX complaints are now in court, according to the Project on the Status and Education of Women of the Association of American Colleges. Project Director Bernice Sandler said rough estimates showed that as of 1973 some 1600 complaints had been filed under Title VII of the 1964 Civil Rights Act, which bans employment discrimination in educational institutions. Title VII complaints go first to the Equal Employment Opportunity Commission and can go to Federal court from there. All told, there are probably 70 or more sex bias cases in the courts, Sandler said."

[8]Illinois *ex rel.* McCollum v. Board of Educ., 333 U.S. 203 (1948).

[9]401 U.S. 1201 (1971).

[10]*See* the *Tinker* majority decision, Harlan's dissent on *Tinker,* and Powell's dissent on *Goss.* See above, Chapter 9, footnotes 4 and 5.

[11]JOHN C. HOGAN, THE SCHOOLS, THE COURTS, AND THE PUBLIC INTEREST (Lexington, Mass.: D.C. Health and Company, 1974), p. 7.

[12]349 U.S. 294 (1955).

[13]374 U.S. 203 (1963).

[14]370 U.S. 421 (1962).

[15]392 U.S. 236 (1968).

[16]330 U.S. 1 (1947).

[17]391 U.S. 563 (1968).

[18]Many observers have commented on the changes brought about by court decisions. Edward T. Ladd writes in PHI DELTA KAPPAN (Jan. 1973, p. 304), "Administrators of our public schools face a dilemma today which they've never faced before: how to regulate student behavior without being sued for violating students' rights or, if sued, without being overruled in court." And *Education Daily* reports, "Schools and colleges are facing a new threat to their already wavering fiscal stability—an increasing number of lawsuits brought by students, employees and teachers in pursuit of damages, back pay and other monetary as well as injunctive relief. The surge has school people worried about whether insurance companies will continue to write liability policies for board members and trustees and what they will cost." *See* "Schools and Their Insurers Keep Uneasy Eye on Lawsuits" (July 21, 1976): 5.

[19]Numerous respondents told us that they were inundated with confusing regulations and reforms. Their confusion and frustration is regularly echoed in articles and letters to the editor appearing in professional education journals. These feelings also crop up in congressional hearings. Some government agency people view the situation a little differently. For example, in testimony on the implementation of the Buckley amendment, one HEW official said his agency was encountering "a major systemic public administration problem—the unwillingness of those affected by the law to exercise discretion and make decisions." *See Education Daily* (Nov. 16, 1976): 3–4.

CHAPTER 11

Teachers and Authority

School teachers function not only as teachers but also as authority figures. Teachers' formal lessons convey information and skills to students, but the lessons teachers informally convey as role models may be equally important. With the exception of parents, teachers constitute the major authority figures for most students. How teachers react to authority—that is, how they deal with administrators, boards of education, and their ultimate employers, the community—can tell students much about how one is expected to behave in society. Similarly, how the teachers embody authority in the classroom, how they behave in the little society they share with students, can teach important lessons about responsibility, tolerance, and many other concepts. Social studies teachers are particularly interesting as role models because, as we have shown in Chapter 3, legislatures have charged them with teaching about the democratic heritage, about appropriate citizen roles, and about respect for constituted authority.

The teacher as a role model of the democratic citizen is the subject of this chapter. We examine teachers' attitudes and behavior in three arenas: the community, the classroom, and the school. According to the literature on the subject, teachers have found their freedom limited at one time or another in each of these areas. For example, teachers have been prevented from active participation in politics,[1] from pursuing free or unlimited discussion of important issues in their class-room,[2] and from the exercise of speech and assembly rights in their schools.[3] Teachers in most localities probably have more options now, but their freedom to act may still be somewhat limited.

The extent to which teachers do act in these arenas, we believe, con-stitutes a model of democratic citizenship which could well have an effect on students. Teachers may be models of active and involved citi-zens or, by contrast, models of citizens who are lethargic, apathetic, or intimidated by authority. From these models in the schools, students derive implicit lessons about citizenship.

Teachers' political/citizenship actions also have direct implications for learning and teaching.[4] For instance, teachers who participate actively in community politics may gain information and skills that they can transmit to their students. In addition, our interviews lead us to believe that teachers who have been active in politics have gained access to law-related resources for their students which would not otherwise be so readily available. Finally, the exercise of democratic skills by teachers may provide an alternative to reliance on authori-tarian behaviors. Blumberg has suggested that teachers who are domi-nated by fear of authority will attempt to dominate their pupils. Students "learn that it is easier to get along by not differing from their teachers' ideas."[5]

Participation in the Community

Although active political participation is one of the ideals of democ-racy, Americans have not been especially active politically. Between 1960 and 1972 the proportion of eligible voters voting in national elections has decreased steadily,[6] and only 36 percent of eligible voters showed up to vote in the 1974 congressional elections.[7] If voting rates are low, rates of other types of participation are still lower. Studies show that fewer than 10 percent of the population generally contributes time or money to a political campaign.

Typically, better educated middle- and upper-income persons par-ticipate more,[8] so one might expect higher rates of political partici-pation from teachers. But working against teachers' participation are some traditional constraints. Many school board members and parents believe that teachers should keep a low profile in the community. They also believe that teachers should be neutral or appear neutral on political issues, claiming that being active politically threatens the ap-pearance of neutrality. These beliefs have in the past worked to constrain teachers.[9] However, as teachers' jobs have become more secure through teachers' organizations, unions, and such job protections as tenure and due process before removal, one might expect increases in their participation.

Today teachers appear to be very active politically. In 1965 an NEA poll found that 66 percent of classroom teachers believed teachers should work actively as members of political parties.[10] Ninety-two percent of the teachers said they had voted in the 1964 election and 14 percent said they had contributed money. An Oregon study of teachers in 1965 found that 90 percent agreed that it was appropriate or proper for a teacher to engage in political activity.[11] Using similar questions, a national study of social studies teachers found similar levels of support for community political activity.[12] Unfortunately, neither the Oregon nor the national study analyzed the extent of actual participation.

Some additional data do indicate teachers are heavily involved in political activity.[13] In 1976, 200 teachers were delegates to the national party conventions and 123 were alternate delegates.[14] The National Education Association and the American Federation of Teachers spent close to a million dollars to support candidates in the 1976 election,[15] and both organizations estimated high voting rates among their members.[16] The NEA estimated that more than 90 percent of its membership voted.

Our interviews with teachers also suggest a high level of political activity. Fifty-six percent of our respondents said they had worked in a campaign or run for office.[17] Most of these teachers had done precinct work, going door to door plugging away for candidates. A few had been officers in a political party or campaign managers. Six percent had run for office, and two percent had been elected to public office.

Compared with the general public, this is an unusually high level of political commitment. Furthermore, teachers in the sample thought this political commitment was appropriate. Teachers who said that they had not been active almost always told our interviewers that it was because they had no time or interest, with only a few saying that they thought it was better to be nonpolitical. The following comment by a suburban Chicago teacher represents only a small minority that believed teachers should stay out of politics:

I have the opportunity but I don't want to get involved in politics. I believe a teacher should be nonpolitical. I'd be first to encourage students to participate, but not teachers.

244

In response to another question, very few teachers in the sample said they had professional reservations about or feared retaliation for being active in the community. When asked if they ever felt that they should avoid taking a public stand outside their class, 80 percent said they felt free to take public stands.[18] The primary reason the minority of teachers gave for avoiding public stands was the feeling they would sacrifice their classroom neutrality. The comments of a teacher in rural southern Illinois highlighted this perspective:

> Yes [I avoid public stands]. I don't want my political affiliations known. I teach American government in a conservative town. I'm independent. One parent called up and said she didn't want her daughter in my class because she had heard I'd flunk anyone who's a Republican. That's nonsense. I told the class it was nonsense. Because I had a Democratic friend doesn't prove I'm a Democrat. Because I was seen with a prominent Republican, doesn't prove I'm a Republican.

The freedom that teachers feel to participate actively in community affairs is supported by their school administrators. Eighty-seven percent of the principals and superintendents we interviewed gave unequivocal support to teachers' political participation, and only two administrators disapproved outright. The comment of a superintendent in a small Texas community is typical of the majority's opinion:

> That is their privilege. I fought for that privilege. I want my teachers to take an active part in community and political affairs.

While defending the right of teachers to participate in public affairs, a few administrators expressed reservations. The main reservation was that classroom presentations must remain balanced or neutral. One administrator said,

> They all do [participate] and they are politically involved but the teacher must be neutral in class.

But some administrators recognized that it may be difficult for teachers to draw that distinction. A second said,

> They need to realize that they'll probably be subjected to criticism. People may think they're doing it [advocating] in class.

In conclusion, teachers in the sample have said they feel free to actively participate in politics, do participate, and receive the support of administrators. Both teachers and administrators were conscious of their responsibility to be politically neutral in the classroom, but only a small minority of teachers thought it necessary to maintain that neutrality outside the class. The great majority of social studies teachers with whom we spoke felt no conflicts between their roles as active citizen and as teacher.

Classroom Constraints

Experienced educators have recognized for a long time that social studies is especially sensitive to community mores.[19] Although math, science, and foreign language training have all been attacked by lay-people at times, social studies is a more common focus of strife since it deals directly with sensitive issues. Courses in the social studies recount the history of the people and their political, legal, and economic systems. Furthermore, as we have shown, legislators have made the social studies the major repository of citizenship training. Therefore, it is not surprising that social studies teachers often confront the social, religious, ethical, and political sensibilities of the community.

Periodically there are well-publicized attempts to influence the curriculum. Most recently, in Kanawha County, West Virginia, a large number of parents with traditionalist religious and ethical perspectives became upset by the introduction of new textbooks with a relativistic perspective.[20] But in addition to such *causes célèbres,* there are always a number of less-publicized instances of community pressure.[21]

Most teachers in the sample said they felt free to participate in community affairs, but those with reservations most often brought up the difficulty of separating their public stands from their classroom roles. One might expect, therefore, that teachers would be hesitant to discuss controversial issues or take public stands in their classrooms. A review of other studies supports this hypothesis. Zeigler's study of Oregon teachers[22] concluded that teachers were unwilling to take strong positions into the classroom. And in their report on a national study of social studies teachers, Jennings and Zeigler stated, "One would cautiously conclude that the prescriptive norms are more constraining in the classroom than in the community."[23] However, they went on to note that teachers who expressed themselves in the community were also likely to express their opinions in the classroom.[24]

Jennings and Zeigler also examined whether criticism of teachers was related to teachers' willingness to express political opinions or take up controversial issues. They found that 68 percent of the teachers in western states recalled criticism of teachers for discussing controversial events in class, compared with about 25 percent of the teachers in the other areas.[25] The fact that western teachers were also among the most expressive suggests some correlation between outspokenness and being criticized. However, a small study of social studies teachers in upstate-rural New York concluded, "Only a small minority feel strong pressure from community groups to stay away from controversial issues in the classroom or teach them according to a partisan viewpoint."[26] Unfortunately, the study did not ask if teachers responded to pressure.

Our concern with teaching about law and with the prospect that law-related issues might be controversial led us to ask two questions of teachers. The first, a general question, asked teachers if they had felt any constraints or problems when they taught about law. A second question pointedly inquired if their teaching or the materials they used had generated any criticism.

Half the teachers interviewed said they had felt no constraints or problems in dealing with law topics, and those who had felt them seldom mentioned constraints resulting from the controversial nature of the subject matter. Only 14 percent of the total sample mentioned this type of constraint, with highs in Texas (23%) and Illinois (17%) and a low in Georgia (3%). Far larger proportions of teachers felt constrained by their lack of knowledge about law-related topics.[27]

The few instances when teachers felt constrained by potential controversy were mainly efforts to avoid offending the religious and ethical sensitivities of the community. The issues were seldom political. The responses of two teachers from Philadelphia and Chicago were typical. The Philadelphia teacher told us:

> There are some issues I just don't deal with in a class of seventeen year-olds. For instance, sex and obscenity. A student could go home and tell her mother she was shocked by the discussion. Once in Sociology the students got into a discussion of Black vs. White, big vs. flat asses, flat vs. big busts. It was a legitimate discussion, but I wanted to get away from it as soon as I could.

In a similar vein, a teacher in Chicago told us,

> Yes, we have to watch what we say in class. For example, in the discussion of sex affairs. There are a lot of Baptist parents here. Once or twice I've talked to a [concerned parent]. I'll give a particular student a library pass [to excuse him from discussing a topic] if necessary.

These moral-ethical concerns are consistent with findings by Jennings in the national sample of social studies teachers.[28] He noted:

One-third volunteered the kind of precautions which must be employed

247

when handling the sensitive areas, primarily the avoidance of taboo topics in the morals [sex] and religious spheres. . . . One-third of the teachers felt there were, indeed, particular topics they definitely should not discuss. Within this set, an astronomical 93 percent singled out topics in the morals-religious domain, with the division being about equal between the two subdomains. Only 13 percent opined that particular political topics were taboo.

Even when the conservative-liberal dimension gets translated into the classroom, it appears much more a religious-ethical than a political concern. As a Texas teacher told us when we asked about problems and constraints:

> [This is] a very conservative red-neck area and I take this into consideration when I talk about the law. To them there is no interpretation of the law. Like morality, it is fixed.

And his colleague down the hall expressed similar concerns:

> To a degree, [I am careful about] any subject contrary to the conservatism of the community. For instance, assigning a research paper on the Kennedy assassination. Some *Playboy* articles are very good but they must be taken out of the magazine and cleaned up. Also, my class requested to salute the flag, but there is one Jehovah's Witness in class, so she is excused. I'm careful not to call attention to her. The community would not accept this.

There are a few other areas where teachers have confronted restraints in their teaching. A California teacher said:

> Once I had my students studying an FTC oil case. We read the case and explored alternatives. A parent who was a school board member complained to the principal that I was attacking business.

Finally, restraints are not always the result of actions by external agents. A young black teacher from Georgia told an interviewer that he tries to avoid civil rights issues:

> My classes are predominantly white. I don't dwell too long on the civil rights era to avoid backlash by some.

The answers to our question about criticism from the community suggest that teachers are sufficiently in control to avoid criticism. Only 13 percent of the teacher sample reported *any* criticism of their teaching of law or social studies, and only 6 percent reported criticism related to the controversial nature of the subject matter.

Although we have dwelled on the negative—those who said they felt constraints teaching about law—this number is very small, and such constraints as there were tended to be religious-ethical more than political. Furthermore, teachers who did feel constrained did not see their self-restraint as a reaction to the threat of censorship. Rather, they saw it as being responsive to the sensibilities of the community. Often, they measured their own effectiveness by their ability to defuse these troublesome areas rather than confront them head-on.

How Teachers React to the
School Authority Structure

The teacher is a member of a hierarchy, subject to rules and regulations promulgated by school administrators and boards of education. Yet the teacher is a professional with responsibility and a large grant of discretion in the education of youth. To explain the tension succinctly, as an employee the teacher is subject to authority; in the classroom he embodies authority. Presumably the two roles are related, and the teacher's sense of himself as an employee affects his relationship to his students. Tracing the precise linkage between the two roles would be enormously complex (and far too costly for this study), but we were able to gather some data on how teachers in the sample perceived their relationship to authority. In the next chapter, we suggest some hypotheses about the possible effect of these perceptions on teaching and learning.

In designing this study, we decided that the already-lengthy interview could not contain questions dealing with all parts of the authority structure that surrounds the teacher. Therefore, we focused on one issue—freedom of expression for teachers—giving respondents the facts of a major court case involving teachers' rights, *Pickering v. Board of Education*,[29] and asking them what they thought could happen in their community in a similar situation. The sequence of questions went as follows:

Suppose a teacher publicly, let us say in a letter to the editor, sharply criticized the board of education or school administration, and the criticism was published in a local paper, how do you think the board or administration would react?

What, if anything, would happen to the teacher? Would they try to fire the teacher, invoke less severe discipline, do nothing official but make life unpleasant, or would they ignore the issue?

Do you know of any laws or legal decisions that would support or protect the teacher?

What laws are those?

The *Pickering* case began when Marvin Pickering, an Illinois high school teacher, wrote a letter to the editor of the local newspaper bitterly criticizing the fiscal policies of the school board. He was fired for action "detrimental to the efficient operation and administration of the schools." The firing was upheld in state courts; however, in a split decision the Supreme Court ruled for Pickering.

The majority of the Court said Pickering had a right to criticize the school board and clarified the conditions under which the expression of teachers is protected. An important consideration was the work relationship between the employee and the employer being criticized. The Court said that if there is a close working relationship, the employee's public criticism of his supervisor could jeopardize the work relationship and justify dismissal. However, in this case Pickering criticized a school board and administration with which he had little direct contact.

In a small study of 86 elementary and secondary teachers, conducted in 1959, Blumberg described a "fear syndrome" among teachers. He observed that a common attitude of the teachers was to fear administrative reprisals if they voiced views that differed from their school's established policy.[30] Our findings suggest that this fear syndrome persists today.

The questions based on the facts of *Pickering* provoked an outpouring of resentment from teachers about their relationship to both administrative supervisors and school boards. Teachers tended to feel that administrators exercised arbitrary power over them. The school was often seen as a petty tyranny.

Twelve percent of our sample's teachers thought the teacher would be fired, and 66 percent expected that the board or administration would impose some kind of sanction on the teacher or make life unpleasant for him. Nine percent felt the teacher would be spoken to, and only 18 percent thought there would be no action against the teacher. (These figures add up to more than 100% because some teachers embraced more than one alternative.)

The following comments show the feelings of three teachers who thought that a teacher sharply criticizing school officials would be fired:

They'd find a way to fire him. They feel that if you criticize you are against them. They can't conceive of helpful criticism.

250

It's happened. If there is a way, they'll get rid of the teacher. They'll make it very uncomfortable. As a result we now have passive teachers.

[Boards could] slowly but surely root out [critical teachers]. . . .

There may not be worse fates than being fired. However, as the following remarks from three teachers indicate, teacher respondents believed that administrators have a variety of alternative means to punish a teacher whose views differ from official policy:

Kill him. Make his life a living hell so he will resign.

Make life unpleasant: A person better have everything down pat; lesson plan, daily activities, schedule, etc. We have some rabble rousers here. They speak whatever is on their mind. I've noticed some subtle things because of it.

As soon as they could, they would build a case to subtly get rid of him. When you stick your neck out, you make sure you protect your ass.

Teachers told our interviewers that administrators have many ways to "get" a nonconforming teacher so that the teacher will either conform or quit. These include insisting that rules be followed in every detail, assigning teachers to different schools that may be hard to reach or hard to teach at, assigning them classes with hard-to-teach students, assigning them classes out of their area of specialization, and giving them unpleasant extracurricular activities.

Of course not all teachers are equally vulnerable. An Illinois principal with obvious "savvy" told us that the administration's reactions to a teacher's expressing views contrary to stated policy would depend on how long the teacher had been employed in the district:

A majority of the board would be very angry. They would want to retaliate somehow. They would send a letter of their own or have a hearing with the teacher. If it was a first-year teacher, he would be dismissed. Second year, if I could substantiate it, also dismissed. A tenured teacher could depend on current procedures.

There is no recourse for a first-year teacher because direct charges are not necessary. Trumped-up charges are possible for second year, since only "cause" and "hearings" are required by law. Tenured teachers are different. If they are tenured, time for remediation must be given. The courts have overturned almost all such dismissals concerning free speech.

Not all teachers expected sanctions. Nine percent thought that it would just lead to bad feelings and that the teacher would be spoken to. The actual language from two interviews of teachers follows:

251

It happened to me. They reacted surprised, hurt. A school board member sent his wife to tell me off.

In this community, the board would be very offended. It's a kind of family. They would be very disappointed and hurt, very upset that the teacher hadn't spoken to them first about it.

Finally, as we noted earlier, 18 percent of the teachers thought that there would be no reprisals. Here are two teachers' opinions:

I've done that several times. There has been no reaction, unfortunately, no reprisals, no response. I'm paranoid enough to think that the administrative underground knows who the troublemakers are.

The school board would not react towards the individual but they would investigate and if the facts were correct they would take action to correct the situation. Ten years ago the teacher would not have been able to give a contrasting view. It was very dictatorial.

How Administrators See It

The responses of administrators when asked the same set of questions were quite different. Only 22 percent expected any sanctions to be imposed upon the teacher. Instead, administrators stressed speaking with the teacher or ignoring the fact that the teacher had been critical.

Teachers and administrators in the sample apparently had very different views of the teacher-administrator relationship. The view from the top down was often different from the view from the bottom up. It may be that what administrators saw as "talks" with teachers, teachers saw as reprimands.

School administrators tended to see the school as a community or a family of which they were the head. They stressed understanding, communication, and adjustment. Many administrators said their reaction would depend on whether the teacher had come in and talked it out before going public.

Superintendents and principals are the main link between the school and the larger community. It is in their interest to solve any conflict before it becomes public. Thus the administrators in our sample stressed school channels for communication and expected teachers to exhaust the remedies provided by the school and the district before they aired grievances publicly.

Informal observations of the schools our interviewers visited suggested that the principal is the closest thing to the father of the school. He wanders through the halls or sits in his office with the now-obligatory open door. He knows or attempts to know the names of all his students and faculty. He participates in chit-chat and oversees his community. He attempts to alleviate teachers' discontent and mediate when teacher-student conflicts arise.

Some of the teachers in the sample suggested that from a principal's perspective at the top it may be difficult to differentiate students from teachers. Both have been placed in his charge. The principal's role of mediating teacher-student conflicts may even encourage him to see students and teachers as equal and similarly subject to his authority. This issue arose several times when teachers in the sample discussed student discipline. Some teachers told us of their admiration for principals who backed them up with difficult students, but others told us of their dismay at a lack of support.

How Do Teachers Think They Can Protect Their Rights?

As we have seen, teachers in the sample said a teacher would be punished if he criticized the school board or administration. Their answers implied that they thought teachers would be intimidated into refraining from criticism. Their responses to another question tend to confirm this hypothesis, at least in part.

When our interviewers asked teachers if they knew of any laws or legal decisions that would protect them in circumstances similar to *Pickering,* a third of the teachers said no. Most of the two-thirds who said yes tended to have a vague and unspecific understanding. Most of them said their rights (unspecified) or the First Amendment would protect them, but only about 30 percent of this group could be more specific, generally saying tenure laws or their contract would protect them. A smaller number of those who could be specific, mostly from Texas and Georgia, suggested that they could invoke organizational support. These respondents generally gave the state teachers' association as a source of support, but a smaller number said the local teachers' organization would protect them.

We do not mean to suggest that teachers' answers show they have no resources when confronted with a possible violation of their free speech rights. The First Amendment, tenure, teachers' contracts, and organizational strength are important protective devices for teachers. However, teachers were not familiar with *Pickering* and other cases dealing with

253

teachers' rights, and they did not seem to have a clear idea of how the law might protect their rights. Generally, our interviewers sensed that teachers' fear and ignorance of their rights made them reluctant to criticize. Teachers expect all hell to break loose if they raise their voice in opposition to the school administration.

It is important to remember, however, that teachers have an alternative to expressing themselves. They can hold on and hope or expect that things will change.

A number of respondents suggested that teachers are not often fired. We might take this as evidence of their reluctance to criticize, for many essentially told us they were willing to suffer in silence. However, sometimes teachers get their way anyhow. A teacher in Pennsylvania gave us an interesting perspective on the teacher-administrator relationship. This teacher had gone public on an issue and, as a result, lost his position as head of the department through a reorganization designed to reduce the power of department heads. But he and other teachers were philosophical. On the wall of the teachers' lounge they kept a list with the names of 11 principals and 10 superintendents who had served in the last 20 years. The former department head had seen them all come and go.

Actual Controversies

To gain further insight into teachers' attitudes toward school authority and teachers' sense of their own rights, we asked them to tell us about actual issues in their district which raised questions of teacher rights. Few teachers recalled controversies at their school which revolved around free speech or academic freedom. Most responses dealt with nuts-and-bolts, job-related matters such as tenure, hiring and firing, unionizing and bargaining, work days and hours, salaries, strikes, and maternity leaves.

These responses may be an accurate reflection of the important issues facing teachers in the sample, but they may also be another indicator of effective restrictions on expression that teachers perceive in the school system. Perhaps speech and academic freedom disputes do not arise very often because teachers' expression has been "chilled"; perhaps they just don't criticize the school in public. Obviously further study is needed to resolve this question.

We can say, however, that the wide range of actual issues teachers mentioned shows that they are hardly bereft of rights. But it may be that their "rights" come down to the opportunity to bargain with their employers over such matters as wages, hours, and working conditions. Perhaps school administrators are prepared to deal with teachers over job-related issues but would find free speech issues beyond the pale.

Conclusion

This chapter has examined several aspects of how teachers react to authority. Generally, teachers in our sample said that they were active, concerned citizens who were not held back from participating in the community out of fear of criticism. Moreover, they did not feel that their classroom presentations were affected by fear of criticism, and the few teachers who did mention classroom constraints said that they were not censored but rather that they chose to avoid (or deal carefully with) touchy moral-religious matters that might needlessly provoke trouble with the community.

Answers to another question also suggest that teachers are not motivated by fear. As we noted earlier, only about 20 percent of the teachers said that they avoided public stands outside the classroom. When we probed further and asked this group "did you discuss this issue [i.e., that they had avoided a public stand] with your class," more than half said yes. Moreover, those who said no generally gave reasons —such as that the matter was private or not related to class—that suggested that they were not dissuaded by fear. Only two teachers said that they avoided talking about their public silence in class because they feared negative administrative reaction.

In contrast to these findings, however, is the resentment and implied fear teachers showed when asked about the fate of a hypothetical teacher who publicly criticized school authorities. Teachers told us that a critical teacher could expect retribution ranging from rebuke to firing.

What consequences do this attitude and the others discussed in this chapter have for teaching and learning? Clearly our respondents did not think of themselves as mousy, timid conformists who modelled a timid version of citizenship for students. And the very fact that so many of them were candid and seemed angry when discussing the fate of the hypothetical criticizing teacher suggests that they have spirit even when confronted by a touchy question. However, their answers imply that they themselves would probably not criticize school authorities. Should this attitude be transmitted to students, it might result in students

255

learning a lesson in conformity that would have implications for their notions of citizenship. All in all, though, teachers in the sample generally seemed to model active and concerned citizenship behavior.

Notes

[1]*See* Sanford D. Gordon and Dennis M. Shea, *A Political Profile of the Rural Social Studies Teacher*, SOCIAL EDUCATION 28 (Oct. 1964): 333–34; Hulda Grobman and Vynce A. Hines, *Teacher as a Citizen*, in LINDLEY J. STILES, ed., THE TEACHER'S ROLE IN AMERICAN SOCIETY (New York: Harper & Brothers, 1957), pp. 126–27; AUGUST B. HOLLINGSHEAD, ELMTOWN'S YOUTH AND ELMTOWN REVISITED (New York: John Wiley & Sons, Inc., 1949, 1975), pp. 92–95; ARTHUR J. VIDICH AND JOSEPH BENSMAN, SMALL TOWN IN MASS SOCIETY (Princeton, N.J.: Princeton University Press, 1958), pp. 60, 195, 270. A review of court cases suggests how school boards have tried to circumscribe teachers' activities. In each of the cases noted in this and the next two footnotes, the teachers were ultimately vindicated by the courts, but it is quite likely that in other districts similar restraints went unchallenged and teachers' activities were in fact circumscribed. For teachers' political activities *see* Pickering v. Board of Education, 391 U.S. 563 (1968) (teacher dismissed for publicly criticizing school board budgeting policies), Montgomery v. White, 320 F. Supp. 303 (1969) (teacher dismissed for community political activities), and Johnson v. Branch, 364 F.2d 177 (1966) (teacher dismissed for civil rights activities in the community).

[2]*See* Gordon and Shea, *A Political Profile;* HOLLINGSHEAD, ELMTOWN'S YOUTH, pp. 153–54, 248; John P. Lunstrum, *Controversial Issues, School Policies, and Reflective Thinking*, SOCIAL EDUCATION 26 (April and May 1962): 189–92, 244–46; HARMON ZEIGLER, THE POLITICAL LIFE OF AMERICAN TEACHERS (Englewood Cliffs, N.J.: Prentice-Hall, Inc., 1967), pp. 112–13. *See also* Sterzing v. Fort Bend Independent School District, 376 F. Supp. 657 (1972) (teacher dismissed for discussing racial discrimination in class) and Wilson v. Board of Directors of Mollala Union High School District, No. 76–92 (D. Or., 1977) (case is as yet unreported) (political science teacher dismissed for including a Communist among the guest speakers in his class).

[3]*See,* for example, Downs v. Conway, 328 F. Supp. 338 (1971) (teacher dismissed for soliciting opinions of other teachers on potential health hazard on school grounds) and James v. Board of Education, 461 F.2d 566 (1972) (teacher dismissed for wearing armband to school on Vietnam Moratorium Day).

[4]ZEIGLER, POLITICAL LIFE, p. 108: "Taking an active part in the political process is obviously related to a substantial reduction in reticence and to a desire on the part of the teacher to want to express his values and to create controversy within the class."

[5]Nathan Blumberg, *Are Teachers Doormats?* EDUCATIONAL ADMINISTRATION AND SUPERVISION 45 (July 1959): 215–29.

[6]Source: THE U.S. FACT BOOK: THE AMERICAN ALMANAC FOR 1976, *Participation in Elections for President and U.S. Representatives: 1930 to 1974,* p. 450.

[7]*Ibid.,* p. 450.

[8]Angus Campbell *et al.* have written:

> . . . increased participation at upper levels of the society probably results less from motivation to protect status position than from the fact that people at upper-status levels are better educated and better equipped cognitively to maintain political interest.
>
> Only a small fraction of the adult population engages in much political activity beyond the act of voting itself. But in the various other types of participation that we record, there is some visible upper-status bias within this fraction. . . . Generally, however, education serves as the best predictor of these forms of participation among status dimensions. Perhaps the strongest relationship with education appears in the tendency to talk informally with others with a view toward influencing their vote decision. . . .The "opinion leader" role in political choice is not widely sought, but it is more likely to be sought by the more highly educated. Educational differences are less marked in some of the other forms of participation: membership in political organizations and campaign work are less clearly dependent on status lines.

(THE AMERICAN VOTER [New York: John Wiley & Sons, Inc., 1960], pp. 476–77.)

[9]Grobman and Hines, *Teacher as a Citizen,* pp. 126–27, write:

> It is thought that any sign of political preference by the teacher will be reflected unfavorably in his general pupil contacts and in his teaching of social studies in particular. . . .
>
> Political activity has a connotation of immorality or sinfulness. Jaynes [1951] . . . found that a substantial minority of a representative group of over 500 Washington state citizens categorized political activity with drinking, smoking, and dancing as activities disqualifying a person for public school teaching.
>
> Many teachers are required by contract or school board regulations to adjure [sic] not only politics but all things that might be construed as political. And doubtless even where there are no written regulations, there may be unwritten regulations. In a recent [1950] survey of three Midwestern states . . . the school board members ranked political speaking or running for office second only to drinking or dating students in seriousness of offense.

In a small study of social studies teachers in the New York Catskills, Gordon and Shea (*A Political Profile,* p. 334) found:

257

Few feel that they would be interfered with if they participated in political activity in the community. However, many feel that such activity would be frowned upon, particularly by boards of education, parents, and school administrators.

[10]*Teacher Opinion Pool: Teachers and Politics,* NEA J. 54 (Oct. 1965): 64.

[11]ZEIGLER, THE POLITICAL WORLD OF THE HIGH SCHOOL TEACHER (Eugene, Ore.: The Center for the Advanced Study of Educational Administration, University of Oregon Press, 1966), pp. 228–29. However, in POLITICAL LIFE (p. 108) Zeigler reports that "only about 9 percent of the teachers are active in the electoral process. . . ." This is consistent with the conclusions of Grobman and Hines (pp. 121–22); drawing largely on a review of studies of teacher political participation in Detroit (1950), Gainsville (1954), and Tampa (1954), they conclude:

> What little concrete data are available on voting and registration habits of teacher political participation in Detroit (1950), Gainsville (1954), and
> that of other college graduates or those with comparable professional standing, even if teacher voting performance is somewhat better than that of the general public.

[12]M. Kent Jennings and Harmon Zeigler, *Political Expressivism Among High School Teachers: The Interaction of Community and Occupational Values* (paper, 1968), p. 6.

[13]In a study of upstate (Catskill area) New York secondary social studies teachers in 1964, Gordon and Shea (*A Political Profile,* p. 333) found:

> In regard to their experience in and attitudes about politics, most confine their political participation to voting (96.5 percent vote most of the time), an occasional letter (most have written to public officials, but 23 percent think it is of little value), and an occasional petition (about half have signed several, but 13 percent never signed a petition and only 10 percent have circulated petitions and feel they are quite effective). . . . Although 60 percent have never given any money to a political party or a candidate, a third have given more than once and over 17 percent feel they have an obligation to support parties, candidates, and issues with money. A sizable majority would be willing to serve as an appointed official (86 percent), hold a political party office (78 percent), or run for political office (61 percent) if they had the time and were asked to do so.

[14]Lists of delegates and alternates supplied by the NEA, Washington, D.C.

[15]*Education Daily* (Oct. 7, 1976): 4.

[16]*Education Daily* (Nov. 11, 1976): 2–3.

[17]In response to the question, "Have you ever worked in an election campaign or run for an elective office yourself?"

[18]In response to the question, "As a teacher in this community, have you

ever felt that you should avoid taking public stands on community, state or national issues outside of class?"

[19]Lunstrum (*Controversial Issues*, pp. 245–46) recounts a variety of efforts to pressure schools in Indiana to include anti-Communist propaganda in school courses in the late 1950s.

[20]*See* Todd Clark, *The West Virginia Textbook Controversy: A Personal Account,* SOCIAL EDUCATION 39 (April 1975): 216–21.

[21]Donald Layton, *Scientists Versus Fundamentalists: The California Compromise,* PHI DELTA KAPPAN (Dec. 1974): 696–97.

[22]Zeigler (POLITICAL LIFE, p. 98) writes, "It can readily be seen that teachers do not regard the classroom as a suitable forum for the expression by teachers of controversial opinions, or for that matter of noncontroversial opinions."

[23]Jennings and Zeigler, *Political Expressivism,* p. 7.

[24]*Ibid.,* p. 8.

[25]*Ibid.,* pp. 13–14.

[26]Gordon and Shea, *A Political Profile,* p. 334.

[27]Eight percent felt constrained by lack of materials; 39 percent by lack of knowledge about law-related topics. Another question highlights just how small the number of teachers who feel political constraints is. We asked, "Have there been any issues in the district which raised the question of teacher rights?" Sixty-five percent of the teachers answered affirmatively. However, few of these issues involved censorship or political rights. At most 7 percent of the respondents mentioned this type of incident. The majority of teachers' rights issues concerned working conditions.

[28]M. Kent Jennings, *Observations on the Study of Political Values Among Pre-Adults,* paper prepared for the Center for Research and Education in American Liberties, Columbia University, Oct. 21, 1966, pp. 19–20.

[29]391 U.S. 563 (1968).

[30]Blumberg, *Are Teachers Doormats?*

CHAPTER 12

Students and the Authority Structure of the School

As citizens of their schools students are subject to a wide variety of rules designed to govern their behavior. These rules suggest a great deal about the attitudes and values of rulemakers and the larger community, including the concept of citizenship these adults have and what values and behavior they prize. In planning this portion of the study, we decided we could not further extend the lengthy questionnaire to ask about the complete range of rules governing students in the sample's high schools. Instead, we focused our questions on controversies between students and adults over school rules, going on the assumption that these instances might tell us (1) about value conflicts in the school and (2) about mechanisms for dealing with conflict. These mechanisms, we felt, would in turn provide information about the authority structure of the school and about its implicit lessons for students.

We began by asking respondents an open-ended question about controversies over rules in their school. However, controversies are not comparable from school to school, and some schools have not even experienced any controversy, according to some respondents. To permit comparison of responses about controversy, we added a question about what sort of reaction might be engendered by a student demonstration such as that conducted by the Tinker children. These anticipated reactions gave us an additional insight into the way school authorities regard student citizens.

Controversies Over School Rules[1]

Respondents' reports suggest that although the issues vary from place to place there is a sameness to student controversies. Students, constrained by school regulations, challenge the restrictions. Administrators work mightily to head off large-scale conflict by individualizing and defusing the protest. They negotiate with the student or students and compromise or give a little. Reports from respondents suggest that students have made important gains on rules governing grooming, smoking, and speech and assembly.

Negotiation strategies and concessions to students on specific issues have convinced about 25 percent of the sample of teachers and administrators that they have lost control over their students. This feeling comes out strongest in discussions of discipline problems—that is, direct challenges to authority. But it also is part of some respondents' reaction to a wide variety of concerns, including dress codes, rules on smoking, and issues dealing with student expression.

However, these controversies must be kept in perspective. There was great variance in the perceptions of what constituted a conflict or controversy. Slightly more than half of the sample's teachers and administrators reported no controversies, suggesting that the 1970s are hardly a period of massive student protest. On the other hand, at least one teacher in 78 percent of the schools in the sample said there had been a student controversy. In 37 percent of the schools, a majority of the teachers interviewed said there had been a controversy. Teachers vary in their awareness of conflicts, their sensitivity to conflicts, and their willingness to discuss conflict. It is, therefore, not surprising that in 53 percent of the schools teachers disagreed over whether there had even been a controversy. (In 25% of the schools teachers agreed that there had been controversy, in 22% that there had been none.) But even when there was agreement on the occurrence of controversy, it was rare for teachers to report the same incident. This suggests that student protests are generally not schoolwide and are not well publicized even within the school. Rather, students and adult school personnel are engaged in a series of skirmishes that are small but nonetheless revelatory.

Judging from our sample, we can say that many schools of the 1970s confront a quiet crisis of authority. Many teachers and administrators we interviewed were engaged in a dispute with students over the issue of who sets the rules. Although this debate has little of the shrillness of the demonstrations of the 1960s, it is nevertheless a real issue, and it emerges again and again in the guise of a variety of specific issues.

In the 1960s many high schools were shell-shocked by a revolutionary spirit among students who demonstrated their commitment to change. These students actively opposed the Vietnam War, participated in Eugene McCarthy's campaign for the presidency, and committed themselves to racial and social justice. Although they emphasized larger social issues, students also organized to increase their role in setting school policy. School boards and school administrators varied in their response to the wave of student activism. Some schools accepted and adjusted to the change while others came down hard on the students, suspending or expelling the rebels.

Authority disputes of the 1970s appear to be very different from those of the 1960s, primarily because of changes in attitudes both in the larger society and in the schools. According to our respondents, students seem to have lost the group consciousness they displayed in the 1960s. They tend to see problems as individual rather than group based. In addition, the concern for broader political and social issues has waned. Dissatisfaction and rebellion are almost exclusively focused on the school's authority structure. Finally, our respondents said that school authorities have altered their approach to student rebellion. In dealing with students school authorities attempt to individualize complaints and thereby further reduce group consciousness. Also, they have developed a certain coolness, a willingness to listen and find a basis for agreement. Today the biggest administrative sin is overreaction. Why have administrators adopted this moderate stance? Some school administrators, as we have noted, feel the impact of court decisions that have expanded student rights and prescribed certain due process standards. However, it may also be that administrators are adapting to fit new conditions in the school and a new generation of students.

Generally, this quiet revolution is manifesting itself sporadically in a variety of issues, many of which have been or are being resolved in favor of the students. Respondents suggest that court decisions have generally increased both knowledge of and respect for student rights and have also generated a certain timidity that has made teachers and administrators more receptive to student complaints.

The conflicts and controversies reported by respondents are so familiar and mundane that they provoke one to wonder if things ever change. When asked about the issues involved in recent school controversies,

262

teachers and school administrators most frequently mentioned dress codes, student expression and assembly, discipline problems, and smoking. (See Table 58.) In addition to these issues, a few respondents mentioned conflicts over grading, attendance, open-campus policies, student records, integration, and locker searches.

TABLE 58
CONTROVERSIES OVER SCHOOL RULES REPORTED BY TEACHERS AND ADMINISTRATORS

SCHOOL RULES	TEACHERS* (N = 213)	ADMINISTRATORS* (N = 115)
Dress and hair codes	15%	13%
Rules on student expression and assembly	15	13
Disciplinary policies	11	13
Smoking rules	7	3
Other controversies	13	9
No controversies	51	56

*Percentages are based on more than one response and add up to more than 100%.

Dress and Hair Codes

The most frequently mentioned area of controversy in the schools was dress and hair codes.[2] Schools have traditionally imposed some restrictions on the clothes students wear to school. Dress restrictions that provoked conflict in the sample's schools include: boys hair length, facial hair, and weightlifter-style T-shirts; girls' skirt lengths, pants, bared midriffs, and see-through blouses; and everybody's blue jeans. The following incidents are typical:

> The dress code is enforced, although in actuality only in extreme cases. See-through blouses are forbidden, but we were told not to send a girl to the office for indecent exposure. If a boy disobeyed the dress code, he would be more likely to be reprimanded. [California teacher]

> Last year a student cut all his hair off. He was told to wear a wig or get thrown out of school. He wore a wig until his hair grew back. [Illinois teacher]

> This is a cowboy community and students like to wear cowboy hats. I collect the hats. They [students] thought I was abusing their rights, but I checked with the administration and had their support. There would be no hats worn in buildings. If the students did not know how to be gentlemen, I would teach them. [Texas teacher]

263

Why do schools have dress codes? Some teachers and administrators said that certain types of dress and grooming are disruptive. They told our interviewers that the schools required an atmosphere that they described as clean, orderly, businesslike, and work oriented. Long hair, jeans, and other violations of the codes were sometimes viewed as indicators of slovenly attitudes and lax behavior. In addition, some respondents said these modes of grooming provoked reactions from other students which led to disruption. (When the courts have supported school dress codes, it has usually been because of their willingness to defer to professional educators' arguments about the educational necessity of such codes.)

However, many more respondents took a more relaxed attitude toward dress codes. They felt that student grooming was irrelevant to teaching and learning. But within this group many had a strong sense that the community favored a dress code, and those who mentioned dress codes often said they would be changed if the parents sought a change. This sense of parents' wishes persists despite the fact that students apparently leave their homes in the morning looking much the same as they do when they appear at school. Obviously, the students do not grow hair or change clothes *en route.* Then why don't the parents enforce dress restrictions? They do—through the school. As one teacher from Illinois stated the situation,

> We do what parents want. Last year the parents rescinded the dress code. Girls had to wear dresses, but now girls can wear slacks. There still can be no patches on certain parts of the anatomy.

For parents the clothes their children wear make one more hassle they would rather not deal with, especially at 7:00 in the morning. Dress codes create the illusion that it is not the parent but the school that is restricting students' choice. Of course, when students attend school improperly dressed, the illusion becomes reality, and teachers and principals are placed in conflict with students.

Educators' resentment of this police role has been one element pushing for change in dress codes. A superintendent in Georgia told us that he had been sued over a hair and dress code. The school code was upheld in court, but the superintendent decided that the issue was "wasting too much time and energy"; his staff was tired of measuring dresses and hair length. When he polled students and teachers, both recommended elimination. He felt that dropping the dress code had increased morale.

That school district's experience is fairly typical. Dress codes were moderated in most sample schools where they provoked controversy, although there remain some schools with elaborate codes and strict enforcement. Many schools removed dress restrictions, and other eliminated strict enforcement. Rules specifying hair length and length of girls' dresses have been replaced by rules requiring cleanliness and neatness. Restrictions on nudity and suggestive clothes were the last vestiges of the code in most schools.

Smoking

Although similar to dress codes in some respects, restrictions against student smoking are more complex. Whereas dress codes are usually arbitrary and mostly a matter of fashion, smoking rules are related to state laws, fire codes, and health and environmental issues.[3] Furthermore, while few students appear concerned about what others wear to school, many students resent the smoke-filled washrooms. The smoking issue is not easily resolved to everyone's satisfaction. Some of our responses illustrate its complexity:

> This school is very liberal in its approach to problems. They look first to the legal aspects of the case. They don't react traditionally. For example, in dealing with the smoking of students, the principal checked with the state. [teacher in large Georgia community]

> I just got myself into trouble with the faculty and town. The students wanted a smoking room. I'm in charge of the newspaper. I'm against smoking, but I told them to write to the editor of the school paper. [teacher in small Illinois town]

There have always been restrictions on student smoking, and there have always been students who smoke in school. This again has placed school personnel in the role of enforcement agents. Teachers are assigned to patrol the halls and washrooms for smokers during class breaks. Meanwhile, on their own breaks, the teachers can go to their lounge for a comfortable smoke. Everybody knows that teachers are adults and students are minors, but that does not reduce the guilt feeling in all but the most insensitive teachers and administrators, nor, according to our respondents, does it reduce students' resentment over the double standard.

Many of the sample schools continued to discipline students who smoked in or around school, but of those teachers who mentioned a smoking controversy, 43 percent said it had resulted in a loosening up

265

of restrictions. The schools that allowed smoking have either developed a designated area, usually out of sight of the community and visitors, or have unofficially designated smoking washrooms. One principal said he tacitly allowed upperclassmen to smoke in designated washrooms with the understanding that they would keep underclassmen out. Underclassmen smoking in other places were disciplined.

Expression and Assembly

A third major area of conflict reported by our sample has been student expression and assembly. Most issues of this sort revolve around student newspapers. Several teachers told us about administrative efforts to censor the school paper. In some schools, students had brought out alternative newspapers and distributed them to other students. In one school, students distributed handbills. Other controversies dealt with speech. In one school in California a principal insisted that the class valedictorian "tone down" her speech, which he characterized as derogatory to Mexican-Americans.

Expression and assembly issues in the sample schools were generally resolved in favor of the students. For instance, the week before our interviewers visited a school in Pennsylvania, some students had published an alternative newspaper. According to the superintendent and principal, the students claimed the school paper did not represent their views. The teacher who advised the school paper was afraid the new paper would compete for ads. The controversy was resolved by allowing the students to distribute the alternative paper after school. Another instance occurred in a sample school in California. The school paper planned to publish an article criticizing a teacher. The principal spoke with the editors, explaining that the teacher's professional code of ethics would not allow him to answer their charges and asking the students to reconsider publishing the article. They decided to go ahead and publish the article.

Not all is sweetness and light when it comes to free speech. It was only as a result of a court decision that students in a California school we visited were allowed to pass out handbills. And several teachers told us that their school newspapers persisted under severe restrictions from administrators who wanted a supportive and docile student press.

Disciplinary Policy

There have always been students who are unruly and disrespectful of authority. But many educators believe the number of such students

266

is increasing.[4] In many sample schools, "discipline" has become a code word for the felt loss of authority in dealing with students. And many conflicts and controversies come down to a question of discipline. Here are some of the opinions of teachers concerned with discipline:

> Court decisions have caused a lessening of school discipline. The more freedom you give kids, the more trouble you have. How low do you go in lowering voter laws, 16? 14? birth? Many forget why age levels were originally set. We're in trouble when the court says what I can't do but not what I can do in class. [teacher in small Illinois community]

> Court action limits the weapons available to disciplinarians. It leads to disruption because some students should not be in school and the administration cannot easily get rid of them. Lateral transfers to another school are used to get rid of headaches. [teacher in large Pennsylvania city]

> We don't go to the bathroom without asking HEW permission. Students now have too much freedom. They [courts] have ruined the students. Everyone has a boss in life, but teachers can't boss students. [Georgia teacher]

In our sample, discipline was a greater problem in urban school districts than in rural or suburban districts. Urban teachers often presented themselves as front-line troops defending civilized society from the hordes of abusive students. They wanted administrators to back them up in the battle, and they often judged administrators on how tough they were with unruly students. Several teachers expressed chagrin at the failure of administrators to provide this type of support. Others expressed admiration for a principal or administrator who had been "strong" or had backed them up on a decision. Still other respondents felt that both teachers and administrators had been deserted by outside authorities. As one teacher told us,

> Teachers won't say anything about anyone even when they know they're right. They are afraid that if they discipline students they will lose their jobs. Now the assistant principal is accused of suspending seniors at random. And there is a lot more swearing than before. This frightens a lot of teachers. There is no way to discipline students unless they are cought cold with a knife.

A major aspect of the discipline problem in the schools we visited was formulating suitable ways to exercise authority. School administrators have a range of tools including special schools for troublemakers, corporal punishment, parent conferences, suspensions, transfers, and expulsions. Although the Children's Defense Fund and others have asserted that schools get rid of difficult students one way or another,[5] many school administrators in the sample emphasized the importance they placed on keeping students in school. This has led them to favor alternative education programs specifically aimed at students who present a discipline problem. Especially in urban districts, administrators now frequently have the option of assigning students to schools that specialize in educating difficult students. Here is how a teacher in the sample saw the suspension question:

> We were given a directive on suspensions. Students have to be given more written notice. Half the time, if we suspend the student they end up in the juvenile justice department and we don't get to see them anymore. So we don't like to suspend. [teacher in large California city]

Corporal punishment is another alternative, one used in many sample schools. One of our interviewers got a chance to observe the "board of education" in action in a school he visited. Some respondents said corporal punishment is a quick-fix method of discipline—immediate, direct, and not requiring a lot of paperwork. These respondents felt that the threat of corporal punishment was a deterrent to misbehavior. Some respondents viewed it as an alternative to suspension and said it was offered to students and parents as an alternative.

> Some localities have had this policy, which is in effect the law, that the teachers or administrators cannot use a paddle. I feel that when you take that threat away from the school, students stop being afraid. Sometimes students are expelled in lieu of paddling. That's much worse. [Georgia teacher]
>
> I don't think punishment of any kind is the answer. It's like taking an aspirin for a headache. I look at paddling of students as brakes on an automobile. Something gets it started rolling downhill, you use the paddle not as a cure but attempting to slow down behavior. [Georgia teacher]

Other Controversies

A little over 10 percent of our respondents told us about conflicts varied enough to defy additional categorization. Locker searches, grading, exams, and open-campus policies have all been the subject of controversy. For example, one teacher said,

> We have had some controversy over locker searches. It's not something that happens frequently but it has touched on some students' sensibilities. I'm not certain of the law. I don't think kids fully internalize

the fact that they have recourse to action—they have a concept of hopelessness. A climate of fear exists.

Then there's the business of not having to stand when saluting the flag. The principal has said they must stand. That's in direct violation of the law. He's heavy on law and order, and the students know he is in direct violation of law.

The Absence of Student Controversy[6]

One way to gain a better understanding of the school's authority structure is to examine the absence of conflict. Why has authority not been challenged in some sample schools? Teachers and administrators gave several different reasons for a lack of student conflict, and they differed in their emphases. Administrators stressed three factors: the administration's respect for student rights, administrators' skillful handling of students, and the atmosphere of the school. Although teachers acknowledged these reasons, they also frequently mentioned students' apathy and ignorance of their rights.

Of those respondents who said there were no student controversies, 60 percent of the administrators and 25 percent of the teachers said that this was because students' rights were respected. Essentially, they said challenges to authority were eliminated by sharing authority. A teacher in California told us:

> The students came out with their own district-wide constitution and bill of rights. It was devised by the students and accepted by everyone.

A department head from Georgia provided a slightly different emphasis:

> Students are given resonable freedom with restraint. If you cause problems, you'll be dealt with accordingly.

A number of administrators credited their interpersonal skills in dealing with student problems before they reached conflict proportions. Teachers also mentioned this aspect of administrative skill. A teacher in California told us:

> Give the administration credit. The principal bends over backwards to help students individually so that collective problems don't arise.

A Texas teacher noted there had been student-related controversies but

> not as a group, but rather as individual protests. I sometimes encourage students not to protest but to communicate with the administration.

269

Another teacher thought the administration so skilled that teachers were unlikely to hear about controversies:

> The discretion of the administration is such that there may well be issues which are never made public. When one student's in trouble, the superintendent and principal prefer to keep it as confidential as possible.

Thus both administrators and teachers often credited administrators with defusing and individualizing student controversy.

Both administrators and teachers, although twice as many administrators, thought that the atmosphere of the school played a role in reducing controversy. Many told us that the smallness of the school, the homogeneity of students, or friendly relations between students and school personnel eliminated the potential for controversy. In addition, a small number specifically credited the "conservative" views of the students. These educators said there was no trouble because students respected authority and understood the importance of order.

Although teachers in the sample generally shared many of the perspectives of the administrators when attempting to explain the absence of student controversy, some pointed to students' apathy and ignorance of their rights. As a big-city teacher in Pennsylvania put it:

> Students are not aware of their rights. They have a student bill of rights, but they lose it or don't read it. Since they're not aware, they don't know when their rights are infringed upon.

(He added that *his* students were different. "They are active, so they know what's going on.")

A final reason given by a few respondents for the lack of student controversy was community disapproval. Administrators and teachers offering this explanation saw the community as conservative and unwilling to condone student agitation. As one western Illinois teacher put it, "This is a small Christian community with a lot of small Christians."

In general, respondents who saw no controversies over rules in their school supported many of the points made by those who did see controversies. Both groups agreed that administrators' skillful handling of students and the climate of the school were important. They differed mostly in that one group saw these factors as important in avoiding conflict, the other in dealing with it.

270

The Resolution of Student Controversies[7]

Most of the student-related conflicts that respondents told us about have been resolved, and, according to the teachers and administrators we spoke with, many have been resolved in favor of the students. As Table 59 shows, the most frequent response to the question about how controversies were resolved was that they had been worked out with the students through a negotiation process. About 10 percent of the respondents reported that a procedure or committee had been set up, probably another form of negotiation and conciliation. However, 10 percent reported that the issue was decided by the courts.

In addition to discussing the process by which controversies had been resolved, many respondents mentioned outcomes. As Table 59 shows, respondents said that in a few instances students and the issues they had raised had simply been ignored, and in some cases students had been punished or rebuked. But the most frequent outcome reported was that the regulations in question had been loosened up or eliminated.

TABLE 59
TEACHERS' AND ADMINISTRATORS' PERCEPTIONS OF RESOLUTION OF CONTROVERSIES OVER RULES

MANNER OF RESOLUTION	TEACHERS* (N = 95)	ADMINISTRATORS* (N = 48)
Worked it out with students	25%	42%
Loosened up (eliminated dress code, allowed smoking, etc.)	24	21
Occuring now, no resolution	22	17
Students punished, rebuked	12	15
Set up a procedure, committee	12	10
Courts decided	9	10
Ignored, tabled, left unresolved	8	4
Other	6	0

*Percentages are based on more than one response and add up to more than 100%.

Teachers' Advice to Students Seeking Change

As a means of gauging both the attitudes of teachers and the relationship of students to school authorities, we asked teachers what advice they would give to students who came to them seeking guidance on changing a school policy. The vast majority said they would advise

271

students to seek changes, with only two percent saying they would tell students to drop the idea. One teacher from a large Illinois city was in that small minority:

> I would tell them to forget it. I'd like to see kids adjust here and in the outside world. But I send them to the principal if it's a serious issue.

Those advising students to push ahead suggested a variety of closely-related strategies that involved working through the accepted authority structure. For example, the largest number would urge students to see the principal, the second largest number would suggest taking the matter to the student council, and the third largest would just tell them to follow channels. Not one respondent said directly that he would encourage a demonstration or any other nontraditional activity.

This preference for working through channels may suggest a certain amount of apprehension in teachers who were asked to put themselves in the uncomfortable position of advising students bent on change. This supposition is strengthened by a look at some of the actual answers of teachers.

> I don't think that a teacher should put himself in the position of advocate for something that is against established codes. Teachers shouldn't be the leaders of protest. See the board, attend meetings, raise qustions there. Check with other schools for data in comparable situations. [teacher in small California town]

> If something is wrong they [students] should set up an appointment with the principal and ask to discuss the issue. If that fails and they still want to change something, I would not get involved. I won't jeopardize my job by recommending any other kinds of action. [teacher in southern Georgia]

Other respondents implied that teachers had little power:

> If I was in favor and if it would work, I would tell them to talk to the counselor or the principal. A classroom teacher can't do much. . . . [teacher in small Texas town]

> I would tell them to tell their parents. Parents run the school. Teachers work for parents, so students should learn to realize how much power the parents really have. [teacher in large Texas city]

Without knowing more about the actual practices of the sample schools, we cannot extensively interpret the data developed in response to this question. For example, in some schools telling students to see the principal or the student council would be the same as telling them

272

to forget it; in other schools, that advice might lead to real change. About all we can say is that the responses to this question are generally in line with other answers, suggesting that in most sample schools administrators are receptive to listening to complaints and possibly doing something about them.

Tinker Revisited

Students have confronted the schools with such a variety of specific challenges on such a range of issues and policies that it is very difficult to gain from general questions a good sense of the general status of students in the schools of the 1970s. Rather than attempt an investigation of the whole range of students' rights issues, then, we concentrated on the issue of free speech for students, in the hope that it would cast light on some general relationships among students, administrations, and the community. Without mentioning the name of the case, we gave respondents the essential fact situation of *Tinker* and asked how administrators and school board members would react to such a student demonstration. Most respondents said they expected a neutral response, neither approval nor disapproval of the demonstration. Many in this group said it would be okay for students to wear armbands as long as they did not disrupt. Others in this group said there simply would be no reaction, except perhaps curiosity.

Although most respondents expected a neutral reaction, some teachers and administrators in the sample thought the demonstration would meet with disapproval. Teachers were somewhat more inclined to anticipate disapproval than administrators were. Some teachers and administrators suggested that the demonstration would meet a mixed response, some approval and some disapproval. Here again, however, teachers were more inclined to expect that disapproval would predominate.

All in all, however, respondents said that their schools would not discourage students from demonstrating. This suggests that the school climate has probably changed significantly since the 1960s, when student demonstrations often seemed to meet resistance. If there has been such a change, court decisions such as *Tinker* have no doubt been partially responsible. For example, when we asked respondents specifically about the case, most at least knew the general direction of the finding. However, awareness of court decisions alone probably cannot explain the lack of resistance to student demonstrations. Our respondents suggested many times during the interviews that the basic relationship between students and adult school personnel has changed

273

greatly in recent years; the anticipated reaction to student demonstrations is probably more a recognition of this change than a response to judicial scrutiny of the schools. What caused this change in the relationship between students and educators? The possible causes are many, ranging from television and working mothers to court decisions. Although outside the scope of this study, determining the precise causes would be a fascinating subject for further study.

Citizenship Values of Teachers and Administrators

Examining the citizenship values of teachers and administrators is important because it is reasonable to assume that their values influence both the formal and the informal curriculum. Certainly educators' citizenship values may influence the values they consciously try to foster in students, through the courses and books they choose to offer and the actual classroom lessons they present. Furthermore, the values of educators may well affect the climate of the school and thus affect students' behavior and the implicit lessons they receive about citizenship.

Several studies suggest the importance of educators' values. Hess and Torney have shown that the citizenship values of students change through the school years and become more like adult values.[8] However, they did not determine whether this is a result of school teaching, maturation, or some other factor. Levenson has shown that teachers' and students' citizenship values are closer to each other than are those of parents and students.[9]

To measure teachers' and administrators' ideas of citizenship values, we handed them the following list of 11 citizenship categories.

Good Citizens Are Those Who:

_____ A. Obey or respect the laws and legal authorities.

_____ B. Take part in community affairs or help in local community matters.

_____ C. Stand up for principles or what they think is right.

_____ D. Register and vote.

_____ E. Are interested and informed about what's going on, about public affairs, government, etc.

_____ F. Are tolerant and respectful of the rights and beliefs of others.

_____ G. Are loyal to the country or government, stand up for the country.

_____ H. Try to improve the country or make the country a better place to live.

_____ I. Take part, actively participate in public affairs.

_____ J. Help other people, the less fortunate or needy.

_____ K. Are independent and self-sufficient. Take responsibility for their own actions.

We then asked respondents the following question:

I have a list of things social studies teachers have identified with good citizenship. Would you look at these and rank order the three you think are most important for being a good citizen? Now which do you feel is the least important?

The question and categories were based on previous studies by Jennings[10] and Levenson.[11] Using interviews with a national sample of high school seniors, their parents, and their social studies teachers, Jennings and Levenson were able to identify 39 specific categories of citizenship values. Despite this large number, the responses were greatly clustered: two-thirds of the categories were endorsed by not more than five percent of the respondents, leaving only a dozen or so categories with relatively wide acceptance. Among the three groups of respondents, the greatest homogeneity of response was among teachers. For our question we selected the 11 categories of values chosen most often by the social studies teachers.[12] These ranged in acceptance from 37 percent to 6 percent.

Table 60 shows the choices of our respondents and those of the teachers in the 1965 study. We begin by examining our findings and later compare the responses of our teachers with those of the sample in the earlier study.

Comparison of Teachers and Administrators in Our Sample

Perhaps the most striking result shown in the table is the rank-order similarities of the values of teachers, principals, and superintendents.

To analyze these findings, we have made use of Levenson's four "criteria" (general clusters of values) that might be associated with citizenship.[13]

1. Participation: The good citizen is cognitively and behaviorally involved in political decisions.
2. Allegiance: The good citizen is loyal and takes pride in his nation.

275

TABLE 60
COMPARISON OF CITIZENSHIP VALUES OF 1965 SAMPLE AND OF FORD STUDY SAMPLE

	1965 SAMPLE	FORD SAMPLE (1976)		
CITIZENSHIP VALUES	TEACHERS* (N = 385)	TEACHERS* (N = 207)	PRINCIPALS* (N = 41)	SUPERINTENDENTS* (N = 69)
Are tolerant and respectful of the rights and beliefs of others	6%	53%	66%	44%
Obey or respect the laws and legal authorities	29	50	52	58
Are interested and informed about what's going on, about public affairs, government, etc.	37	41	28	39
Are independent and self-sufficient. Take responsibility for their own actions	10	33	30	29
Register and vote	33	28	25	24
Stand up for principles or what they think is right	9	27	17	15
Try to improve the country or make the country a better place to live	9	24	31	21
Take part, actively participate in public affairs	37	16	14	12
Take part in community affairs or help in local community matters	22	13	13	24
Are loyal to the country or government, stand up for the country	12	10	15	27
Help other people, the less fortunate or needy	6	7	8	5

*Since respondents picked several values, columns will add up to more than 100%.

276

3. Obedience: The good citizen complies with legally established rules and regulations.
4. Non-political considerations: The good citizen is a good person. (Non-political values can be divided into social values such as tolerance or helpfulness and personal values such as inner fortitude and morality.)

Tolerance (a nonpolitical value in Levenson's scheme) and obedience were chosen most frequently by all three groups in our sample. Participant criteria of citizenship were chosen less frequently:[14] only 24 to 28 percent among all groups chose "register and vote" as one of the three most important citizenship values, and only 12 to 16 percent chose "take part, actively participate in public affairs." The most cerebral and most passive of the participation values—"are interested and informed"—was chosen more often than the other two by all three groups. "Are loyal to the country or government," an allegiance criterion in Levenson's scheme, was chosen less frequently than the other values.

Some interesting findings emerge when the data are examined further. For example, although either tolerance or obedience was chosen by most respondents, few respondents chose both. (As Table 61 shows, an examination of selected intercorrelations of the citizenship criteria of teachers shows a large negative correlation, Tau-b $= -.26$, between those choosing obedience and tolerance.)[15]

Respondents who chose obedience were also *unlikely* to choose independence and actively participate, and they were *likely* to choose loyalty and registering and voting. These respondents seemed to possess a rather traditional notion of democratic citizenship.

The respondents choosing tolerance, on the other hand, were *likely* to choose independence and *unlikely* to choose register and vote. Their ideal citizen seems intellectually active but not necessarily active in the political arena.

There were also some differences among the groups in our sample. For example, superintendents seemed more concerned with obedience than principals were. Twenty-two percent fewer superintendents than principals chose tolerance, and superintendents chose obedience as their most important value. Their choices may well reflect their positions. Principals are located in school buildings, in the midst of students and teachers. Often they are accessible to parents also. Anyone who has been in a high school recently knows that a successful principal must be a consummate human engineer. It is not hard to see why principals

TABLE 61
INTERCORRELATIONS OF SELECTED CITIZENSHIP VALUES OF TEACHERS

	Loyal	Tolerant	Independent	Register and Vote	Actively Participate	Interested and Informed
Obedient	.13	-.26	-.25	.10	-.21	-.08
Loyal		.01	-.30	-.02	-.19	-.08
Tolerant			.17	-.26	-.10	-.09
Independent				-.26	-.10	-.16
Register and vote					-.01	-.15
Actively participate						.02
Interested and informed						

would preach tolerance. By contrast, superintendents are usually located at central headquarters, directing from afar, relatively isolated from teachers, students, and parents. Tolerance is important to them, but obedience and respect for authority are more important.

Although only a quarter of the superintendents picked "loyalty to country" and "take part in community affairs," they were more likely to pick these than were teachers or principals. Loyalty would seem to be another reflection of their position of authority. Their emphasis on community participation may reflect their leadership role in the community. (It is interesting that principals and teachers more often chose a broader context for their participation: they chose to improve the country and to take part in public affairs more often than they chose to take part in community affairs.)

There were also some differences among respondents from the different states making up our sample. California teachers most often chose tolerance (59%) and independence (52%). Illinois teachers most often chose tolerance (58%) and interested and informed (46%). Pennsylvania teachers chose tolerance (62%) and obedience (57%). Texas teachers picked the same two but reversed the order—obedience (56%), tolerance (54%). Georgia teachers overwhelmingly chose obedience (68%), with interested and informed second (43%) and tolerance fourth (30%).

The age of respondents also seemed related to the choice of values. Teachers 35 and younger chose tolerance (60%), interested and informed (48%), independence (35%), and stand up for principles (30%) more often than teachers older than 35. By contrast, the older teachers chose obedience (54%), register and vote (37%), take part in public affairs (20%), and loyalty (15%) more often than younger teachers.

The differences suggest a generation gap between older and younger teachers. Younger teachers showed more support for the nonpolitical citizenship values of tolerance and independence, and they favored the passive participation of being informed. Older teachers put more emphasis on voting and actively taking part, and they also gave greater stress to obedience and loyalty.

The differences between younger and older teachers are similar to the differences between teachers and superintendents; that is, the responses of teachers over 35 look more like those of superintendents than do responses of teachers 35 and younger. Earlier we suggested that some of the superintendents' value preferences could be explained by their position. Their age or political generation may also explain some of the differences.

Teachers 1965—Teachers 1976

Comparison of the results of our study with those of the 1965 survey of social studies teachers is complicated by certain differences in the questions. The earlier study relied on respondents to supply their own answers to an open-ended question on citizenship. Our study, on the other hand, provided 11 categories from which teachers were asked to choose the 3 most important.[16] The role played by the different questionnaire methodologies will be considered in our comparison of the two groups.

As Table 60 shows, the single largest difference between the two groups appears in the category of tolerance. In 1965 tolerance was one of two values mentioned least frequently (only 6%); in 1977 it was the value chosen most frequently by the teachers (53%). Teachers in our sample were also much more likely to choose obedience and independence. The 1965 teachers ranked obedience well below the participation values, but the 1976 teachers ranked these values in the reverse order. For example, participation in public affairs and the local community had far fewer adherents in our study than in the 1965 study.

These differences are striking and merit consideration. If they reflect changes in the citizenship values of teachers, they show a shift toward less emphasis on participation values, especially active participation, and more emphasis on nonpolitical criteria, such as tolerance and independence. Out teachers also were much more inclined to see obedience as a citizenship value. (In both studies allegiance was not an important value.)

These differences probably derive partially from the different methodologies of the two studies. The open-ended question in 1965 brought forth participatory criteria. Perhaps these are the values teachers think of first when they think about citizenship. But by giving them the options of choosing tolerance, obedience, and allegiance in our study, we may have opened up for our sample teachers a more rounded picture of the good citizen, enabling them to tell us about other values.

However, we think a good case can be made that the changes are not due solely to changes in methodology but represent changes in teachers' concepts of citizenship during the intervening years between the two studies. We have already shown that there are differences be-

280

tween older and younger teachers. In our sample, older teachers (who probably were teaching in 1965) are somewhat more like the teachers in the 1965 sample; they chose tolerance and independence less frequently and voting and taking part more frequently. There may well be a generation gap along these dimensions.

Younger teachers in our sample were probably high school or college students in an era of unprecedented participation, the 1960s. In that period political participation included nontraditional forms such as demonstrations, sit-ins, and protest marches, and young people took the lead in political activism. However, in the late 1960s and early 1970s, many young people began to withdraw from participation, and demonstrations and protests subsided. Recently enfranchised young people failed to vote in significant numbers. Perhaps those who had once participated in political action were tired or frustrated, and many who concluded that political activism was unlikely to accomplish anything may have dropped out of politics. The disaffection of this political generation and age cohort may be reflected in the responses of the younger teachers in our sample.

These indications that this political generation and age cohort has, since the end of the 1960s, turned from social participation to personal development could explain why the younger teachers in our sample are different from both the older teachers in our sample and the 1965 teachers. First, the emphasis that social studies teachers of the 1960s (as represented in the 1965 study) placed on active participation might have contributed to student activism in the 1960s. But if this former student generation, appearing as younger teachers in our study, tried active participation and became disenchanted, then it is understandable that they would turn away from direct political participation and instead recognize nonpolitical values and such relatively passive political values as being informed. Moreover, the traumas of Watergate might have reinforced their withdrawal from political activism but perhaps have had less effect on older teachers who have kept their faith in traditional forms of political activism such as registering and voting.

The Effect of the Informal Curriculum

As we noted earlier, it would be impossible, with the resources available to this study, to systematically evaluate how students' perceptions of law and citizenship are affected by the informal curriculum, that is, the way schools formulate and administer rules, and the attitudes and expectations of teachers and administrators. All we can do is briefly review our findings on this informal curriculum and make some tentative hypotheses on how they might affect students.

Our findings do not generally confirm the hypothesis of those who argue that American schools are dictatorial institutions that routinely trample the rights of teachers and students.[17] To be sure, we did not speak to students, but the teachers and administrators we talked to did not paint a picture of a repressive institution, either for students or for themselves. In general, as we pointed out earlier, most respondents felt that there were few controversies over school rules and that such controversies as did occur were usually resolved through negotiation, frequently with the result of loosening up the rules and giving students at least part of what they wanted. When respondents looked at teachers' rights and the relationship of teachers to the authority structure of the school, they again did not find repression. Teachers told us they felt free to actively participate in politics, to take stands outside of the classroom, and to discuss topics fully within class.

It is easy (perhaps too easy) for those who believe the schools are repressive to find all sorts of dire consequences for education. However, our findings suggest a far more complex picture of the schools, and we must generalize very cautiously.

Our data on how respondents view education law (Chapter 10) show the difficulty of determining consequences for teaching and learning. For example, it is clear that teachers are often uncertain about education law (more than 70% said they wanted to know more about one or more aspects of law affecting students and school people), but it is far from clear what the consequences are for law-related or citizenship education. Surely a creative teacher could turn his own uncertainty into a chance for the class to fully explore law-related issues.

To take another example from that chapter, about 25 percent of our respondents felt confused and frustrated by new laws and court decisions, and, in response to another question, about 25 percent (perhaps the same respondents) said they felt that these laws and court decisions had worsened conditions in the school. It is possible that these critical respondents would as teachers misrepresent the role of law and the courts and undervalue the law's protection of rights, but although it is true that respondents who did not understand two key Supreme Court decisions were more critical than those who did, we do not have enough evidence to support this contention. Certainly eminent jurists and law professors have been equally critical of such decisions without losing their understanding and appreciation of the role of law. As for how teaching might be affected by educators' attitudes toward court decisions concerning schools, the only contention our data support is that since most respondents say that such decisions have had little impact, it is probably safe to assume that their attitudes do not affect their teaching much one way or the other.

Chapter 11 contains data that are somewhat easier to generalize about. If our teachers' self-reports are accurate, then teachers would seem to model active and concerned citizenship for their students. However, other data in the chapter resist easy interpretation. For example, one could argue that the reluctance of a minority of teachers to discuss controversial issues in the class might be a desirable model of tact and sensitivity to diversity, but it might instead be an instance of chilled free expression. And, as we pointed out in the conclusion to the chapter, teachers implied that they were fearful of criticizing school authorities, and this fear might cause them to model timidity for students and thus affect students' developing notions of citizenship. But this interpretation is pretty problematical, resting on several assumptions—that teachers in the sample were themselves fearful, that this attitude would be conveyed to students, and that this attitude, which after all deals with the relationship of employee to employer, might affect students' attitudes toward the relationship between citizen and state.

Nor is much clarification provided by the responses to the two questions that attempted to trace the effect of teachers' attitudes on their classroom teaching. As we pointed out in Chapter 11, of the fairly small minority of teachers who said they had at times felt they should not take public stands on issues, more than half said they had discussed their not taking a stand with students, and those that did not said they were not dissuaded by fear but rather claimed a variety of professional reasons (e.g., that the instance did not pertain to the course, that they would act unprofessionally by discussing it with students, etc.). This response suggests that teachers are not intimidated and often do introduce controversy into the classroom, though one could argue that the professional reasons teachers offer might be a camouflage for such real reasons as fear of getting into trouble with school authorities.

Answers to a series of questions about using student controversies as topics for study also suggest that teachers are not intimidated. Our interviewers asked those respondents who said there had been conflicts over student rights or other issues in their school if they would favor or oppose making a study of this issue a part of their course. By a two-to-one margin, teachers said they would favor it (39% said they favored it, 25% said they favored it and were doing it now, and another 5% said they would not oppose making such conflicts a subject of study).

In response to a follow-up question asking why they would favor or oppose studying such conflicts, those in favor said either that student controversies are relevant or that they teach students to think. Only one of those opposed said he feared the administration would disapprove, but most of the others gave reasons that implied a certain amount of apprehension about how their supervisors would react: they said that such issues were too emotional, that students were too immature, or that such issues promoted controversy. Here is some of the actual language these teachers used:

> The kids would become involved in the personalities of the issues rather than the law. They would look to see if their friends were involved and would use their personal feelings about the administration to examine the issue. [teacher in small California town]

> I don't thing it's right to let students solve problems. In school, they do what they are told. I may be an old fuddy. [teacher in small Texas town]

And an administrator in a small California district said that it all depends on how it's handled:

> There is no such thing as a neutral person. If the teacher was an ultra-liberal and a rabble-rouser, no. If he was impartial, yes.

As we have noted, the data presented in this chapter generally suggest that schools today are relatively tranquil not because students are successfully repressed but because they are treated with respect and their complaints taken seriously and often acted upon.

If one searched, of course, one could find some suggestions of a darker underside. About a quarter of the respondents (many located in cities) complained that the schools were undergoing a crisis of discipline. If they are right, perhaps students are learning lessons in institutional disarray and personal irresponsibility. Perhaps, as a few teachers suggested, students are ignorant of their rights and are learning lessons in apathy. And of course it is possible that respondents are seeing the school through the proverbial rosy glasses. Perhaps interviews with students would disclose a very different picture.

Can we draw any conclusions from this array of data? All in all, the pitcure suggested by these chapters is that schools are reasonably open institutions and that the informal curriculum is teaching students some good lessons about citizenship. To be sure, there are many problems in interpreting the data, and several pieces of data suggest that the schools are not yet democratic utopias. Obviously, many unanswered questions remain, calling for further research; but our findings suggest a set of hypotheses very different from those offered by much of the critical literature appearing in the 1960s and early 1970s.

Notes

[1] This section is based on responses to the following question: "Have there been any conflicts over student rights or other controversial issues in this school?" If respondents answered yes, they were asked, "What happened?"

[2] DAVID SCHIMMEL AND LOUIS FISCHER, in THE CIVIL RIGHTS OF STUDENTS (New York: Harper & Row, 1975), provide a lively chapter on the numerous school-related personal appearance cases that have been considered by the courts (pp. 142–81). See, for example, their discussion of Pugsley v. Sellmeyer, 250 S.W. 538 (Ark. 1923) and Karr v. Schmidt, 460 F.2d 617 (1972). There is also some confusion both as a result of inconsistent rulings by judicial circuits (SCHIMMEL AND FISCHER, p. 181) and as a result of Title IX. On November 23, 1976, *Education Daily* reported (p. 4):

> Federal law prohibits school districts from prescribing hair length standards for one sex and not the other, but it may or may not bar a different standard for each sex, according to the Office for Civil Rights.

> In a letter dated October 14, to Sen. Robert Taft, R-Ohio, OCR Director Martin Gerry explained that staff members were currently studying whether or not a school can set different hair length standards for boys and girls under the Title IX anti-sex discrimination law.

> [Gerry wrote:] "Reasonable differences in clothing standards for males and females are permitted so long as the goals of such standards are the same—maintenance of order, modesty or cleanliness."

> [Gerry continued:] "It is our position that under Title IX, school districts may prescribe non-discriminatory rules relating to facial hair, although we recognize that such rules will only effect [*sic*] male students."

[3] A legal memorandum of the National Association of Secondary School Principals (March 1972) notes:

> Smoking is an increasingly serious problem which plagues a vast majority of secondary school administrators. . . .

> Most communities and school systems have ordinances and regulations

relating to health and safety that include no-smoking laws. The enforcement of these laws, however, has become progressively more difficult. In public schools, the smoking problem has become a serious administrative and legal problem.

State laws generally regulate smoking only indirectly. . . . In some states, however, smoking is regulated directly through laws which forbid it in areas where food and beverages are prepared and stored. Most states, too, explicitly prohibit the sale or giving of tobacco to minors. Twelve states make it illegal for a minor to smoke. Local fire safety ordinances, on the other hand, nearly always regulate smoking directly by prohibiting it in certain public and private places. . . .

Although several states have laws relating to smoking and minors, few statutes expressly prohibit minors from smoking on school property.

[4]*Education Daily* (March 18, 1976, p. 1) reports that

Educators rank school violence and disruption among the top five problems they face, and generally feel that they don't have the knowledge or resources to cope with it, according to a government funded study. . . .

In its 150-page report, RBS notes that violence in 1972–73 cost the schools $500 million or $10.87 per student, about half spent to recoup vandalism loss and half paid for security services. In 1974–75, the costs for some urban areas were "incredible," the report said—$15 million for security in New York City, $3.5 million budgeted for Los Angeles.

There are hidden losses, too, the researchers observe. "The cost of school violence and disruption in educational terms may be higher in the long run than the financial costs—and more important—yet these costs are impossible to estimate.

School people are doing what they can about violence and disruption, but along with drug use it's on the upswing in urban, suburban and rural districts.

See also Jack Slate, *Death of a High School*, PHI DELTA KAPPAN (Dec. 1974): 251–54.

[5]According to the Children's Defense Fund there is "rampant use of suspensions and other disciplinary devices to throw children out of school." CHILDREN'S DEFENSE FUND OF THE WASHINGTON RESEARCH PROJECT, INC., CHILDREN OUT OF SCHOOL IN AMERICA (Cambridge, Mass.: Children's Defense Fund, 1974), p. 5. An analysis of data for five states reveals that "during the 1972–73 school year, at least 152,904 children were suspended at least once for over 575,000 school days or 3,200 school years" (p. 124). The Defense Fund's report continues:

Hundreds of thousands of children lose millions of school days every school year because of a range of disciplinary devices. While suspension is the most commonly used disciplinary device, as a result of unclear policies and vast school principal discretion, a wide variety of disciplinary actions have been developed to exclude children from school. . . . They are even more invisible than suspensions. Most are informal and checked solely by the restraint of the excluding official. Few contain basic elements of due process, though many result in children being put out of school for as long [as] or longer than many suspensions. Many border on illegality. Almost none are justifiable in terms of the best educational interests of children.

Many districts still have the power to expel children. But school officials prefer to use other means of permanently excluding children. Tantamount to expulsion is "voluntary withdrawal." Technically no blight remains on the child's records and the child (theoretically) may not be precluded from re-enrolling in another school in the district after a while. But it often results in permanent exclusion. (pp. 118–19)

[6]We asked respondents who said there had been no conflicts over student rights, "Why do you think not?" This section is based on their responses.

[7]We asked respondents who said there had been a conflict over student rights, "How was it resolved?" This section is based on their responses.

[8]HESS AND TORNEY, THE DEVELOPMENT OF POLITICAL ATTITUDES IN CHILDREN.

[9]George Levenson, The Public Responsibilities of the Private Man, unpublished Ph.D. thesis (University of Michigan, 1971), p. 74. Levenson also has found that the citizenship values of parents of students in 1965 are similar to values of a 1925 sample of students (p. 92).

[10]M. Kent Jennings directed the original study and collected the data in 1965. For additional information about the study, see JENNINGS AND NIEMI, THE POLITICAL CHARACTER OF ADOLESCENCE, Appendix. The question used by Jennings in the original questionnaire was open-ended. It read:

People have different ideas about what being a good citizen means. We're interested in what you think. Tell me how you would describe a good citizen in this country—that is, what things about a person are most important in showing that he is a good citizen.

[11]George Levenson did an extensive analysis of the citizenship aspects of the study. See The Public Responsibilities.

[12]The order of the categories on the hand card was random and did not reflect the order found by Levenson.

[13]Levenson, pp. 57–58.

[14]Note, however, that there were four participation values—"are interested and informed," "register and vote," "take part in public affairs," and "take part in community affairs"—a larger number of values for this criterion than for any of Levenson's other criteria. That means that respondents had more chances (4 of 11) to choose a participation value but also that they were

less likely to pick any particular one (i.e., if they thought participation was important they could spread their vote among four values). It is possible that if they had fewer to choose among, one participation value would have received greater acceptance, perhaps rivaling "tolerance" or "obedience."

[15]The larger the negative number of Table 61, the fewer respondents who chose both values; conversely, the larger the positive number, the greater the number of respondents who chose both values.

[16]Although we planned to compare the results of the two studies, we decided not to exactly replicate the original citizenship question. The open-endedness of the original question enabled Jennings and Levenson to identify citizenship values without imposing their own preconceived ideas about these values. This is a standard technique, which we employed extensively in our own questionnaire. However, it relies on the mental agility of the respondent and obviously works best when respondents are asked about something they are familiar with and ideas they have already thought through. The open-ended citizenship question forced respondents to bring to mind the myriad of citizenship possibilities, accepting some and rejecting others. Social scientists like to think that the respondents bring forth their most central notions as well as their complete set of notions. Rather than replicate the question, we decided to build on the results of the previous study. We did this because a fruit basket approach placed before respondents a full range of citizenship values, from which to pick some and reject others. A second reason for repecting the open-ended question was that typically some respondents only give one response but others give three or four. However, the multiple responses may result in differences that are as much a function of verbal facility and quickwittedness as they are of different values. Indeed, Levenson found that an increase in the number of responses was related to the likelihood of mentioning participatory citizenship criteria (p. 138). Fixed response alternatives give the researcher more control.

[17]See, e.g., JERRY FARBER, THE STUDENT AS NIGGER (New York: Contact Books, 1969); JOHATHAN KOZOL, DEATH AT AN EARLY AGE (Boston: Houghton Mifflin, 1967); HERBERT KOHL, 36 CHILDREN (New York: New American Library, 1967).

PART IV

CHAPTER 13

The Territory Ahead: Some Future Directions for Laws and Regulations Affecting the Curriculum

As we noted in Chapters 2 and 4, law-related education has succeeded, in relatively few years, in creating a beachhead in the school curriculum. In 63 percent of the sample schools for which data are complete, respondents told us there was at least one course specifically devoted to examining law-related topics. That does not mean that there is a law course in 63 percent of all American high schools. As we have pointed out in several places, there is reason to think our sample may be somewhat unrepresentative. After all, we chose the five states in part because each harbored at least one major law-related education project and because we hoped to find a wide range of law-related education activities in those states. However, the sample may not be entirely unrepresentative of the national picture. YEFC's recently published *Directory of Law-Related Educational Projects* lists more than 35 states with a least one statewide project, suggesting that states with at least one important project are in the majority.

The data themselves suggest another caution. There were only 71 courses devoted to law reported in the 48 schools that contained any courses devoted to law—less than one and a half courses per school. Moreover, law courses were almost always electives. Of course, it is possible that students could get extensive law-related instruction in other courses, including such required courses as civics, government, and

289

history, and indeed virtually all teachers of these courses told us they included law-related instruction. Moreover, about a third of these teachers told us that law topics had been added to their course in this decade, suggesting that teachers are making law a more important component of such courses. However, we could not determine how much law-related content there was in these general courses, and therefore we think it safest to simply note that there is the possibility that students receive extensive law-related instruction in such courses, but the only place we are sure they receive a detailed look at law is in scattered elective courses on the subject.

This suggests that extensive law-related education is reaching only a small fraction of the students in the sample high schools (and may be reaching no students in the 37% of the sample schools without a course devoted to law). Clearly a beginning has been made; just as clearly, much remains to be done. The central question of this study is what effect education law has had to date on the spread of law-related education and what effect it can or should have in the future.

As we have noted, respondents usually told us that education laws and regulations such as mandates and textbook laws have not been a major factor in shaping the curriculum in their school. This finding is underscored by the response to a general question asked late in the interview, which was specifically intended to measure the law's effect. When we asked respondents, "Is there some way the law has resulted in your doing something you would not have done otherwise or dissuaded you from doing something you might have done?" only 35 percent told us that law had had such an impact.

A brief review of our findings on curriculum mandates suggests why two teachers out of three said that law had not required them to do anything they would not otherwise have done. Our legal analysis found that mandates are often vague and general, more like loose guidelines than marching orders. Although statutes may require that a particular course be offered, they almost never suggest a detailed content or method of instruction. State departments of education usually do not follow through with detailed curriculum regulations, but rather produce curriculum guides that are explicitly designed to help local educators create their own programs. State departments often explicitly disclaim the role of enforcer of curriculum laws. Rather, they see themselves as facilitators for local districts.

Our respondents seemed quite comfortable with the mandates they had. Two-thirds said that mandates were a good thing—helping, reinforcing, and directing their efforts. Although most did not find that mandates were very important to their work, the majority would not change them. Moreover, three-quarters of those who would change them would like to *increase* rather than decrease the number of mandates. All in all, our respondents did not chafe under the mandates of their states, and they seemed to support the principle of the mandates—that the state has a right and duty to make certain subjects required for schools.

In general, what is true for the mandates seems true for the other areas of law we looked at. Legal analysis suggests that these areas of law generally permit much latitude for local districts, and respondents did not seem to find them constraining or seem eager to change them.

That being the case, why should mandates and the other laws be changed? If they provide general guidelines from the state without stifling local autonomy and initiative, if they maintain the principle that in a democracy the people and their representatives have a voice in education but do not derogate the role and responsibility of professional educators, then why not leave them as they are?

To put it another way, can laws dealing with teaching and learning do more? Can they be made more detailed and specific? Can they provide more direction to education without imposing a stifling uniformity on local efforts?

A good way to begin answering these questions is to consider the basic purpose of the system of laws dealing with teaching and learning. John W. Meyer and Brian Rowan have suggested that a principal function of education law is to represent some centralized and enforced consensus about which students, teachers, and topics of instruction constitute "schooling" in any particular jurisdiction.[1] For example,

1. *Students* are those persons of a certain chronological age who are eligible, indeed required in all states but one, to attend school.
2. *Teachers* are those persons who have met the specified legal requirements for a credential, including a bachelor's degree, a mandated array of preparatory courses designed to assure a level of general educational accomplishment, a familiarity with some particular subject matter, an ability to work with children, and some additional nonacademic requirements such as good health and good moral character.
3. *Subjects of study and instructional materials* are those either mandated or permitted by law and then enforced by funding and accreditation mechanisms, by promotion and graduation requirements, and sometimes even by criminal penalties.

All of these elements—students, teachers, and topics—are assembled into constellations and become the core ingredients of the larger term "schooling," whose meaning is captured by the legal definitions. As Meyer and Rowan point out, these categories give meaning to the whole education enterprise. They index and validate education. Hence, students leave school documented by particular degrees, teachers are hired on the basis of their credentials or certificates, schools are evaluated by accreditation standards.

Besides defining schooling for particular jurisdictions, the law provides consensual definitions for American education in general, furnishing a language of exchange and recognition for educational institutions. The structure provided by law permits the 15,000 school systems and the hundreds of teacher education institutions to operate within standards that are similar from state to state, permitting educational institutions to recognize the credentials of teachers and students from different regions and creating something like a national structure of education.

Finally, law promotes the legitimacy of schools and helps build support for public education. This seems a minimally necessary, even inevitable role of law in regard to education. For the legitimacy of schools, their ability to obtain resources, and their capacity to mobilize public confidence and support depend in large part upon maintaining congruence between their organizational structure and the socially shared categorical understandings of education. As Meyer and Rowan ask, "How could parents or the state legitimately extend broad powers over their children to random, strange adults? What sensible person would devote years and money to study without an understanding that this is 'college' or 'economics'?"[2]

If this theory of the underlying purpose of laws dealing with schooling is accurate, then lawmakers do not intend to regulate the content of education or to substantively shape what happens in the classroom, but rather seek to minimally define schooling and provide a threshold of public understanding and support. The legal analysis conducted for this study provides some backing for this theory, suggesting that lawmakers have rarely sought to govern the actual learning process.

Laws generally impose only nominal controls on the primary educational activity—instruction—and even more casual controls on the outcomes of schooling. Actual educational work occurs in the isolation of classrooms, largely removed from the impact of substantive rules.[3] Hence, the law might demand that a student be denied a graduation certificate if he has taken too many units of government and not enough of history, but it largely ignores the issue of whether he has succeeded in learning the subject matter. The legal design permits teachers to advance through levels of certification, to attain salary increments, or to acquire tenure based on educational attainments or duration of employment. Yet legal provisions may never submit a teacher to any serious evaluation of performance competency, or any assessment of the extent to which the teacher's abilities coincide with the school district's instructional needs. Funds may be withheld if a mandated subject is not offered for the specified quantity of time or credit units, but no sanctions exist to assure any particular content or quality in the curricular offering.

The laws governing schooling focus almost exclusively on the formal appearances of education, impinging very little on the actualities of teaching and learning. If the school satisfies the categorical rules that give meaning to the educational enterprise, then the law traditionally has not demanded concern for the quality of instruction or ultimately for what the students learn and are capable of doing. The only test of compliance has been whether the schools manifest visible adherence to the external classifications. Are the teachers certified, the students enrolled in appropriate courses, the school accredited, the physical plant and facilities adequate?

Once the law has erected a framework delimiting the acceptable perimeters of actual educational activity, it relies on a host of implicit assumptions about what occurs within the approved structure. The curriculum mandate that "history" be studied is largely implemented through confidence in certified teachers. The teacher is assumed capable of teaching the required course because he has completed a certain number of semester hours in history at an accredited college. The accrediting agency does not inspect the quality of instruction at the college but instead relies on the soundness of administrative organization, the number of volumes in the library, the expenditures per student, and other concrete indicia of academic excellence. Thus all depends on a sequence of confidence, on a series of assumptions. The state relies on the teacher's preparatory program to provide good teachers for certification; it assumes that the district will require the teaching by that teacher of something called "history"; the district and community rely on the schools; and the schools in turn rely on the teacher. The chain is endless because it is circular. Each link is forged by implicit and unquestioned assumptions.

However, this pattern may now be changing. For many years the public had confidence in and gave support to public education, but it appears that the public is now taking a closer look at schools. In many states, this has resulted in proposals to change the law, to measure what

293

students and future teachers have actually learned. This has inevitably raised the spectre of "outcome measures," standardized tests to gauge what students have actually learned. Many educators doubt the validity of such tests and question whether they should determine the success or failure of students or educational systems. Many educators believe that such tests may threaten the autonomy of local districts and jeopardize a long tradition of curriculum flexibility in American education.

This reaction suggests that attempting to move education law beyond its function of minimally defining schooling brings us close to the horns of a dilemma. On the one hand, one could argue that the unassailable character of legal categories of schooling and their disconnection from actual instructional activity may constitute a blessing. Laws must of necessity be somewhat removed from the precise content of teaching and learning because much of the beauty of those processes rests in their variety and spontaneity. Perhaps rules can regulate only the general structure of schools, leaving the actors within the schools relatively free to practice multiple realities and follow diverse educational philosophies. Moreover, actual instructional change can often occur without any reform of the categorical rules.

And consider the risks of attempting by law to grapple with the substance of teaching and learning. There is the risk that a current majority of lawmakers might attempt to impose an orthodoxy or uniformity that could stifle the experimental dynamic in education.[4] Respondents in our five-state sample expressed such misgivings. Our interviewers thought that respondents were unwilling to recommend changes in laws affecting the curriculum because they felt that instituting changes would only jeopardize a good set of laws or make a bad set worse. Perhaps latent in this attitude is the distrust professional educators may feel for state legislators who tamper with education matters. Furthermore, in a pluralistic society built on principles of individualism, there is built-in resistance to the very notion of a governmental program of character and intellectual formation. The intensity of current controversy focused on the schools highlights the issue. What is the extent of governmental prerogative to monitor the messages transmitted by society's primary socializing institution?[5]

On the other hand, the state's interest and the appropriateness of the law's role seem clear. After all, education performs the important function of socializing citizens for the state. It is a central means for determining status and respect, for incorporating society's human material into its formal structure. Since education is such a critical and

294

controversial force in the ultimate shaping of American life, why should not the law, our basic social ordering device, have a greater potential role in guiding the responsiveness of schooling to societal needs? If the government has a sufficient stake in schools to justify compelling students to attend, then surely it has the lesser power to decide what values and what information should be transmitted to students.

A glance at the empirical data from this study suggests that this is indeed a dilemma with sharp horns, that there is some validity in both lines of argument. Our research suggests that many problems can and do arise because educators are uncertain of relevant laws, do not know what these laws require them to do, and are unsure about how state law generally affects them. Some of our data suggest potential problems for a more directive role for education law; other data suggest that the alternative system of loose guidelines may be ineffectual.

If education law is made more directive, if it attempts to closely monitor the content of education, it may impinge strongly on the classroom, reduce teachers' fredom to act, and encourage a rather mechanical compliance with the law. A possible example is provided by a substudy we did that measured how a very small group of Texas eighth-grade teachers reacted to a legislative mandate dealing with a unit on law. (We are aware that the number of respondents is too small to permit any hard-and-fast conclusions. Rather, we offer these findings as a case study of compliance that may have general implications.)

In 1967, the Texas legislature passed the following resolution requiring the Texas Education Agency (TEA), the state's department of education, to develop a 16-hour teaching unit on law for the eighth-grade American history and citizenship course:

> RESOLVED by the House of Representatives of the State of Texas, the Senate concurring, that the Texas Education Agency . . . be, and is hereby, directed to develop a course of instruction, of at least 16 classroom hours in length to be taught in the sixth or seventh grades,* to teach the basic elements of good citizenship, stressing the importance of the law, the rights and responsibilities of citizens under it, and the possible long and short term consequences of violating it;

---

*It has been assured that the intent of this Resolution was to apply to the junior high school level. The Agency, therefore, has been given permission to develop materials for this unit for the eighth grade at which level the State adopts textbooks in civics with focus on citizenship. (TEA, *Framework for the Social Studies, K-12* [Austin: TEA, 1970], pp. 27–28.)

The *You and the Law* materials developed by the TEA include a guide for teaching the unit, a correlation guide to show how the new topics relate to the traditional course of study, a set of overhead transparency posters, and a set of audio tape recordings. In addition, the Dallas Junior Bar Wives Club prepared a resource manual in cooperation with the TEA. These materials were distributed in 1973. According to the TEA, eighth-grade teachers are not required to adopt the law unit. However, if they choose to do the unit, they must commit the minimum 16 class hours to it.

Because of our interest in law-related studies and the effects of law on the curriculum, we interviewed 12 Texas eighth-grade teachers in addition to the regular sample. These teachers taught in junior high schools closest in distance to the high schools in our sample. All these teachers were aware of the mandate on the law unit, but it is significant that they appeared to be under the impression that the unit was required. All taught it and none suggested that he or she had an option. The following comments are representative:

State law requires two weeks of *You and the Law*.

The superintendent came down and said you're required by law to teach this, and I did.

The TEA made a group of 15 tapes. . . . We would adopt the various materials. . . . We were forced to use what they gave us. Now we are on our own. We branch out now.

The state sent word it was going to be required. They sent us materials.

Of 11 teachers for whom the data are complete, only one claimed to have initiated or planned the law unit. This teacher had participated in a pilot program for the unit and said he "started from scratch." Seven teachers said they implemented the decisions of others. When they were asked the importance of their own role, seven said they were personally unimportant.

This appears to be a mandate that has been communicated to teachers (however imperfectly), and it seems to have had an effect. But what kind of effect? Below are two respondents' views of the way the unit has been implemented.

How did this unit originally come to be introduced into this school's social studies curriculum?

Respondent A	Respondent B
The superintendent came down and said you're required by law to teach this and I did. I play one or two tapes a day and discuss them. I understand they've revised the tapes. If we get new tapes, it would be a better unit.	I teach a citizenship quarter which contains law. State law requires two weeks of *You and the Law*. This starts things off wrong. I don't teach *You and the Law* in concentration anymore. I found that kids were bored by two weeks of it crammed down their throats. Only two films are worth anything; the tapes are boring; the simulation game is good but time consuming.

How would you describe your role in introducing these law topics to the curriculum?

Respondent A	*Respondent B*
Unimportant	*Decisive*

How did you decide what law topics to include and how to teach these topics?

Respondent A	*Respondent B*
I didn't decide. I just had the set of tapes and played through the entire set. They go from old-time law like in old-time England to out-West law, to modern court cases. I make appropriate questions based on the tapes and ask students those questions.	I looked at *You and the Law* as much broader than the state requirement and material. I don't leave anything out but I don't use the manual word for word.

Of the 12 eighth-grade teachers we interviewed, Respondent A is the rule, Respondent B the exception. The passive compliance reflected in the adoption of *You and the Law* is striking. It stands in marked contrast to our general findings on how law studies enter the curriculum, which suggest that the largest motivating factor is the interest and enthusiasm of the individual teacher.

It is important to note that the resolution establishing the unit is not prescriptive (it does not *require* schools to offer the unit) and the resolution does not expect teachers to implement the unit without help (it asks the TEA to create materials). Moreover, the TEA has followed through with a very wide variety of materials for teachers and students, and, in this unit and in its other curriculum documents, the TEA has not suggested that its materials represent the only or best way to teach but rather that the materials are designed to help Texas educators plan their own approach to the subject.

But somewhere along the line the signals appear to have jammed before they reached the 12 teachers in the substudy. They thought they had to teach the unit and had to use the TEA materials. They did not think they had any latitude. Not surprisingly, all but one of these 12 teachers seem to have complied passively—to have played the tapes, asked students some questions, and let it go at that.

As we noted in introducing this example, we do not know to what extent the 12 respondents are representative of other Texas eighth-grade teachers. However, the substudy does suggest that one possible consequence of more directive laws governing instruction is that educators might be confused over how much latitude the laws permit, or assume that the existence of a mandate and state materials binds them to a particular approach.

On the other hand, a looser, less directive system might have very little effect. A likely result, according to our findings, is that teachers will often be unaware of general, unconstraining laws. In every state in our five-state sample (including Texas), we found that a majority of respondents were simply unaware of many requirements. It is possible, of course, that the mandated topics found their way into the curriculum anyhow, through such means as curriculum guides, texts, or departmental syllabuses, but we found no evidence that this is the case. In fact, we think it very possible that unless teachers know about the topics, the topics may simply not be taught. Moreover, teachers who were aware of mandates knew only that they were to teach a course on this or that topic. They usually did not know about the values, skills, and attitudes that the legislature and state department of education indicated they wished to foster. In contrast to the illustration provided by the Texas eighth-grade teachers, then, the responses of many educators

298

in the sample suggest that nondirective mandated topics may not be getting through and may not be having any effect at all.

Are we left then with two paradigmatic influences of law on education? Laws that minimally define schooling—touching on the structure, organization, and categorical terms of education—seem far removed from actual educational activity. Laws controlling the content of instruction are replete with pitfalls—uniformity, orthodoxy, and intellectual stagnation. Or is there some holistic legal approach to education which can foster rationality, quality, and accountability of schools, while preserving diversity and spontaneity?

A third type of law affecting schooling might begin with a new look at the many laws dealing with the educational process, with the result of introducing a measure of consistency and rationality into a disparate series of laws that have rarely been considered as interlinking parts of a system, a portion of an ecology of law and education. Our legal research suggests that states have infrequently examined how one type of education law—social studies mandates, for example—affects other parts of the code (such as general goals of education, teacher certification, and materials selection) or affects teaching and learning as they actually take place in the schools of the state. Legislatures have reacted to particular needs, and have *added to* the education code from time to time, but have rarely taken a long look at the system of laws governing teaching and learning.

A first step might be to enact systematic planning, involving a wide spectrum of interested parties in an effort to consider and arrive at a consensus about educational goals. There are a few possible examples suggested by current education laws. The South Dakota legislature recently created a public involvement plan encouraging local districts to meet with students, teachers, administrators, parents, and community leaders to determine educational philosophy and objectives.[6] Educational priorities were agreed upon in Wyoming after extensive discussions coordinated by a state "sounding committee" and were presented to the state board for endorsement.[7] A thoughtful approach in Georgia involved commissioning several papers on the future of education in that state. These papers formed the basis for debate over the derivation of educational objectives.[8] These processes, though not universal, seem to represent a significant trend, and they might provide a model forum for reassessing goals and reconsidering the curriculum. Obviously, deliberations about what the schools ought to be doing will be useful in coordinating a school curriculum that is congruent with those goals. Once goals were decided upon, it would then be possible to move on to the question of how each area of relevant law could best advance these goals.

It would clearly be presumptuous for this report to suggest the goals and changes in the law which should emerge from such deliberations. These would no doubt differ greatly from state to state. However, we can suggest some considerations affecting the place of law-related education.

Should law-related education be explicitly mandated? In several states, proponents of law-related education have worked to add law studies to the series of mandated subjects, on the assumption that it will become part of the curriculum of every school once it is mandated. Our research suggests that there are many slips between passing a legislative act and getting a mandated subject into the curriculum.

As we noted in Chapter 4, much depends on whether a mandate has a specific action component—a requirement that the subject be offered for so many hours (or for a semester or a year), a requirement that students pass the course for graduation, or a requirement that students pass a test on the subject before they are permitted to graduate.

However, while a specific mandate of this sort is apt to be needed, the results may not be all that proponents had hoped for. Educators sometimes feel that there are too many mandates already, that schools are bombarded with new requirements with no indication of what is to be dropped. (Mandates may quietly fade away, but they are almost never legislated out of existence.) A new law-related mandate might therefore be met with some resentment, or, as the Texas case study suggests, with rather mechanical compliance.

Since law-related education could easily be made a component of history, government, and civics courses—indeed, since law-related content is almost inevitably present in these courses already—another alternative might be to provide that law-related topics be emphasized in such courses. If this approach were taken (or even if a separate course were mandated) it would be wise to link the requirement to teach about law with directives designed to help teachers do the job successfully. Mandates could be accompanied by provisions for pre- and in-service teacher education, by provisions enabling local districts to assess the success of their efforts, and by special resource allocations designed to enhance the quality of instruction.

A bond might be forged between what is to be taught and those primarily charged with teaching, between curriculum laws and laws governing those who will communicate the curriculum. Hence, certification requirements might be made more a function of school needs and teacher responsibilities. Exceptions to the certification requirement might be expanded, perhaps along the lines of the Pennsylvania regulation providing that noncertified experts can teach up to 300 hours a year or the California law that permits those with special qualifications to receive eminence credentials. The formidable task of such exceptions to certification would be to make it possible for schools to secure a resource for students without going through extensive red tape and without jeopardizing teaching standards or threatening the job security of teachers. In-service education might be triggered by evaluating teacher performance. Professional advancement and job security might be based on assessment of teachers' contributions to schools' instructional needs rather than on the accumulation of credits at the university.

Finally, it would be important that teachers understand why some subjects are mandated and how much responsibility they themselves have for making them work. In short, teachers would not only need help offering mandated subjects, they would need motivation for doing so. They will probably not be motivated by the fear of sanctions (only 20% of our respondents spoke of enforcement provisions), but they may be motivated by professional interest if the mandates arise out of a broad-based review in which educators themselves play an important part. Also, much would depend on how teachers learn of mandates. In the five sample states, respondents had learned of the mandates themselves in a rather hit-or-miss fashion, but they learned of changes in the mandates rather systematically, usually from their supervisors. Perhaps this delivery system could be embellished by extensive teacher education programs designed to introduce the new curriculum, in which classroom teachers who participated in pilot demonstrations of the program would introduce some creative possibilities to other teachers. Perhaps the state department of education could coordinate special newsletters for teachers, through which teachers would be encouraged to share their successes and frustrations with the new curriculum. Through such means teachers might come to see the new curriculum not as an imposition from above but rather as an educational enterprise to which they can contribute. To convey this sense of possibility and flexibility to teachers in subsequent years, as well as to prevent mandates from becoming outdated, perhaps the mandates could have "sunset" provisions, keeping them in existence only for a set number of years, after which, presumably, they would be refashioned as part of new systematic reviews of relevant laws.

We have dealt so far only with considerations that would arise if the principle of mandated curricula were retained. But isn't it possible that one result of full-scale reviews of laws governing teaching and learning might be a sharp cutback in the number of mandates or total elimination of them? For many people, state mandates smack of compulsions imposed on local school districts. Thus the creation in Arizona of a State Basic Concepts Commission for social studies was accompanied by acrimonious protest against the imposition of detailed instructional guidelines.[9] In North Carolina, the legislature recently rewrote the state's curriculum law, over objections from teachers and the state superintendent of public instruction, to encourage the teaching of "the free enterprise system at the high school level and its history, theory, foundation and the manner in which it is actually practiced." Opposition centered on the argument that the state should not legislate what to teach.[10] Even leaving politically-charged instances such as these aside, it is not unlikely that one result of a systematic look at curriculum law could be the elimination of many outdated mandates and the consolidation of others that overlap.

Our research suggests that proponents of law-related education might find the reduction in the number of mandates to their advantage. Our interviewers found that in many schools law-related courses came into being as a result of local curriculum revisions, especially those accompanying the shift from a semester to a quarter system. These changes opened up more opportunities for elective courses, and apparently teachers and students were sufficiently interested in learning about law to add law-related courses at this time. This finding suggests that reduction in the number of state mandates might lead to an opening up of the curriculum and the addition of law courses in many schools throughout the state. Since these courses would come into being because of local assessments of needs and interests and because of the enthusiasm of local teachers, we believe they could well be educationally exciting examples of the potential of law studies.

Of course, a logical corollary of reducing or eliminating mandates might be to provide more flexibility in many other areas of relevant law. Perhaps instead of subject matter requirements for future teachers, candidates for teaching certificates could be asked to develop competencies in certain broadly defined areas relevant to the state's educational goals. Perhaps other requirements for teacher certification could be liberalized. Perhaps laws dealing with materials selection could be revised to leave the maximum of discretion in the hands of local districts.

Whether states determine to add new directives, retain their present laws governing education, or make the system less directive, we believe that state education laws and regulations should explictly encourage the full use of the community. We pointed out in Chapter 8 that the area of education law appearing to alarm teachers the most was their possible liability for injuries suffered by students, especially while on field trips. When we asked teachers a general question about which laws had had an effect on their actions, they mentioned fear of liability more frequently than mandates, teacher certification laws, textbook laws, or any other area. As we pointed out, this is not so much a legal problem as a problem of communication. The principles of tort liability are the same on off-campus activities as they are inside the classroom. Legislatures might put teachers' fears to rest by explicitly encouraging the use of off-campus learning activities and by spelling out certain general guidelines for educators in charge of students off the school campus. State departments of education could follow through by encouraging off-campus activities, holding special teacher education programs that would at once explore the educational value of these exercises and explain to teachers the law governing them.

We have one final recommendation, this one for proponents of law-related education. We have suggested that a thorough review of relevant law might provide a more rational structure for education, perhaps hastening the adoption of curricular innovations such as law-related education. We do not wish to imply, however, that changing the law is essential to bringing about curricular reform, or that it is an easy and automatic way to do so. Our research shows that law has not been the primary determinant of curriculum change in this field. Rather, in our sample schools law-related education has entered the curriculum because of the interest and enthusiasm of students, teachers, and administrators. Educators in our sample appear to have been aided in many ways by teacher education programs and by the materials and services offered by law-related projects. That reservoir of commitment and interest constitutes one of the real resources of the law-related education movement.

We urge, therefore, that projects continue to work with individual educators and offer them assistance. These services will be all the more needed if states do mandate law-related studies. If there is one overriding lesson suggested by the research for this study, it is that there is no simple and easy way to change the curricula of the public schools.

Under any legal structure, much will depend on the energy and creativity of the individual teacher. Law-related education has shown that it can appeal to teachers, and that appeal is its greatest source of strength today.

Notes

[1] *See* John W. Meyer and Brian Rowan, Notes on the Structure of Educational Organizations, paper presented at the annual meeting of the American Sociological Association, San Francisco, August 1975. Much of the discussion on categorical rules affecting schools is adapted from that paper, although with a quite different focus.

[2] *Ibid.*, pp. 4–10.

[3] *Ibid.*

[4] *See* THE DANFORTH FOUNDATION AND THE FORD FOUNDATION, THE SCHOOL AND THE DEMOCRATIC ENVIRONMENT (New York: Columbia University Press, 1970), which includes numerous comments on the general theme.

[5] BERNARD BAILYN, EDUCATION IN THE FORMING OF AMERICAN SOCIETY (Chapel Hill, N.C.: University of North Carolina Press, 1960); PETER BLAU AND O. D. DUNCAN, THE AMERICAN OCCUPATIONAL STRUCTURE (New York, 1967).

[6] Concurrent Resolution No. 511, adopted by the legislature in 1972, discussed in Cooperative Accountability Project, *Legislation by the States: Accountability and Assessment in Education* (Denver, 1973), p. 42.

[7] EDUCATIONAL TESTING SERVICE AND EDUCATION COMMISSION OF THE STATES, STATE EDUCATIONAL ASSESSMENT PROGRAMS (Princeton N.J., 1973), pp. 5–6.

[8] *Ibid.*

[9] M. M. Gubses, *Accountability as a Smoke Screen for Political Indoctrination in Arizona*, PHIL DELTA KAPPAN (Sept. 1973): 64–65.

[10] *School Law News* (April 2, 1975): 2.

APPENDIX I:

The ABA's Special Committee on Youth Education for Citizenship

In 1971, when the ABA established the Special Committee on Youth Education for Citizenship, it was clear to educators and lawyers involved in law-related education that the burgeoning programs in the field required national leadership and direction. Activities of varying quality had been undertaken largely on a piecemeal basis, with minimal communication and coordination among them. There were no guiding standards and much needless duplication of effort. Recognizing this, a group of leading educators urged the ABA to assist law-related education programs, promote coordinated activities, establish standards of quality, and serve as a catalyst for further activities in the field.

In order to carry out these objectives effectively and objectively, the Special Committee has not established any proprietary interest in any particular programs, materials, or approaches in the field. Rather, it works closely with interested individuals and groups in developing programs best suited to their special needs and interests. In particular, it tries to serve as a bridge between the legal and education professions, providing encouragement and assistance to lawyers and educators who work together to plan law-related education programs.

The Special Committee is a clearinghouse of information in the field, frequently provides consulting services to law-related projects around the country, and serves as a national catalyst for law-related education.

Under a grant from the Office of Juvenile Justice and Delinquency Prevention (OJJDP), the Special Committee has recently embarked on many activities of widespread impact, including an annual seminar for leaders in the field. Under a grant from the National Endowment for the Humanities (NEH), the Special Committee is conducting a program to strengthen law-related education in the elementary grades.

The Special Committee has conducted 12 regional conferences, at which a total of more than 2,000 lawyers and educators from neighboring states have come together for two days of action-oriented workshops on the rationale for and strategies of law-related education. In addition, the Special Committee has conducted hundreds of workshops at legal and educational meetings.

The Special Committee's publications include three curriculum catalogues—the *Bibliography of Law-Related Curriculum Materials: Annotated* (second edition), *Media: An Annotated Catalogue of Law-Related Audio-Visual Materials,* and *Gaming: An Annotated Catalogue of Law-Related Games and Simulations.* Each lists and describes a wide variety of curricular materials in the field, including both elementary and secondary materials. In addition, the Special Committee has published *Reflections on Law-Related Education,* a collection of rationales; *The $$ Game: A Guide to the Funding of Law-Related Education Programs; Teaching Teachers About Law: A Guide to Law-Related Teacher Education Programs;* and the *Directory of Law-Related Education Projects,* a listing of more than 325 projects active in the schools.

The Special Committee also publishes *Update on Law-Related Education,* a periodical providing information on recent Supreme Court decisions, articles on classroom strategies, and up-to-date reports on funding, curricular materials, and the activities of law-related education projects.

The Special Committee's research activities include this study and report, funded by the Ford Foundation, and a study under a grant from the Law Enforcement Assistance Administration which resulted in the book *Law-Related Education in America: Guidelines for the Future* (St. Paul: West Publishing Company, 1975). That book analyzes survey research that YEFC conducted in 1973 and 1974 and contains recommended guidelines for project developers and funding sources.

APPENDIX II:

The Methodology of the Empirical Research Phase

Designing the Sample

The sample design reflects the varied interests of the research committee, the financial constraints on the study, and the constraints imposed by the many variations among school systems within and among states. Empirical Research Director Leigh Stelzer sought to create a sample that would balance these various interests and constraints, one that would permit our interviewers to visit a wide range of schools in as economical a manner as possible.

In Los Angeles in October, 1975, Stelzer met with YEFC's research subcommittee, Terry Saario of the Ford Foundation, Project Director Joel Henning, Legal Research Director Michael Sorgen, and Assistant Project Director Charles White. The group decided that the sample had to include several states so that the impact of a variety of laws and regulations affecting the curriculum could be analyzed. They also agreed that the sample had to include representatives of several levels of the school hierarchy, such as teachers, department heads, principals, and superintendents, to determine how various actors believe information about law is transmitted to teachers and to help us better understand how educational innovation takes place.

As mentioned in the preface, Henning, Stelzer, and White selected five states for study—California, Georgia, Illinois, Pennsylvania, and

307

Texas—because their education laws differ considerably, because law-related education has been implemented differently in each state, and because the states provide geographic and demographic diversity. The study concentrated on high schools because a previous YEFC study had shown that law-related education was more apt to take place there than in elementary schools and junior high schools.

Stelzer employed a three-stage random sample technique to choose secondary schools, first randomly selecting counties within the five states, then school districts within the selected counties, then high schools within the selected school districts.

The use of counties rather than school systems as the first stage rested on the following reasoning: a sample drawn from all school districts in the state would have been composed of widely scattered school districts. By using counties as the first selection stage, our interviewers were able to deal with school districts from relatively few counties. Although these counties were often scattered geographically, through this type of clustering our interviewers could study more than one school system per county and thus save a great deal of time and money.

For the first stage of sampling, Stelzer stratified the counties in each state by their population density. The purpose of stratification by population density was to insure that the sample would reflect the spectrum of urban-rural community styles. Choosing a range of counties by population density guarantees that cities, suburbs, small towns, and rural areas will be represented in the sample. Of course, this also provides for a sample that will reflect differences in cultural styles, amount of money spent per pupil for education, and many other characteristics.

The criteria for determining the strata varied among the five states. To have imposed the same mathematical formula—for example, to have determined that counties of from 100 to 5,000 persons per square mile would constitute the low density stratum in each state—would have been to ignore the very real differences among the states and to negate one of the reasons for choosing states with different characteristics. Instead of imposing a uniform criterion, then, Stelzer examined density figures for each state and grouped counties by criteria appropriate for each state. When counties in each state were rank-ordered by density, they conformed to two patterns. Counties in California, Georgia, and Texas fell neatly into three natural groups—high, middle, and low density—and counties in Illinois and Pennsylvania fell into four groups—high, moderately high, middle, and low density.

Within each stratum Stelzer randomly selected between one and

308

three counties. Since in every state the high density stratum contained no more than two counties—Georgia and Texas each had a single high density county—he selected only one county from this stratum. He would have preferred to draw two counties from the "moderately high" group in Pennsylvania and Illinois, but the small number (three in Pennsylvania, nine in Illinois) and the financial limits of the study convinced him to select only one. In general, he selected two counties from the middle density and two counties from the low density strata in each state.[1]

As Table 62 shows, this process resulted in a pool of five to seven counties in each state. The next step was to select school systems within each county. Stelzer ramdomly selected between two and four school systems from each of the selected counties that had more than one school system. He followed three rules in selecting school systems:

1. selection of the school system of the central city of the high density county (to assure that urban schools would be represented);
2. selection of up to three additional school systems in the high density county (to assure representation of suburban school systems);[2]
3. selection of two school systems in all other counties (to assure representation of schools from middle and low density counties).[3]

As Table 62 shows, these criteria resulted in 10 to 15 school systems in each state's sample, for a total of 64 systems in the sample.

In most school districts in the sample (54 of 64) Stelzer randomly selected one academic (as opposed to vocational-technical) high school. In the remaining 10 school districts, he randomly selected more than one academic high school. These school districts included:

1. five central city districts in high density counties (because the diversity of these districts could not be represented by only one school. It may seem that Stelzer's criteria for selecting school systems and for selecting high schools give undue weight to the cities, but this is not the case. The high density counties do, in fact, contain a large proportion of the state's population);[4]
2. three county-wide school districts in Georgia;[5]
3. one county-wide school district in Pennsylvania; and
4. one county-wide school district in California. (Stelzer chose more than one school in the five county-wide districts because a goal of the study was to study at least two high schools in each county. In most cases, there were two or more school systems in a county, so our interviewers could cover one high school from

TABLE 62
STATISTICAL SUMMARY OF SAMPLE

STATE	SAMPLE				COMPLETED			
	COUNTIES	SCHOOL DISTRICTS	SCHOOLS*	NUMBER OF SUBSTITUTION SCHOOLS	SCHOOL DISTRICTS	SCHOOLS	TEACHERS	ADMIN-ISTRATORS
California	7	15	18	1	15	18	47	24
Georgia	7	10	16	2	9	14	37	25
Illinois	6	14	16	1	14	16	44	22
Pennsylvania	6	12	15	1	12	14	43	22
Texas	5	13	16	0	13	16	43	23
Total	31	64	81	5	63	78	214	116

*Our interviewers were denied access to two schools in the sample for which no substitutes could be found. These two schools are not shown in this column.

310

each of two systems. Where there was only one school system, however, it was necessary to study two high schools from the same system.)

This resulted in a sample of 15 to 18 high schools in each state, for a total of 83 schools in the sample.

Our interviewers were very successful in obtaining access to the schools in the sample. The great majority of superintendents and principals welcomed our interviewers and provided adequate time for the interviews. We were allowed access to 76 of 83 schools. (In percentage terms, our interviewers were allowed access to 92% of the schools in the sample.)

There were, however, a few schools that refused to participate. The reasons varied. One school was in the middle of an accreditation review, and another had just been through one. One superintendent thought the bar should put its own house in order before it tried to reform education. Another said his teachers taught classes every period and thus had no free time to speak with us.

Stelzer and the interviewers did not detect any pattern in the schools that demurred, and we think the wide range of schools to which they gained access attests that there was not any systematic bias in our sample. Our interviewers visited schools where teachers were happy and others where teachers were bitter; schools that appeared loose and informal and others that appeared rigidly organized; schools with many law-related studies and schools with relatively few.

In five of the seven cases in which schools or districts would not participate there were obvious alternatives, and Stelzer was able to make substitutions. Generally, he selected another school in the same school system. In two cases there were no reasonable alternatives for schools that were dropped.

Selecting Respondents

Our counties, school systems, and high schools were selected randomly, but not our teachers. At each high school in the sample our interviewers specifically sought out social studies teachers engaged in law-related studies and attempted to interview a minimum of two regular teachers plus the social studies department head. Most of the department heads (55 out of 61) were full-time teachers as well. A total of 214 teachers and department heads were interviewed. (See Table 63 for a state-by-state listing of teachers and administrators in the sample.)

Our interviewers identified teacher respondents through the school

311

TABLE 63
SAMPLE OF TEACHERS AND ADMINISTRATORS BY STATE

	CALIFORNIA	GEORGIA	ILLINOIS	PENNSYLVANIA	TEXAS	ALL
TEACHERS IN SAMPLE						
High school teachers	33	24	33	32	31	153
Department heads	14	13	11	11	12	61
Total	47	37	44	43	43	214
ADMINISTRATORS IN SAMPLE						
Superintendents	6	11	8	8	10	43
Principals	18	14	14	14	13	73
Total	24	25	22	22	23	116
NOT INCLUDED IN GENERAL SAMPLE*						
Curriculum coordinators	3	2	2	3	6	16
Eighth-grade teachers					12	12

*Not included in the general analysis except where specifically mentioned.

312

principal. They contacted the principal and told him (there was only one female principal in the sample) that they wished to speak to social studies teachers. They emphasized the interest of our study in law-related education, civics, and citizenship. Some principals chose the best day for them to come to the school and arranged for them to meet with the social studies department head and, usually through the department head, the appropriate teachers. Other principals simply directed them to the department heads, who then arranged the best time to speak with the teachers.

Usually, it was obvious to everyone who the appropriate teachers were. Teachers, department heads, and principals were conversant with topics, materials, and activities of teachers, and they steered the interviewers to appropriate potential respondents. The evidence for the appropriateness of the repondents will be found in the data. Our interviewers never received even a hint that they had been misdirected. To the contrary, teachers and administrators were completely responsive to the needs and interests of our study.

Our interviewers' first preference was for teachers who taught identifiably law-related courses in the social studies, going under such titles as "You and the Law," "Youth and the Law," "Law," or "Criminology." When there was no such course, they spoke with teachers who dealt with law-related topics in such courses as history, government, and civics.

Because of the way the interviewers chose teachers, the data should not be taken to represent a random sampling of social studies teachers. They represent, rather, a sampling of teachers who identified themselves, or were identified by others, as offering law-related education.

Teachers and department heads constitute the sample of teachers. The sample of adminstrators includes 73 principals of the schools at which interviews were conducted and 43 district superintendents. In a few cases, an assistant superintendent, usually the person in charge of instruction, was substituted for a superintendent whom the interviewers were unable to see.

In large cities, where it was clear that the superintendent was far removed from the concerns of the study, our interviewers conducted informal, truncated interviews with curriculum specialists. In addition, when they came upon curriculum specialists in the schools they visited, they conducted brief and informal interviews with them. They received helpful information from the curriculum specialists, which we have discussed at appropriate points in the report, but the specialists are not

313

included in the sample statistics. (See Table 63 for a state-by-state breakdown of the curriculum specialists interviewed.)

Also not included as part of the regular sample were some interviews conducted in Texas, where the state encourages the teaching of 16 hour-long units on law and citizenship in the eighth grade. To gain further information our interviewers made an effort to interview some eighth-grade teachers of law, selected from elementary schools closest to sample high schools. Data derived from these interviews have been discussed separately in the report.

Interviewing took place in the late winter and early spring of 1976. Our interviewers used two interview schedules, one for teachers and one for nonteaching administrators. The administrative questionnaire included some questions asked of teachers and additional questions designed to identify the role of administrators in curriculum development and information diffusion. Both schedules were lengthy, generally resulting in interviews of a half-hour to forty-five minutes for administrators and an hour to an hour and a half for teachers.

Designing the Interview Schedules

The interview schedules were tested three times. In December 1975 Stelzer used them as the basis of interviews with three teachers and a department head in a south-suburban Chicago high school, and afterwards he, Henning, and White revised them considerably. In late January, Stelzer used them with three teachers, a department head, and a principal in a west-suburban Chicago high school, and afterwards discussed the questions with them. This pretest led to minor revisions.

Originally, we planned to use the state of Illinois as a pretest of the sampling procedures and the interview schedules. Stelzer drew a sample of Illinois schools, and in the third and fourth weeks of February a team of four interviewers, including Stelzer himself, conducted interviews in six high schools in downstate Illinois and three high schools in the Chicago suburbs. Upon evaluation of the interviews, we decided to make some minor revisions in the interview schedules. These included consolidating and eliminating some questions, making some changes in wording, and adding two questions. We decided at that point to make those changes in the instruments and give Illinois equal status in the study by incorporating data from interviews for this final pretest into the Illinois statistics, along with data from further interviews in the state.

314

Notes

[1]Stelzer selected three middle-density counties in Georgia because there is only one school system in most Georgia counties, and he felt it important to have at least three school systems represented from this group. He drew only two low-density counties in Georgia because he believed that counties of this density were relatively homogeneous, since the range of density from this stratum was far lower in Georgia than in the other four states. In California, he selected three counties from both the middle and low density strata because of the heterogeneity of California and its pivotal role in the study.

[2]In one of the five states (Pennsylvania) there were no additional school systems in the high density county. In that state, Stelzer chose three additional school districts from among the other counties in the sample.

[3]Stelzer's reasoning for selecting two school systems from these counties illustrates his attempts to balance several factors in designing the sample. Because of the financial constraints of the study he wanted to save money by choosing more than one system per county. However, he also wanted to choose a number of counties. Hence, he decided to choose two systems from each of five to seven counties per state, as opposed, say, to four systems from each of a smaller number of counties (more economical but not providing enough variation).

[4]The following counties contain the designated proportions of their respective state's population: Cook County, Illinois (49%); Los Angeles County, California (35%); Harris and Dallas Counties, Texas (27%); Fulton and DeKalb Counties, Georgia (22%); Philadelphia County, Pennsylvania (17%). About 30 percent of the sample comes from these counties, so the proportion of the sample from these counties is approximately equal to the proportion of the states' population from these counties.

[5]Among the sample states, Georgia was unique for its organization of school districts. Most of Georgia's school districts are county-wide. In addition, it has some independent (mainly city) districts. Four Georgia counties in the sample had independent as well as county school systems.

315